OUT OF QUATRO

From exile to exoneration

LUTHANDO DYASOP

Kwela Books,
an imprint of NB Publishers, a division of Media24 Boeke (Pty) Ltd
40 Heerengracht, Cape Town, South Africa
PO Box 879, Cape Town 8000, South Africa
www.kwela.com

Copyright © Luthando Dyasop 2021
Copyright © All artwork Luthando Dyasop

All rights reserved.
No part of this book may be reproduced or transmitted in any form
or by any electronic or mechanical means, including photocopying
and recording, or by any other information storage or retrieval system,
without written permission from the publisher.

Cover design and typography: Wilna Combrinck
Editor: Pam Thornley
Proof reader: Sean Fraser
Set in EB Garamond
Printed and bound by CTP Printers, Cape Town

First published by Kwela Books 2021
ISBN: 978-0-7957-1042-1
ISBN: 978-0-7957-1043-8 (epub)

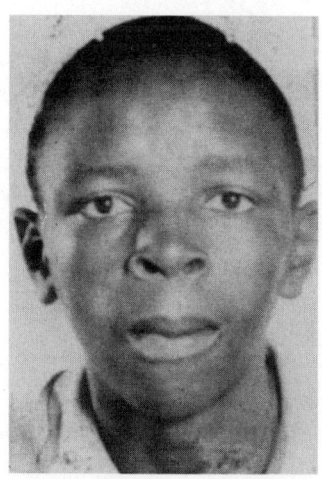

In memory of Sipho Phungulwa (1957–1990), and in appreciation of support mainly to my wife, Connie, and my whole family.

Above: Mugshot of Sipho Phungulwa.
Photo: The National Archives and Record Services of South Africa.

CONTENTS

Author's note   9
Introduction   11

PART ONE: GROWING UP
Chapter 1   17
Chapter 2   22
Chapter 3   27
Chapter 4   32
Chapter 5   37
Chapter 6   43
Chapter 7   49

PART TWO: INTO EXILE
Chapter 8   57
Chapter 9   61
Chapter 10   63
Chapter 11   70
Chapter 12   76
Chapter 13   80

PART THREE: MILITARY TRAINING AND THE EASTERN FRONT
Chapter 14   87
Chapter 15   94
Chapter 16   100
Chapter 17   112
Chapter 18   120

PART FOUR: QUATRO
Chapter 19   137
Chapter 20   149
Chapter 21   156

PART FIVE: EAST AFRICA
Chapter 22 — 167
Chapter 23 — 176
Chapter 24 — 186

PART SIX: RETURN TO SOUTH AFRICA
Chapter 25 — 197
Chapter 26 — 202
Chapter 27 — 209
Chapter 28 — 217
Chapter 29 — 225

PART SEVEN: MAKING A NEW LIFE
Chapter 30 — 233
Chapter 31 — 239
Chapter 32 — 246

PART EIGHT: THE TRC AND AFTER
Chapter 33 — 255
Chapter 34 — 263

Coda — 268
References — 274
Acknowledgements — 275
About the author — 276

AUTHOR'S NOTE

I write this book with great concern within the parameters of a historically racially divided society. I use terms to whose connotations I do not subscribe.

Terms like 'African', 'blacks', 'whites' and 'coloured' are discomforting due to their exclusivity, though they are loosely used in conversations and in government circles. To some people they are acceptable, while to others they are derogatory.

In present post-apartheid South Africa, the political dispensation is aiming to do away with all forms of racialism. It is a protracted process that will not be easy to attain after the centuries of racial segregation and subjugation.

So, though I may find it difficult not to use these terms in their present context, they are inappropriate and have no room in future discussions when social cohesion actually takes place.

Also, in keeping with our African culture of respecting the elderly by preceding their names with the titles 'Mama' and 'Tata' for female and male respectively, where I do not mention the titles does not mean I do not respect them, because I do.

INTRODUCTION

Finding one's mission in life can be difficult.

In my case, the arts have made a lasting impression, so much so that I knew from an early age that my life was destined to revolve around them. It is all about the talents, the accompanying passion and the ultimate happiness derived from engaging in them. In this way, the challenges, the hardships and the obstacles one encounters are overridden and dismissed when focus on the bigger picture is not shifted.

In this book, I go to lengths to reveal the twists and turns into which life ushered me for choosing to follow my heart. It is about the struggle to keep my head above water when rip currents seized me and tossed me into life's deep end.

Surviving for the umpteenth time can only be humbling, to say the least. I felt that given another chance I should write an autobiography, though for certain reasons, from time to time, I abandoned the project. Having once had the itch to write the book meant one thing for me, though: the knack to do it was there after all. Once I realised this, I decided I was going to write it.

Yet being a fellow mortal meant I could take only so much of what the universe threw my way during a time when the world was at war with apartheid.

Writing now, in the time of the Covid-19 pandemic, is like living through a war. All the ugly features of war, both psychological and physical, are there. In hindsight, this corroborated my decision to write my story, resonating with tensions and anxieties and fear for one's life.

Unlike the Covid-19 pandemic, the causes and origins of which are not yet known, the origins of wars can be identified more easily. This is a story not only about my life, but also about a certain time in South Africa's history when the African National Congress (ANC) reached a crisis point; when some of its policies were being questioned, and no one could predict the tragic outcome. Some would prefer this history to be forgotten. So why do I tell it?

Many of those who died in the Umkhonto we Sizwe (MK) mutiny in Angola in 1984 would have wished to be understood and I, being a survivor, am left no option but to put things in perspective. It would be unfair to history if we assume that this part is unimportant, as the source of many recent events – such as the groundbreaking ruling of the Constitutional Court in June 2020 that the present electoral system is 'unconstitutional' – can be traced back to that period.

Though this might appear to be an attempt to exonerate myself, in essence I am aiming to set the record straight and elucidate some grey areas in my life that have tended, time and again, to be used against me. My family, friends and everyone close to me (or not) all deserve clarity, and this book might assist.

The then ANC spokesperson, Zizi Kodwa's comment on the Emmy award-winning documentary about Marikana, just about says it all:

> [T]he ANC encourages South African voices to continue telling the story of South Africa, as difficult as some episodes of it may be and with all its trials and tribulations. It is our strong belief that the arts ... [are] an important voice in the definition of a South African narrative by South Africans themselves.[1]

My earnest wish is that all those who went through similar tribulations may tell their stories. In that way I believe they will have done

---

[1] *ANC takes flak for 'cast member' statement about Miners Shot Down doccie.* 20 November 2015. News24. https://www.news24.com/News24/anc-takes-flak-for-cast-member-statement-about-miners-shot-down-doccie-20151124\ Last accessed 29/04/2021.

themselves and humankind a huge service, while simultaneously freeing themselves from psychological captivity.

What follows, I want to believe, is an account of my step-by-step path towards opening up about my life. May every reader embrace my story without prejudice and find encouragement to hold on to their chosen path, no matter what.

PART ONE
GROWING UP

When I saw the child in wonder, I knew he must have seen the change in me. I was ready. Wiping a tear of joy, I said, 'Do you want to hear a story? It is a story about my life that I wish no one will ever experience. It goes like this …'

CHAPTER 1

I love the town of Mthatha, the town of my birth, and I have always loved the people there. I so love the place and its inhabitants that I would rather die somewhere else than there. For me that would be tantamount to bringing a 'guilty' decision to a sacred place. That is how deep the connection was and still is to this day.

Life must have been one sweet dream with minimal concerns and worries on my part until my first day at school. That day jolted me into real life! I was not admitted because I was not going to be six until 21 September of that year, 1964. Back then, they turned down any child whose right hand didn't reach the left ear when stretched over the head.

'You are still too young to attend school, come next year,' the principal said. 'Next!'

So, on that unfortunate day, my mother had to comfort me all the way home, promising I would definitely be in school like the rest of my friends come 1965. To me it didn't make sense as I grappled with the fact that I would be without my friends – something I hadn't anticipated at all.

Our place at 1043 Bokolo Street, New Look Location, had a thatched rondavel where my family of five lived. There was also a six-cornered thatched hut and three flat-roofed flats my parents rented out. In that rondavel was a big king-size bed in which we all slept. It was later that my father decided, at my mother's insistence, to build a kitchen, another bedroom and a dining room, all attached to the rondavel.

On one of the walls in the dining room hung a print of the painting,

Aragonese Dancer: The Fandango, by RS Clemente. It was the pride of Father's life and it had been presented to him by a friend of his. Due to its enormous size no one could miss its unusual and imposing beauty. Facing the kitchen door was my mother's pride – her chicken-run beside a small vegetable garden. In front of the yard was a big mulberry tree whose shade, on a hot day, would be enjoyed not only by us but by passers-by for a minute or two. The rambling rose on the front fence added some aesthetic value to our humble, but warm, household.

I had a brother, Mnyamana, who was born with a mobility impairment. He was either in bed or on a wicker chair, and he needed round-the-clock care. If my mother, his eternal caregiver, had to go anywhere Mnyamana would be in the care of my sister Nomzekelo.

That year, 1964, my parents were arranging to find Mnyamana a place at Ikhwezi Lokusa, an institution for the physically handicapped that was not far from our location.

Now that my friends were all at school, I had more time to spend with my brother than ever before. I tried to entertain him, but he must have sensed the sadness behind my efforts and mostly he was the one comforting his little brother. And when we embraced joyfully, fraternal love melted any yearning to attend school for a while. Given the new-found strong bond between brothers, anything could wait.

But the wait wasn't too long. During the Easter school holidays, my friends and I conjured up a plan for me to attend school when class resumed. Like the rest of the class, I would just enter the classroom and sit down; the teacher might ask questions, as they are wont to do, but I had to be there in my uniform with a slate and a pencil at the ready. It seemed so simple and I was prepared to take a chance.

The evening before that special day my mother washed me thoroughly until she was satisfied I was as clean as could be. She did the same the following morning. Although Mother was apprehensive of the plan my ingenious friends and I were about to execute, I must give it to her that she was eager for me to take the plunge. This she showed by giving me a slight pat on the back when I was ready to go. I didn't look back as I took those three or four strides to the gate, opened it and broke into a run to my next-door friend, Vuyani Makhalane.

'Yes, today I'm going to school,' I said to myself.

The school was actually a community hall, Rotary Hall. There hadn't been a proper school built at that time. For the intermediate phases, classes were conducted in churches while secondary schools were old schools spread over the Transkei. St John's College in town only admitted those with exceptional academic achievements.

When my friends and I gathered outside with the rest of the school for morning prayers, I prayed with my eyes open, looking at their every move for guidance: if they twitched a thumb, I did the same.

Our class was in one corner of the hall with three other classes in the other corners. It was ridiculous because of the noise of all the children inside the hall. The teaching resumed and hadn't progressed much when the teacher, Miss Nomonde, drew on the blackboard mounted on an easel what she said was a human being. I chuckled until I was coughing uncontrollably. I couldn't help it: that, to me, was a bad drawing. But this caught the attention of the teacher and, for the first time, she became aware of my presence.

She asked, 'What is your name?' and I told her. She then asked me my surname and I didn't know it. My friend Vuyani nudged me and whispered, 'Say Gaba.' Gaba is my clan name and not my surname, but to avoid saying, 'I do not know my surname, teacher', I decided to reply: 'Gaba is my surname, miss.' The teacher accepted me as one of her pupils without probing any further. She was more interested in seeing me draw something better than her own drawing and so I drew what I thought was an ideal human being. She was impressed and I was happy ever after on the day I was admitted to school.

I was actually taught to draw by my father. Among other things that he taught me, drawing became my favourite pastime. I would draw for my family and friends. No doubt I can say that I could draw before I could write. It came effortlessly and naturally. I wouldn't struggle with any shape as long as I had seen it before. My father, on the other hand, wasn't as passionate as I was despite having shown me the ropes. To me, everything in front of me was a picture waiting to be drawn. I loved seeing the picture take shape and this made me feel great, but in no time I would give up one drawing and start on another, and another. I was living my dream and the world couldn't have been a better place.

When I came home from school in high spirits, my mother and brother were happy for me. The teacher had said I should bring five cents for the monthly school fees and also bring my date of birth. Somehow, that teacher had taken it upon herself that I was to be admitted to her class and to education in general.

We hadn't finished the academic year when that teacher left us; the rumour was that she was marrying a man from a faraway place. Another teacher took over, but I knew that had Miss Nomonde not been there I wouldn't have attended school until the following year. It was strange, but I felt I had lost a special part of me when she left. Of course, that was unfair to the other teachers who taught me later because they, too, imparted knowledge in their different ways.

Now, knowledge was the primary factor that pushed me to yearn to attend school. The world, in my eyes, was this enchanting place with many opportunities to fill me with delight. Around each and every corner there must surely be some surprise or something I didn't know that was waiting to be learnt, to be explored, and I was going to learn and explore it!

In that same year, 1964, my brother, Mnyamana, was accepted at Ikhwezi Lokusa, the home for the physically handicapped. My parents and I could walk there as it was not far from our home.

Ikhwezi Lokusa was situated on top of the hill to the right of our location. As my parents walked slowly up the hill, I was always ahead of them, alternating between brisk walking and breaking into a run. As I was safely in their view, they did not mind my show of excess energy. The more I ascended, the more appealing was the view of my location sprawling in the valley before me.

Whenever Mnyamana saw us approaching he became very jovial, fidgeting in his wheelchair and lifting his arms in an open declaration of joy. There were many who shared his condition, some older and some younger. What differentiated life there from home life were the facilities and games that were suitable for them to play.

The place was always spotlessly clean, and the caregivers were totally committed to their work. Their patience and their motherly affection were exceptional. Those angels in their starched white uniforms were all a-flutter in different directions when attending to something urgent, and always at their patients' beck and call. What altruism! They had sacrificed so much in prioritising the health and well-being of children like my brother. It was a testing and challenging job, not for the selfish among us.

I was always sad to leave my brother. I could not help feeling pity for all of them, although they seemed to have accepted their fate. I had to pull myself together and try not to cry lest it spoilt his day. Be that as it may, it was heart-warming to see that my brother was in good hands, however poignant the atmosphere was.

Then in 1965 we heard the news that Mnyamana had passed away. We were told that he had succumbed after a short illness. The thought of never seeing him again brought tears to my eyes. Tears that had been welling up during our visits and which I had held back came gushing out as though someone had opened the floodgates. I must have been a sorrowful spectacle. The loss drained me emotionally and the void was unexpected and sudden.

Never before had I had attracted such attention from my family, with both my parents and my sister all making efforts to soothe my aching heart. It was comforting to realise that I was surrounded by loving souls and that I was the same as everyone else in a time of grief: we are all prone to moments of heartache and misery at times in our lives. The intervals between those moments should be cherished while retaining the lessons learnt, and noting the differences as one takes another step on the ladder of life.

CHAPTER 2

School progressed unhindered. To me, it was not just an option but the best thing to do. But what I found unpleasant was the readiness of the teachers to lash out at us, pinch or whack us if they deemed we deserved it. I wouldn't tell my parents how ruthless they could be because they would assume I wasn't a good boy at school. Back then it was common for parents also to smack their offspring once the teacher hinted at their bad behaviour.

Given this bittersweet school life one had to endure, I could not help comparing it to the treatment my brother had received when he was at Ikhwezi Lokusa. I asked myself, how on earth could some people be so mean towards children while others, not far away, were so kind and full of goodwill?

Once my parents realised that I could go to school unaccompanied, they had me join the Methodist Church Sunday School, which was located in the opposite direction to the school. This time I was to be registered as Luthando Dyasop, since Dyasop was my correct surname. The Sunday-school teacher, Mrs Jonas, decided to spell my name as Jassop. The point here is that Mrs Jonas resented it when referred to as Mrs Dyonase, which to some people sounded more African. So now she insisted that my surname was Jassop and I had to grin and bear the fact that I was Gaba at school, Dyasop at home and Jassop at the Sunday school. I felt I didn't know who I was. My father had to explain it to me so I could be clear of my identity.

The explanation I got didn't make sense to me back then. I was young and any mention of a word like Khoikhoi was beyond my comprehension. It was only later when I had been taught history at school that my origins became clear to me. According to my father, my great-grandfather was a Jassop, of European origin. He was in the British-German legion that had initially been assembled to fight in the Crimean War but was sent to the Cape to assist in the frontier wars against the Xhosa people following the end of the Crimean War.

During the ongoing frontier wars, the German soldiers were given land by the Cape Governor, Sir George Grey, and so places with names like Berlin, Stutterheim and Hanover came into being.

It was at that time that Jassop met my great-grandmother who was Khoikhoi and they had a son, Tom. Tom married a Xhosa woman of the Mkwayi clan and chose to be naturalised as Xhosa.

Having worked on farms under near-slavery conditions, Tom finally found a place for his family of ten children at Shiloh Mission. This is a Moravian Church Mission near Whittlesea – a town some 45 kilometres or so from Queenstown. It was and still is a community of both isiXhosa and Afrikaans-speaking people. There had always been one church – the Moravian Church – but later another church, diametrically opposed to the Moravian church, was established. This was the Israelites Church, formed by evangelist Enoch Mgijima. The Israelites had a rebellious history regarding issues pertaining to land which resulted in the 1921 Bulhoek massacre of about 200 congregants who had occupied land that the British claimed as theirs.

The Shiloh Mission was where my father, Gibson, grew up. He was the second last of the ten children, born in 1918. When my father started school he was already ten years old – something that was not out of the ordinary at that time. But on that first day at school, the teacher beat him 'for a little thing like talking'. He was cross about that and bolted out of the class and ran to report the incident to his mother. There and then, his mother told him not to bother about school; he could learn many trades at the farms in the area and be an Orlam just like many others.

In the jargon of that area and that era, an Orlam was someone who was a handyman. He could fix any problem on a farm household, from plumbing, painting and bricklaying to tending to the animals. In short, an Orlam was an all-rounder and a go-to kind of guy. The term 'Orlam', in this instance, was a misnomer – the real Orlam were people of mixed Khoikhoi and Afrikaner blood. They were more advanced culturally, and many farmers depended on them for the smooth running of their farms. They were the envy of the hard-working menials. Most Orlams relocated to join others in the then South West Africa, now renamed Namibia.

To my father, the option of being an Orlam instead of getting a formal education was more appealing. In no time he learnt the ins and outs of farm life, was hands-on and gained experience in the 'ambagte' – jobs requiring special skills.

When the Second World War broke out, many Xhosa people around Queenstown enlisted. My father left the farms and Shiloh to become a tinker in Queenstown. After the war he, along with a friend, decided to go to Port Elizabeth for better earnings, but he did not stay there after his employer relocated with him to East London. That was where he met and worked for a Mr Bergman.

A constant pattern in my father's work history was his need to be independent and to be taken seriously. He longed for a friendly atmosphere between him and whoever he was working for. If this element was not present, he would be very miserable and would never ever work for that person again. In Bergman he found a friend he could learn from, talk to and be listened to. Such a friend was worth more than the pay to Father, when he looked at his background of poverty. There was this man Bergman who treated him as his equal and was not being ashamed of it, even though he was white: a man whose friendliness came straight from his heart.

It was a companionship that was to remain unbroken even when my father decided to remain in Mthatha, where Bergman had a chain of stores he was leasing. For the first time in his life, Father experienced a cordial relationship between people of European descent and African people. The laid-back ambience, as opposed to the cut-throat life in places like Port Elizabeth and East London, bowled him over. People in Mthatha went about their business with their heads held high, unlike on the farms where one had to grovel just to earn a living and where one's pride could not be nurtured.

'When I came here, Luthando, in 1947, and saw Mthatha, I fell in love with the place and its people,' he often reminded me. The large tracts of land owned by black people of course made him wonder if he could put to use his farming knowledge, but this time for himself.

It was while he was contemplating this that he spotted a gap in the local job market: there were literally no house painters among the Xhosa community. It was perceived that painting was an alien job mostly associated with coloured people; and the coloured community, in a way reciprocating the gesture, left working in the mines for the Xhosa people. My father decided to take up house painting as his primary profession, and his dreams of becoming a farmer went out the window.

In that year, 1947, the British King George VI, Queen Elizabeth and their two daughters, Elizabeth and Margaret, came to South Africa and Mthatha featured on their itinerary. A banquet for their reception, which was open to the public, was held just outside the town. I assume everything else came to a stop in the little town as everyone wanted to get a glimpse of the royals. That visit not only set Mthatha on a pedestal as a special destination, but everyone relished sharing the same air, the splendid weather and their open space with a royal family. For my parents it was to remain a memorable day because it was at that event, so I was told, that they met for the first time.

My mother, Jongiwe Jane Spondo (née Nunu), was born in 1922 at Tsolo, a town next to Mthatha. She also came from a big family, but her background was fundamentally different from my father's. Hers was village orientated, in a solely subsistence rural economy. She, at least, had elementary education.

She had previously been married, but her husband had died in the mines, leaving her with a daughter, Nomzekelo, who was born in 1941.

For as long as I remember, my mother loved letter writing and choral music. She wrote letters almost every week to my father's siblings both near and far. What my mother detested was people mixing Xhosa with English or Afrikaans words when talking around her, and my father was the main culprit because he had grown up in an Afrikaans-speaking environment. In Mthatha he tried his best to perfect his English, to the detriment of his Xhosa. So, as he would be regaling us with his exploits of the day at work, my mother, in anticipation of the conglomeration of Xhosa, English and Afrikaans in my father's account, would break into a choral song so loud it would drown Father's voice, thus discouraging him from continuing with whatever he was going to say. In return, Father would wink at my sister and me – another way to say he understood.

After my parents decided to stay together, they were taken in by a Mr Orenjstein. Mnyamana and I were born in the Orenjsteins' house in Blakeway Road. Mother worked as a maid (now called a domestic worker) while Father helped around the house while doing his house painting around the town. The family stayed there until Father got his own place at New Look Location, in what is now called Ngangelizwe Township, just outside the town of Mthatha.

Mrs Orenjstein, I was told, had a floral dress that I loved so much that I would stare at it in delight. If I was crying, they would show me the dress and all the world would be fine. When my family moved to our own place, Mother was given the dress, just in case ... Then, when the Orenjsteins relocated to East London, all that was left were the memories my parents kept of that supportive family. Sometimes it was as though my parents needed a chance to extend a word of gratitude once more for the hospitality they enjoyed at their hands. This taught me a lesson: kindness goes a long way.

CHAPTER 3

I hinted earlier about the sudden concern of the family about my well-being after the passing on of Mnyamana. I was ready to wallow in it as much as I could. That was when Father took me under his wing – he became the best friend I ever had.

During school holidays he insisted that I accompany him to wherever he was working. This could be around Mthatha, on the Wild Coast, Maclear, East London and other places. Or we would visit our family in Queenstown and Whittlesea.

Every visit there would be preceded by Mother buying me clothes and Father buying hats both for himself and me – a straw hat for me and a Battersby hat for himself.

On landing at Queenstown, after a few steps from the station, Father would always say, 'Luthando!' and I'd respond, 'Tata?' 'We have forgotten something,' he would say. I would look at our light luggage and assure him that everything was there. He would then smile and say, 'We are in Queenstown – and that's what we have forgotten!' I would lighten up because I knew what would follow: hats dropped to one side of the head and walk with a swagger as we strolled down to the town centre. We did that throughout the visit.

What struck anyone upon arriving in Queenstown was the cleanliness of the place. Littering was a foreign concept, and a sense of hygiene and self-respect must have been inculcated in the minds of citizens from time immemorial. But that's just scratching the surface, for Queenstown's claim to fame must be its love of jazz. Queenstown – the 'little jazz town' – was renowned for producing world-class musicians like the Matshikizas, Mongezi Feza,

Victor Ndlazilwana and others. Besides these household names, there were local jazz bands and singers who never got international coverage, among them the Transistors and the Queenstown Jazz Sextet, both alternating in backing Iris Windvoel. They kept the home fires blazing each and every Saturday.

Father and I attended those jazz sessions. There was something about jazz that was enchanting, but I couldn't tell what it was. Whatever it was, or is, it had to be something found in the combination of certain factors: the dress code (dressed to the nines, shoes shining, shirts and ties all crisp and fresh – everything elegant); the talk that would vary from sports, boxing, international jazz and, in undertones, politics; and finally the music itself, associated with the breaking of boundaries, freedom of individual self-expression, rebelliousness towards mundane musical limitations and norms; and ... liberation.

Back then, South African black folk found a high in music more than in alcohol, which may be the case today. Maybe it was because alcohol laws had barred black people until 1962 from indulging in liquor. But the whites must have realised that keeping us black people sober all the time was a big mistake: they could let us destroy ourselves while thinking we were enjoying ourselves. Fortunately for me, my father never indulged at the time, though some of his friends, to a very limited extent, sipped glasses of the stuff now and again. Father always wanted to know if I was okay and I would say I would be if only he would dance for me the foot-tapping, finger-snapping and hip-swaying thing I loved seeing him do. And when he did, you should have seen the way he hopped onto the dance floor with agility, and I would find myself next to him jigging and jiving. What a way to show I was okay!

Father believed in having his freedom to come and go whenever he could. You see, we were meant to be gallivanting with no restrictions. And so, after hopping from one jazz session to another and retiring to a guesthouse, we would, two weeks or so later, return to Mthatha. On arrival back in Mthatha it would be the same drill: 'Luthando, we've forgotten something.' This time I would know that our hats had to be in the right position. 'Yes, Father, we are at Mthatha!' I would say. It was not said with a sinking feeling, believe me, because however out of the world the visit to Queenstown had been, I was happy to return home safely. To me, a safe return completed any successful tour. To Father it meant no more looking for fun but putting his nose to the grindstone.

It was during one of those school holidays – I was ten or so – when my dad said I should come with him to where he was working. It sounded so important that I should be there, and I really wanted to find out why especially me, because he could hire anyone to assist him.

It turned out that we were going to the Wentzels' little farm just outside town. My father had taken me, not to assist him, but to play with the Wentzels' child. I didn't mind playing with a white child, but I was astonished to find that it was a girl. I was not used to playing one-on-one with a girl, let alone a white girl! I remember standing there in the sun, and watching her approach. I was like hypnotised prey about to be swallowed by a slowly advancing viper. It was her greeting me in my language, Xhosa, that made me feel at ease. It transpired that the whole family spoke Xhosa fluently, to the extent that they had even been given Xhosa names by their workers. Her real name was Belinda – Cherrytjie to her parents – but Qhips to everyone else.

Qhips had a sister. The problem with her sister – I forget her name – was that she was so into animal husbandry that she would spend any day, every day and the whole day in the company of the animals while Qhips stayed closer to the house. This was why I now had to be her playmate and friend. That didn't take hours to happen.

Once our friendship gelled, we went bicycle riding towards town and off the road, winding through the trees beyond a pond where we stopped for a break. I had had a question in my mind all along and I couldn't wait to ask her.

'Qhips,' I said, 'do they beat you at your school when you come late or don't know the answer to a question?'

She looked at me, startled, and said, 'Why should they beat me when they can talk to me? Or they can tell my parents if I'm not behaving.' She then said it was time we went back.

All the way back I ruminated on her response to my question. Of course, there was no issue of them coming late to school as their parents all had cars. There was a school bus for each white school: the Hoërskool Transkei for the Afrikaners and Umtata High School for the English. Besides that, some cycled to school. They were unlike us who didn't have those advantages and had to walk to school, sometimes barefoot in winter. The distance and the weight of the books on our backs were our daily challenges.

Back at the Wentzels, Qhips brought out coloured pencils and drawing books for us. She was casual about the way she went about her drawings, while I was trying to be perfect in my work. When she saw how good I was, she went inside and showed her mother. Her mother came out and said we shouldn't be sitting under the pear tree – why didn't we get into one of the family cars? Just then an overripe pear hit me on the head. I was startled, but Qhips's mother was not amused. 'That's why I said get inside a car!' she said, gesticulating. Qhips chose a black left-hand-drive Cadillac.

Their fleet of cars boasted big, imported American cars that just idled and were seldom driven. The family was obviously wealthy, though they had a humble disposition. Human values were nurtured in the children and no one could argue with that. I remember, for instance, one poor white vagrant they had taken in so he could find his feet. That man turned out to be an incurable racist: he had manhandled many black farmhands and had gone on to brutalising another. That was Mtshateni – the guy no one should mess around with because he was the most reliable handyman with the most experience in how to run the farm. Everyone loved him; his big smile and affable disposition made the very sun shine.

When this news of Mtshateni having been brutally assaulted came to Sbhozo – Qhips's father's Xhosa name – he was livid with anger. It was 'Vat jou goed en trek!' (pack up and go!) and no sweet goodbyes. The man couldn't believe his ears. To him Sbhozo was a verraaier – a sell-out – how could he side with an African? Well, it turned out that where he came from, the Eastern Transvaal, treatment of African people as human beings was not the norm.

I dearly loved that family. Or, let me be specific, I loved Qhips. Now, in retrospect, I can surely say she was my first girlfriend. All the romance with no kisses. At the time we were so immersed in each other; our compatibility reigned supreme. Things like kisses seemed so trivial – we were young, not black and white, and someday we would find a way. Such fine minds together were not meant to part except when it was time to go home, or when my father's work at her home was done. Even then we made ways to connect with each other. It would be at the Cab Car Race in town every Saturday.

The Wentzels took part in that race and naturally I would be rooting for team Wentzel. Qhips's feisty uncle, Boetietjie, was the driver. Among team Wentzel's engineering crew were two mechanics: Ogies, who was coloured, and Six Toes who was an African – named thus on account of his physiological anomaly. Both of them could have participated in the races perfectly well had it not been for their skin colour. Those cars had been stripped of everything save the necessary mechanical parts and the driver's seat. The race took place on a muddy surface. The cars skidded, collided with each other or capsized, but because they were so light the team members would flip the car back into position and the race would go on. It didn't matter who won; what mattered was that we were entertained.

Those were the days my friend,
We thought they would never end ...

That Mary Hopkins song played loudly from the speakers as we headed to our various abodes – hers on the farm, mine on the other side of town.

CHAPTER 4

The town of Mthatha, on the banks of the Mthatha River, was the capital of the Transkei, which got its self-rule from South Africa in 1963. This was the result of the co-operation of the Paramount Chief of the AbaThembu, Kaiser Daliwonga Matanzima, with the South African government.

Matanzima had an overly ambitious plan of having Transkei attain the sovereign status enjoyed by the three British protectorates – Lesotho, Botswana and Swaziland. Unfortunately for him, the Democratic Party, led by Victor Poto, and the vast majority of the people in Transkei were opposed to being separated from the rest of the country. With Transkei-born people like Nelson Mandela imprisoned on Robben Island for fighting for the liberation of the entire country, such plans were doomed to meet resistance. So, for Matanzima to go ahead with his dream, opposition had to be repressed and eliminated.

While this was happening, those of European descent – the whites – were enjoying their privileges just like those in other parts of the country. The colour bar existed: whites had exclusive amenities like a public swimming pool, golf course, squash courts, bowling club and even a separate entrance to the local cinema. On Sundays they attended church services in their own churches and when dead they would be buried in their own cemetery. Everything was separate. One could be forgiven for concluding that they had their God and we ours – theirs being better than ours.

Anyway, their High Commissioner, by the name of Mr Abrahams, ensured that these privileges were safeguarded while Matanzima, on our side, made sure we recognised his efforts towards the building of his own nation in its own country. His Transkei National Independence Party (TNIP) was against the ANC and its liberation struggle, which it thought was doomed to fail.

Whichever way Matanzima tried to hoodwink everyone, it was obvious that Transkei did not have opportunities for the locals to realise their professional goals. We depended on the South African mainland for almost everything: brain drain was the main feature as the cream of the 'homeland' left for greener pastures, while young men would seek work in the gold and coal mines of South Africa in a system of migratory labour that made sure they forfeited any right to settle in the white man's land of South Africa.

In trying to make up for what he was failing at – that is, politically wooing us – Matanzima brought entertainment and sports closer to us. I was quite young when there was a Bantu Trade Fair (Batfair) held at the Rotary Stadium in our location. There came a myriad musicians from near and far who played a South African kind of jazz. To our great joy, Matanzima brought the newly formed, though illustrious, Kaizer Chiefs Football Club to play a Transkei Invitation Eleven at our Rotary Stadium. Orlando Pirates, Zulu Royals, Mangaung United followed suit. The games would be preceded by Matanzima kicking the ball clumsily to the centre of the field, to everyone's amusement. Then we would be overjoyed to see our stars gracing our humble stadium. Talk of Kaizer Motaung, 'Chippa' Moloi, or 'Sugar Ray' Xulu! It should be understood that they did not support the separate development promoted by the apartheid system, but were showcasing their skills to us, their great fans. For us, the locals, Matanzima's good intentions started and ended with the arrival and departure of such teams – our view of his political goals never changed.

There was no development in our location. Ironically, the superintendent was white – Mr Goss – and his offices were at the entrance to the location. The white community was not allowed to enter without permission from Goss: another irony. This was to protect them from any potential attack by us, so it was for their safety. The only time, and the nearest that whites came to entering our vicinity, would be when they were visiting the Umtata Falls, which were adjacent to us. Even then, there was never any incident of robbery or assault directed at them. We were, after all, not the savages we were purported to be.

Just before finishing my higher primary I decided to change my surname from Gaba to my real surname – Dyasop. My principal, Mr Mapipa, decided to write it as Dyasophu. I was incensed, but could do nothing about it. I remained Dyasophu till my matric.

In 1975, just before my last year at school, I had not yet made up my mind which career was suitable for me. A chance meeting in town with a draughtsman, who was also an artist, turned my life around. He told me that had he not been black, he would have studied to be an architect, but that this faculty was reserved for whites only. He took time telling me of the marvels of architecture and that there was room for us Africans to develop our own architecture to world standard.

It was an intriguing conversation that left me with many questions. I did not see any reason why politics should interfere in one's educational pursuits, but that's how things were. Blacks were limited to being only civil servants, factory workers, mine workers and menials. My parents, I knew, wished I could become a white-collar worker and not an artist, because in those days art did not seem to be a rewarding profession. Though I strongly needed to uplift my family to better living conditions financially, anything other than being an artist did not sit well with me.

That year a new English teacher, Mrs Dwane, joined our school. She had been teaching in England. She was very stimulating, and we all liked and enjoyed her classes. At that time of my fixation with architecture and knowing very well that I would never be studying it, she was a breath of fresh air.

What was odd was the range of essay topics she assigned to us – they were tough. They ranged from writing about science to propaganda. I remember writing an essay on propaganda. To me, propaganda was a tool used by the evil government of South

Africa and its stooges in the Bantustans like Transkei. In retrospect, I think my sincerity was so scathing that it was a crime I was ready to commit if only I could impress her.

As a result of my outpouring of feelings towards the whole system and its education, she singled out my essay and read it aloud to the whole class. And the more she heaped praise on me, the more I felt pressured to do better. I just loved her.

I even went to the extent of visiting her at her home in the Anglican mission in town. I volunteered to prune a hedge there when she asked for anyone 'to come and help me ... for a bit of pocket money'. Gardening has been one of my enjoyable pastimes. The hedge was overgrown and a shabby background to a patch of well-looked-after lawn, so it was with pleasure that I started clipping away at the shoots to create a nice tidy shape. Her husband, who was a reverend, was the quiet studious type, always reading something in his study.

Their two daughters' understanding of what was happening in the world was astonishing. They were so young to be that knowledgeable! For instance, they knew about the happenings in Formosa, using the name Taiwan when the new name had not yet registered for most people. Out of their earshot, I commented to their mother that her children displayed such wonderful knowledge. I asked her, 'How does this happen?'

She said, 'They read. You must read too, Luthando.' Then when we had finished everything, she pushed an envelope towards me and thanked me for a job well done.

Then she said, 'Now it's time for my afternoon nap.'

I said, 'A siesta?'

She looked so bewildered when she heard me say the word.

She said, 'Luthando, so you know that word?'

'I do read,' I said, and after a moment of silence we both laughed.

Yes, I did read. From an early age I read out of interest and for fun. Fortunately, I had friends who were avid readers, and we did not restrict ourselves to setwork books at school, but everything across the board. As time went on, we read the novels of James

Hadley Chase and John Creasey before we graduated to Isaac Asimov's serious stuff.

Unfortunately, as fate would have it, the Dwanes' stay in the Transkei did not last long. Their political proclivities must have been noticed by the Transkeian intelligence and they had to leave unceremoniously for Pietermaritzburg. Now that was a paradox: how does one find refuge in apartheid South Africa? Maybe the imminent danger to the family was so overwhelming that anywhere was better than the Transkei.

CHAPTER 5

It was with a distraught feeling that I entered my final year at Ngangelizwe High School in 1976. I felt as though I was being pushed towards the gallows. No one but me knew my feelings about the politics of the day. I was on autopilot, with no enthusiasm at all. Teachers weren't as interesting as Mrs Dwane had been. I realised then that she had been a buoy that had kept me spiritually and emotionally afloat.

Throughout my school days I had been the youngest or one of the youngest in class due to my early admission to school. Then suddenly I did not care whether I failed or passed. I became the class clown, unfailingly finding something to make the class laugh ... Then love walked in.

She entered the class in mid-February – quite an awkward time to commence an academic year. We had all settled down when I saw her beautiful face. I was taken aback by her exceptional charm. There was no desk for her so the principal, Mr Dontsa, said I might as well share my desk with her 'in the meantime'.

Now that she was close to me, I felt I had to do something ... and fast. While the teacher was going on about something, I applied my tried-and-tested skill – drawing – to win her over. I drew a lovely couple next to a sports car, kissing, with roses strewn all over them. The moment I became aware that she was watching, I went on to add a nice villa in the background and two beautiful children playing together. Of course, that drawing took the best part of the period but had resounding results: I had won her heart.

Even after a desk had been organised for her, from time to time she came over to share my desk with me. It was a romantic break for her, she confessed. She was, you see, bored with everything – which meant keeping up with the expectations of her wealthy family.

'So, I am the woman in the drawing?' she asked, but before I could answer, she added that I should add more children because she loved them a lot.

I said, 'I also love them, but raising children will need a lot of money'.

She promptly and confidentially said, 'Money is not my problem; my problem is how to use it.'

That was the first time I had ever heard that cliché. I was to learn later that her father had won the Best Black Businessman Award in 1975. He had thriving businesses at Lusikisiki – a town on the Wild Coast. He was one of the co-founders of the now defunct Afribank. Along with the award was the offer of a tour for him and his family to any destination of his choice in any southern African country. They chose to see Zambia and that explained her late arrival at our school.

Nothende – that was her name – ticked all the essential boxes. She was against the political set-up in the whole of South Africa, the inequality gap between the rich and the poor concerned her, and the imminent so-called independence of Transkei brought only strong revulsion from her. I was captivated by her vast wisdom and I loved her all the more. We were always together throughout the days of the week. When we parted, we would remind each other to listen to the jazz programme on the radio at 6 pm every day, except Sundays.

Whether we liked it or not, talk would eventually veer towards our personal goals in life. I made it categorically clear that the art world was my calling. That, to her, was not a problem and her family would be supportive. If I didn't make it I could assist in the family businesses. In that way I would be able to sustain her high living standards. It seemed easy to her, but I felt it a bit opportunistic from my side to accept such an arrangement. I thought to myself: a man must have his pride. If what attracts her to me today is not there tomorrow, what would be the point of ever being together in the first place? How would I spoil her, if I depended on her family? And what about my family?

You see, my mother had once perched me on a stool in front of her, way back when I was fifteen or so. She warned me about this thing called love: how many hearts had been broken in its name. She took her time in delivering the message. She had been watching my growing love for Qhips Wentzel and was concerned. I did not seem to be aware, she said, that we could not be together as husband and wife due to my being black and her being white. 'It is the way it is, my child, and no one can help it.' She had uttered the words with difficulty and unease – helplessness clearly etched on her face.

Mother might have been spot on regarding the racial divide, but what she did not know, or at least did not advise me about, was the class divide that existed within the same racial grouping. We might both be black, but Nothende belonged to the upper class while I came from a poor background. In this case, it was not the clash of races, but a complex of issues: a clash of classes, the conflict on the role of the sexes and a trial for tradition.

Love is a matter of the heart; my meddling mind had trespassed its space and my heart did not let go that easily. As Mother had said, it was broken in the name of love. It goes without saying that I failed my matric and had to repeat it in 1977. That year turned out to be the most boring I can remember. I regretted repeating the class the moment I set my foot inside that same class I had shared with Nothende. It was the worst decision I had ever taken because Nothende wasn't there. I had lost, and I was lost ...

Every day I stumbled into the classroom only to slump down at my desk. My eyes would stray towards the door – maybe in February or March she would charge into the classroom and reclaim her space beside me and in my heart ... *this* time for good. How I let her slip through my hands was something I could not fathom. I pulled my hair out for the best part of the year wondering how she fared, because I still cared. Then I knew: love had wings and it had flown away as quickly as it had come.

In anticipation of failing matric yet again, dropping out of school was a thought I had been toying with throughout the year. That would not mean neglecting educating myself outside the scope of the mainstream education system.

Amassing general knowledge was of paramount importance to me, and that was to be the trend for the next three years. I had joined the library by 1976 and it had been my main source of information for various diverse subjects, art being at the forefront, while exploring other art forms in all their dimensions. It was not easy to break into the art world: lack of formal education in the subject and lack of finance to buy art materials (which are expensive) were the factors standing in my way. But there was one aspect I could afford to do – signwriting. I was good at calligraphy, having been inspired by the only signwriter I knew then – Mr EE Heslop.

In one instance, while assisting my father painting the chain of stores owned by Mr Bergman, we had painted over the letters 'Buffalo Motor Spares' that were on the wall above the veranda. Father was not assigned to do the signwriting, but I was convinced I could do it.

When the paint had dried by lunchtime, I climbed the ladder and, out of my father's sight, repainted the letters. People across the street stopped and watched me in wonder because I was so young and puny-looking. Soon Father joined them, maybe wanting to know what was happening. When he saw me, I was halfway through the task, and he couldn't stop me. Instead, he made a meal out of it. He boasted to all and sundry: 'That's my son up there.'

But he later reprimanded me for pulling that stunt. 'Firstly,' he said, 'you do not ascend a stepladder without someone holding it tight for you because there are those who are unemployed who may push the ladder and while you are rushed to hospital, they take your job.' I had been told that many a time. It was his golden rule – he never broke it, but all the same he would never have let me do the signwriting.

After Heslop came Mr T Pemba from Port Elizabeth, also an artist. He stayed close to my home and I approached him with my drawings. He was also of my Gaba clan. He encouraged me to practise more on a regular basis. But he stayed in Mthatha for only a few years.

It was around the time of his departure that Monde Mngqibisa took over the signwriting and any art-related job. He was also a good piano and organ player. What distinguished him from any artist I had seen previously was his immaculate appearance – a real dandy. With his bell-bottomed trousers, high-heeled shoes, Afro hair and chiffon around his neck, one would think he was a member of the American group, the Temptations. This was when he was playing piano or organ around town.

In 1978 I decided to work with Father. My speciality was signwriting, if it was needed. I just needed to be of help to the family, though my father thought my future was not in art, but in some white-collar job. I was just as comfortable in overalls, despite the status associated with them. We travelled together as far as East London, spending days to weeks there.

And what about those weeks on the Wild Coast – Coffee Bay, Hole-in-the Wall or Port St John's? Father had long before been on those shores, leaving us indefinitely, but a mechanism for us to get by was in place. If we needed anything, Mother would approach the Sparg's Store in town and get it on credit and pay for it when Father returned. She never kept tabs on Father's movements; she was not in an insecure place regarding their relationship. When asked about the whereabouts of my father, she would say, 'If, when he returns, he brings pineapples, then he's been to East London. If it's weird stories of haunted houses and ghost stories, then it's the Wild Coast.' Then she would resume whatever she had been doing around her paradise, our house.

Ultimately, I looked forward to savouring the unbridled freedom to do what I wanted with pleasure, with no constraints and no regrets. Wide-open spaces, thick impenetrable forests, the moon rising over the sea and roaring seas themselves were a fascinating combination that have kept me going repeatedly to the Wild Coast. The beautiful and stunning views and the simple life led by the inhabitants are a combination made in heaven. They are the proud inheritors of this lush world. Their ancestors welcomed shipwreck survivors long before the Dutch landed in the Cape in 1652.

Just like the hulks of wrecks and the unfound treasure lying on the coast's seabed, the people are firmly rooted to this locality of legends and yarns. In the abounding beauty, even atheists start believing there's a God out there!

So going to the Wild Coast to work was an opportunity not to be missed. Painting bungalows and cottages in off-season meant having the spectacular scenery to ourselves, with only a few around in their caravans who could not extricate themselves from the natural charm that is the Wild Coast. With the necessary groceries available, we would embark on the job at hand. Painting interiors and exteriors is time-consuming and being only the two of us meant we had to be prepared for a longer stay – not that we would be complaining.

Working on the surface to be painted is of great importance. The aim is to restore a finish that is exactly the same it was originally. It is costly, but the end product is rewarding aesthetically. Taking pride in our job made every step along the way easier and more enjoyable. But the most welcome part of it would be when the owner praised our work as 'marvellous', 'wonderful' and 'amazing': everything was in its place and nothing had been stolen or was missing.

My dad and I didn't believe it was because of our cleverness, or something similar, that we achieved that excellence. We had a ritual of praying before work – inviting good luck and chasing away evil spirits. In these allegedly haunted houses, Father would paint crosses on the walls while muttering, 'I did not kill you, leave us alone.' At night, after a stroll along the beach, we would retire to our servants' quarters, which Father believed were out of reach of the ghost inside the cottage. Then he would tell me of his plans for the family and, just before I dozed off, he would shake me and say, 'Luthando, let us pray.'

CHAPTER 6

It was not long before the inevitable happened. There was a falling out between my father and me. He was adamant that I was not destined to do what I was doing; that I could do better, and he had given himself time to think about it. That meant henceforward he was going it alone.

Maybe he didn't mean to hurt me, but to me he seemed harsh. I didn't need him to explain himself. At that time, we were painting a squash court in town, it was after lunch and I felt I might as well leave immediately for home.

Thus far I had seen nothing worthy of replacing my passion for working with paints of various colours and producing magic with them. I felt shattered and empty. My self-confidence dipped immediately, and I withdrew from the outside world. I thought long and hard about my situation. I concluded that the root cause of it all did not lie with my father, but with the apartheid regime which had sidelined us black people. All frustrations, I felt, were the result of the political situation in the country. It dawned on me that, though I had been living according to my whims, I had been living a lie – a comforting lie.

It was time I faced the truth, and the truth was out there: Kaiser Matanzima had gone ahead and declared Transkei independence, though it was nominal on all counts. It was recognised only by the South African government, but there was no confusion among the people – the independence was a sham.

After 1976 most of the white community left the Transkei but those who remained continued enjoying those privileges which, even after 1976, seemed inaccessible to the black community. Transkei continued to be the source of cheap labour for the mines and industrial areas of South Africa. Unemployment was widespread.

It would be disingenuous to say no one benefited from or made the best out of the situation. It was at this time that Matanzima offered the ANC and the Pan Africanist Congress (PAC) political detainees on Robben Island freedom in the Transkei on condition that they recognised his state. Surprisingly, some homesick political exiles from the USA, Britain and elsewhere came back and seized government offers in the Transkei cabinet and other institutions with both hands. This was disappointing to say the least, but what was heartening was that leaders like Walter Sisulu and Nelson Mandela were not deceived.

It was then that I made the acquaintance of other school dropouts I had known during my school days. We discussed politics and more politics. There was an abundance of issues worth discussing. The recent killing of Steve Biko and the repression of the opposition meted out by Matanzima supplied us with adequate sources of topics.

The arts, on the other hand, contributed to opening our eyes. Gibson Kente's *How Long* and other plays followed, which also made a political impact on us. On the musical front, Hugh Masekela, Jonas Gwangwa, Caiphus Semenya, Miriam Makeba, Letta Mbulu and others had left South Africa because of its racial and repressive policies towards its black citizens. Johnny Mekoa, the founder of the Jazz Ministers, was detained by the police on arrival back on home soil from the Newport jazz festival for having refused to perform on the deck of a South African warship participating in the celebration of 200 years of American independence. In short, there was a myriad events cropping up almost daily that kept my friends and me obsessed with politics.

The ultimate eye-opener was our introduction to the ANC's underground propaganda machinery – Radio Freedom. It was not easy to access. One had to make certain tweaks in the radio and elongate the aerial. For best results, we would dig a hole in the ground and insert an additional aerial with its end attached to a metal object like a tin. We were transgressing the law merely by tuning in to the station, and we knew that. Defiance and rebelliousness had a soothing effect on us. We even went on to smoke marijuana. Since we were careful with whom we listened to Radio Freedom, if someone smoked with us, then he could be trusted. It should be mentioned here that we viewed smoking pot as better than consuming alcohol, which was legal.

Radio Freedom was where we heard of military training in outside countries and the name of Oliver Tambo, the commander-in-chief of the ANC's military wing, Umkhonto we Sizwe (MK), and the president of the ANC at the time.

Now, imagine the feelings of a young, black, frustrated child when information with such content was at his disposal – it was exhilarating stuff. All this at a time when the Transkeian government under Matanzima's TNIP was increasing its suppression of its main opponent – the Democratic Progressive Party (DPP) led by King Sabata Dalindyebo. It came to light that the DPP was composed mainly of underground ANC members and supporters. They were constantly harassed, detained and tortured by the Transkei special branch. The King himself suffered a lot from these repressive measures and had to flee to exile in Zambia, where he spent his last days.

Some of the children of the DPP leadership were known to us. They were the nucleus of the ANC underground youth movement in the region. It goes without saying that on their side there was the need to be extra cautious, given the brutal treatment of their parents. Plans to 'cross' the border to join MK were afoot among us, but that was not to be an easy matter. So much frustrated me because I was extremely eager to join MK immediately.

It was around late 1979 when I met and befriended Mbulelo, the cartoonist of the *Intsimbi* weekly newspaper. He was staying at Stwayi Village situated on a mountain top south of my location. Our natural love of art was the catalyst that formed the basis of our friendship. Having been to an art school himself made him more advanced in the subject than I was and, given my thirst for more knowledge in art, I was prepared to learn from his experience. As matters regarding joining MK were still on hold – pending 'connections' to get me there – I was eager in the meantime to go with the flow. I felt I had nothing to lose if I digressed towards art.

Mbulelo struck me as someone with a serious persona and came across as being a bit cold. I dearly needed him to show his warm side, which I thought he was hiding, revealing it only in his humorous cartoons. Battling the hardships of life with humour was the constant theme of his cartoons. Somehow, to an extent, this was something he related to in real life: I could see that life had not been an easy stroll for him, though he resolved not to let it show.

On several occasions I accompanied Mbulelo to the offices of *Intsimbi* to present his weekly cartoon. That would be a day or two before publication. *Intsimbi* was apolitical in content and limited itself to the confines of a newspaper highlighting the availability of low-hanging fruit in the new Transkeian political and socio-economic dispensation. Its editor, Father Michael, was a member of the Roman Catholic Church mission in town. Standing tall, always with a camera at the ready, Father Michael's contagious smile and fluency in Xhosa had endeared him to the Mthatha community. His newspaper, unfortunately, didn't stand a chance of competing for sales against the long-established Xhosa newspaper, *Imvo Zabantsundu*.

How much Mbulelo earned was not my business and I wasn't going to pry, but I could tell it was not much. His long walk to town and back evidently proved what I suspected. I later suggested he consider staying at my place, as it would be nearer to town and easier for us to work together.

By around April 1980 he was effectively staying with me. He brought along essential art materials and some clothes. My room outside wasn't big, but with some improvisation here and there, we could work around any problem of space.

We immersed ourselves in drawings with ink, painting in watercolours and more. I also discovered my latent love of writing poetry. In light of my recently discovered political inclinations, my poetry was highly politically charged. I would draw a picture and write a poem on top of it, or start with a poem and then draw a picture on top of it.

I soon realised that something was troubling my friend. It was my insistence on listening to Radio Freedom on my radio. He would trivialise it, making it seem that he had better plans for us. It became immediately clear that we were not on the same page politically. No matter how I tried to ignore this, our differences flared up from time to time. My family was happy for our sake that we were getting along, quite oblivious to our differences. They treated Mbulelo with the best hospitality they could afford without expecting anything in return.

One day things came to a head when, after returning from town, he said, 'These people are saying you are a biblioklept.' He never said who 'these people' were, but he insinuated that they were the library staff. Yes, honestly speaking, I had not returned some books – one on Hatha Yoga and the other on art – but there was no way the library staff could have known that unless he had told them. Anyway, how did they know we were staying together?

Now, being called a book thief, even euphemistically, was not funny and it did not go down well with me. I started remembering how many times Mbulelo had uttered the phrase 'these people'. Once he had said, 'These people are saying your poetry is immature.' I had just brushed the comment aside; someone else's negative opinion of my poetry, or anything else for that matter, would not deter me. I hadn't even asked him at that time who he was referring to when he said, 'these people'. But now I felt that things had gone too far. How could he, of all people, be the one to stab me in the back? But the biggest question was: was he expecting me to roll over and accept staying with a snake?

Maybe I had given him the impression that I was a pushover. Well, I was far from that. I had been friendly but was not going to be manipulated. I had reached the point of giving him a piece of my mind. I was cool when I told him that I suspected he was a government spy trying to win me over, and that I thought it best for him to leave and never set his foot in my place again. When he remained seated, I became angry and aggressive. My mother must have heard my shouting because she came over and asked what the problem was. I told her that Mbulelo was a government spy and that he should leave.

Abruptly and unceremoniously was how the relationship between Mbulelo and me ended. I thought to myself: was he really what I accused him of? I did not want to sneer at the hunch. I might not be psychic, but my analytical mind had come to that conclusion. One evening we had attended an art exhibition at the library in town. I was taken aback when Monde Mngqibisa, the artist, upon seeing Mbulelo, turned to the door and left the exhibition as fast as he could. It was as though he was running for dear life from a house on fire. I had turned to Mbulelo and asked what could have been the reason for Monde to bolt out like that. Were they sworn enemies? But Mbulelo did not give me a satisfactory answer. I knew Mngqibisa to be a people's person and it was hard for me to reconcile that with his immediate reaction to seeing Mbulelo.

CHAPTER 7

After Mbulelo's departure, my mother became extremely pensive. She must have been pondering what I had said about Mbulelo. The fact that I had made my position in relation to the government clear, and the possible backlash from it, compounded the situation. There was a realisation that something, sooner or later, had to give. And this made me panic. That was when I resorted to the book on Hatha Yoga to help me cope.

Hatha Yoga is about poses and postures as one limbers up for yoga itself, which is being beside oneself using breathing exercises to release tension or trauma. The health benefits from practising yoga are numerous, more especially when one meditates. Of all the body postures one can use to meditate, my favourite was the headstand. The book guided me throughout and even recommended fasting to aid detoxing. It was those poses and fasting that made my mother conclude I was either suicidal or losing it. I had not communicated to her the good reasons for embarking on yoga and that omission had dreadful results.

In June 1980 three men entered my room and overpowered me. They were following orders from my mom. They tied my hands behind my back, bundled me into a waiting car and drove me to a medical doctor in town. That doctor recommended that I be taken the following day to a psychiatric institution at Umzimkhulu for evaluation.

In the afternoon of the following day I arrived at the institution in a straitjacket. I was taken to an enclosed place with the word 'Rehabilitation' written on a board next to the entrance. The doctor who came to examine me was of Indian descent and I remember thinking that here was the man who would understand me when I told him about the yoga, and he would discharge me immediately. But that was not to be. I was to stay there for two harrowing months.

That winter we were always barefoot and had only short-sleeved tops and shorts to wear, and nothing else. Even at night the windows were open, and I shivered all night as the single flimsy blanket was of no help. Uniforms were changed every two days. Washing was an appalling event: we undressed, threw the uniform into a container and gathered in the central yard, all naked. The nurses, both male and female, were treated to a voyeuristic spectacle as they sprayed water from a hosepipe at us while we jostled each other for access to the water and a few soap bars. They shouted incoherent orders at us at the tops of their voices. Mostly, they seemed crazier than us. When the whole show was over and we had put on clean uniforms, while still wet, the nurses retired to their office laughing uproariously.

What one learnt early on in that institution was not to raise the ire of the nurses if one did not want to see their unpleasant side. Anyone with a rebellious streak would be manhandled, kicking and screaming into a structure lower down from where we were accommodated. When he came out he would be more like a zombie than a human – silent and terrified – and what they had done to him no one ever knew.

The first thing I resolved to do was to forgive myself, my mother, the nurses, everyone, even the world itself which was unfair. I might never have control over how someone else conducts themselves, but I could map my own way forward. The circumstances I was in should not determine my destiny. I felt I should rise above the harshness and pettiness shown by the staff. My happiness could only come if I made peace with the space I was in. If I did not forgive I would forever be in a cage of self-pity, sadness and anger.

Around me, I found out, most were patients who were depressed as a result of traumatic and shocking incidents in their lives. There was a young man who assisted the nurses as they gave us our medication. He had memorised each and every patient's type and amount of medication and the nurses took his word for it because he was always spot on. I found it incredible that he was kept at this place when he had such an excellent mind. I was later to learn that he was homeless and when outside the place the trauma of returning home from the mines and finding his home razed by fire and all his family dead would come back to him, and he would have to be readmitted. The institution, in other words, had turned into his home.

Then what about an elderly man who had been sending money religiously to his young wife to buy cows, only to find they had never been bought? His younger brother had sprung to the defence of his wife when he wanted her to account for this. He soon found out that she had been cheating on him with his younger brother and they had been spending the money on a lavish lifestyle. He said that the thought of the sums of money he had sent his wife was not as devastating as the thought that the love he had invested in never existed in the first place. His world just caved in and he had been depressed ever since.

Once a week a chaplain came. I immediately recognised him as Reverend Guma – my great friend Lungile's father. I did not know that he had been transferred to Umzimkhulu, and it was years since I had last seen him during my visits to Lungile at his home at the Anglican Mission premises not far from where my teacher Mrs Dwane had resided.

Reverend Guma would not have recognised me because he was always in his study while Lungile and I played our soul and jazz records at a low volume so as not to disturb him. I did not tell anyone that I knew the chaplain because I did not want to draw undue attention to myself.

Reverend Guma would saunter into our enclosure and proceed towards an open space and then we would be allowed to join him for a sermon.

The sermon was not more welcome than the soothing winter

sun warming the place where the sermon was held. Some basked on their backs, or even turned their backs on him so as to face the sun directly. Reverend Guma was not at all distracted by these actions as he proceeded with the business at hand, regardless.

After the sermon, he made his way out of the enclosure as slowly as he had entered and disappeared into the distance. I wondered whether I was right in not approaching him and telling him who I was, but I always concluded it was okay not to do so as it would have evoked nostalgia and left us both sad.

In the seventh week I was told to report at a building some two kilometres away. I was astounded because I was to go there on my own without anyone escorting me. The nurses just gave me a note with the name of the person I should meet there. It turned out to be a psychiatrist. She was very amiable as she welcomed me in and introduced herself. She said I was there for a psychometric test and then she asked me to draw anything that was on my mind.

I wrote the test and then drew a picture of the chaplain conducting a sermon. Two days later, I was to see her again, this time to get my results. She was jubilant as she said I had scored 100 per cent in the psychometric test. She asked me about my gift – art – and I said I was thinking of putting it to good use. She said she hoped my dreams would one day come true. Then she hinted that I would be leaving for home very soon, and she hoped I never again returned to that institution.

And so, indeed, after a few days my name was on the list of people who were leaving. They told us to report to the nearest clinic if we felt that the world was weighing us down. The once hostile nurses had suddenly transformed into caring and concerned professionals as they pleaded, 'Please, never come back again.' I, for one, was sure that not in a million years would I ever go near such an institution.

The bus we boarded left for Umzimkhulu in the morning and I reached Mthatha the same afternoon. It was a relief to be back home. My mother was so happy that tears rolled down her face – tears of joy. I knew she had always loved me, and I loved her too. That was what mattered the most. It was clear they had all missed me.

When my father returned I said I felt like touching base with my relatives in Shiloh, Whittlesea, sometime in August. I had made up my mind while at Umzimkhulu that after returning from Whittlesea, I was going to leave for exile; I would walk all the way to Lesotho if that was the only option I had.

Going to Whittlesea was a way of saying goodbye to my relatives there and paying homage to the deceased. I had a long journey ahead of me and I wished my ancestors to accompany me all the way and back again.

According to our African beliefs, we are here on earth not only to fulfil our dreams, but to represent the departed by being good models in our society and they – the ancestors – would watch over us and be our guardian angels, relaying our prayers to God. Oh! The thought and belief that we each have angels guarding over us was sufficient to turn any sad moment to a moment of contentment and strength. And I needed strength – mental strength – more than ever before.

PART TWO
INTO EXILE

Amaswaiman

CHAPTER 8

Politics affects us all in various ways and degrees, for some even to the point of losing their lives, while others will leave their loved ones and sacrifice comforts for unknown outcomes. Maybe I had been paranoid about what I believed Mbulelo to be, but I was not going to take chances and remain in Transkei (or South Africa for that matter) when I had drawn the battle lines.

My plan to escape to exile was kept close to my chest. I thought it through thoroughly. If I told anyone, they might discourage me by emphasising the austerity of footing it all the way to Lesotho. That would be something I did not need at the time, because the courage I felt I had was great and my confidence in achieving my goal was convincing.

On 25 October 1980 I left home. It was a Saturday and the Transkeian government had decided to hold the celebration of four years of 'independence' on that day instead of on the Monday, which was the actual day. The festivities were held in town. People had been brought by bus from all over the Transkei, but I had remained at home preparing myself for the life-changing journey ahead of me.

To some, hiking is a hobby that is well planned beforehand with a map or a guide to show them the best way to reach their destination. My approach was different. I didn't know what lay in wait for me beyond Maclear district, but I was not bothered. I kept telling myself that I had to do it, and nothing would hold me back.

It was at around five o'clock in the afternoon, when everyone was leaving the Independence Stadium, that I left Mthatha. I dressed warmly and carried a bag with essential toiletries like a toothbrush, toothpaste, comb, face cloth, soap and mirror. Added to that were a matchbox, a torch and also a heavy stick as a traditional weapon for defence. I did not carry much cash as I had faith in human benevolence and heavenly intervention. As I had travelled the length and breadth of the Transkei, I knew of a short cut to Tsolo, the first town on my way. It passed through villages that were familiar to me.

I had passed Ncambedlana and Ncambele when it suddenly grew dark. I had no fear of getting lost because of my knowledge of the byways of the road, but a problem arose with dogs from houses close to the road: they charged at me and the stick became handy in warding them off. It was, however, unnerving because their barking invited unwanted attention from their owners. But fortunately, the dogs were not heeded by the owners, who were either inebriated or had better things to do than bother to find out who they were barking at. Even those who did not believe in the so-called independence of Transkei had found an excuse to indulge in alcohol. The unforeseen encounters with dogs really retarded my progress because I had to slow my pace so as to appear as if I was only passing through the neighbourhood.

When I reached Mjika and Khambi villages no lights showed through the windows; everyone seemed already in bed. A howl from a single dog would awaken all the dogs in that particular village as well as those of the adjoining village. It was not the way I had envisaged my journey – I had overlooked this aspect of harassment by the villagers' canine forces.

In the early morning I reached the last village of Tyeni. It's a sprawling village lying near the little town of Tsolo. I hadn't slept a wink, but I was glad I had passed the first hurdle. The Sunday-morning frost seemed to herald a bright sunny day and when it warmed up I decided to rest. The rest turned to sleep. What woke me was the chill from the shade of the trees nearby. But I was refreshed and raring to go. It was then that I decided never again to travel in the dark. Besides avoiding a repetition of the previous night's harrowing experience, I wanted to take in all the views of the countryside, perhaps for the last time in my life.

What I realised when I resumed my journey was that some of the villages I had passed had a special meaning for me. For instance, at Mjika there was a general store my dad and I had painted repeatedly since I was young. It was until recently the most convenient store for all the surrounding villages as one could get anything there, from a pin to a blanket; from ploughs to chicken feed; have one's maize milled too; and even collect one's post.

My mother's uncle, who was a very kind soul, had once lived at Khambi. At his funeral service the family and mourners in general had shed tears for the loss of such a good-natured person who had not been ill for a long time. He was buried in the bottom left corner of his lush vegetable garden and orchard.

Tyeni village was where an old friend of Mother's, who was married there, still lived. She was the one who gave me the name Luthando. I had once asked her, 'Why Luthando?' to which she had answered, 'Your parents were so in love when your mother was pregnant with you and so, Luthando – which means "it is love" – was the obvious name for you.'

In the distance ahead imposing mountains faced me and I said to myself, 'Tonight, I want those mountains to hug me.' But to reach them I had to increase my pace and once there I would have an ascending, curving road to negotiate. That meant I would be much higher in terms of altitude than where I was then, in the rolling hills of treeless grassland.

Accelerating my speed and having in my mind the sun's intention to set before I reached the mountain, I forgot about my weariness and everything else. My mind was made up and if I held on to the belief that everything is attainable if one gives one's all, I would make it. Being in sync with dear nature and realising the interconnectedness inherent in humans and nature opens us to the abundance of generosity engulfing us.

Sure, as the sun was setting, I was at the foot of Ntywenka Mountain, tired but content with my progress so far. I hadn't eaten a morsel that day but had been drinking from bubbling streams along the way. I was halfway to the summit of the mountain when

I decided to call it a day – I so wished to see the villages I had passed from that vantage point, come following morning.

On the Monday morning, I was awakened by the chirping of birds and a strong whiff of mountain breeze was teasing my nostrils. My immediate response was to stretch my legs and arms and reorientate myself to the captivating scenery around me. I was far from the crowing cocks waking everyone in the serene villages nearby, or alarm clocks' rude shrills in towns and cities far way. I was not going to spoil anything around me by plucking a wildflower or dislodging a boulder to see it roll downwards.

After ascending what was left of the mountain would bring me, on my left, to Schenk's store and still on the left further down would be the road to Ngcolosi – St Cuthbert's Anglican Mission School, where my sister got her weaving skills. I wasn't walking, I was almost trotting uphill in anticipation of seeing these familiar places.

In no time I passed Ngcele village on my right, where my mother's younger sister was married. It was still early in the morning and there was no sign of life there. I might as well move on regardless, I said to myself. It would not have helped any of us if I had dropped in. My aunt would have been excited and would spread the news that her nephew had visited her and later, after a meal, would enquire when I would be leaving. It would break both our hearts to part so soon; for her it would seem that her hospitality had not been adequate to meet my expectations and I would feel cruel for having let her believe I would be around longer, only to up and leave. Passing the village took a lot of effort, but I managed.

What lay ahead was the real challenge as now there was no one I knew I could turn to. From then onwards, I was in the wilderness. That evening I found sleep on the doorstep of Maclear town despite the noise from the neighbourhood. I wanted to see the town in the early morning because I might not see it again for a long time. Funnily enough, the town was part of South Africa, so I had to prepare myself psychologically to be reminded of the realities of being black in apartheid South Africa. After that it would be Mount Fletcher – a town falling under Transkei.

CHAPTER 9

As I entered the town on that Tuesday morning, I saw the road sign directing one to the well-tarred road to Mount Fletcher, but some adventurous vein in me took over: I was not going to take the clear open road, but would take the appealing route through town heading to Rhodes. Little did I know that it was leading me to the Drakensberg by way of one of the highest passes in South Africa – Naudé's Nek.

Adventure – all credit to it – is without any catches, but it is with expectation of hardship ... and more. It is the 'and more' part that entices most of us to risk our lives. What was on my mind as I turned my back to the town was that this would be the last time I was in the region. Some time previously my father had been working at Qhips's grandfather's farm. He had been away longer than we had anticipated, and my mother had been worried. I had gone to find out from the Wentzels in town, as they had a shop in Mthatha. They assured me that father was at the farm and was well; if I so wished, I could join him there. I had then told my mother who gave me the green light. The following day I jumped at the opportunity and hopped on the van to Maclear.

The area was good for sheep farming. Cheese and other dairy products were also produced. The Wentzels' farm was enormous: fields stretching to the horizon; cattle numbering hundreds to thousands; sheep, goats and geese mingling with each other; and the farm workers always busy with something. It was quite clear that old man Wentzel was wealthy and what puzzled me was how he had come to serve as a policeman during his time in Mthatha. He and his wife, who we called Nomacuntsu – the stingy one – had at the time owned a farm outside Mthatha. But they were down-to-earth folks putting hard work ahead of anything else. After the 'independence' of Transkei, the whole Wentzel clan returned to Maclear.

I was recalling the fact that I had found my father busy upholstering every couch on the farm when I heard the sound of an approaching vehicle behind me. It was a long-wheel-based van and I instinctively hitched a ride. It came to a screeching halt just metres from me. I ran to it and jumped onto the back where a black man was sitting. At the wheel was a young white driver alongside whom sat an Alsatian dog that kept its head protruding through the open window for the best part of the journey. Just as the black farm worker knew his seat was at the back of the van, these farm owners' dogs knew that the passenger seat at the front was traditionally theirs – at the sound of the van revving, they automatically jumped in without being called.

I hadn't asked the driver where he was headed to, and he hadn't asked me either. As the van resumed its journey at an alarming speed, I turned to look at my fellow black brother. He was looking at me as though he was trying to remember where he had last seen me. He then said, 'I hope you have not escaped from your farm workplace because once we get to the farm and they discover you have deserted your duties on your farm, you are in for a very severe beating.' Then he turned his face and looked to the front.

I was not nonplussed by those utterances; serfdom still existed in South Africa, although it might not have been institutionalised. What was worse was we black people accepted it as something normal, while our white counterparts believed the stereotype of a black person as dishonest, lazy and thieving. Was it the gush of air into my eyes that was making them water as we sped along, or some emotion getting the better of me, or both? I didn't know!

After fifteen to twenty minutes the van stopped at a turn to the left. Apparently, that was the road to the driver's farm, so I jumped off and bowed, mumbling my gratitude in Afrikaans. He took off at the same high speed while I continued on my path.

CHAPTER 10

For the past two days I had been aware of the upward climb that had been the main feature of the local topography. My pace slowed drastically due to the high altitude and my exhaustion. The biome was rugged and dry. It had not yet recovered from the winter season although there were patches of green here and there between the flat, spreading thorny plants and small bushes. The tussock grass, standing up to a metre high, was still fawn in colour and rustled in the sporadic wind. The panoramic scenery inspired wonder, fear and respect. And the road? That gravel road was only for strong four-by-fours and hikers tough at heart.

The sun set, but I moved on; I would stop only when I was sure that sleep was imminent and I would wake up naturally from my slumbers and move on, although sluggishly at first.

That Wednesday early morning, I had not walked far when a jogger appeared from around a bend – all alone. She was young, lean and blonde. There must have been a farm or holiday accommodation around. The girl flashed me a smile. I continued for a while, expecting to see a settlement or something, but nothing could have prepared me for the sight a few hours up the road …

Imagine reaching a summit and the road turns right and you find there's a deep gorge in front of the curve out of which rise mountains whose peaks, from my position, were way down below – a canyon yawning at my feet! Those mountains, forming a range of their own, rose in the distance to fuse with the clouds as they reached the horizon, or maybe Lesotho. The Drakensberg mountain range at its best, be it summer or winter, can be breathtaking and Naudé's Nek, though challenging, made my detour worthwhile.

I didn't need to see anything better after viewing that awe-inspiring scene and my curiosity was more than fulfilled. Suddenly, I was rejuvenated and it was with added fervour that I diverted from the road leading to Rhodes and turned towards the south east, thus turning my back on the Drakensberg range. I was still in unfamiliar territory, still within the range, but somehow I found a footpath leading me away, hopefully to some human settlement. It was evident the path had long been established but had not recently been used. The fact that the grass was knee high meant that there had been no veld fires during the winter.

I was obsessed with covering some valuable distance before sunset. The path led me uphill and downhill, or around a mountain, then suddenly, on a mountain top, there was mist so thick it turned to a precipitation of flaky drizzle. Fortunately, I had collected some kindling along the way for a night's fire, as I had been doing all the previous days. I looked around for some shelter among the many rocks, got my fire going and then I saw it – a chestnut horse.

It was by no means my Pegasus to fly me to my chosen destination, but maybe a stray horse, maybe in unfamiliar terrain just like me. The horse snorted and stomped the ground repeatedly without intending to move from its spot. Once it looked my way, yet it stayed put. I gazed at it in wonder. Well, a horse to keep me company and me to keep it company was not a bad idea at all. Then it became dark, so I couldn't tell whether it was there or not.

Thursday morning was warm, and the sky an ultramarine blue. The drizzle of the previous evening had left the rocks wet and they glistened in the sunlight. I looked around for my equine friend, but he was gone. The beautiful world around me was begging me to stay longer but, just like my missing horse, I had to go.

Soon I found myself descending to the small town of Mount Fletcher. I could not help thinking that had I not made the detour towards Naudé's Nek, I could long have been past the town. The well-tarred road from Maclear now proceeded towards Matatiele.

Being in Mount Fletcher meant that I was again in Transkei territory. Villages along the way were basically like those of the other Transkei towns – unpolluted by garbage, with a scanty male population due to the migratory labour system in the mines – but the houses were built of stone. Along that route to Matatiele the Drakensberg can be seen, a formidable background in the distance to the left of the road. There were also villages and expansive fields to the right. Later in the afternoon I saw a shed out in a field and decided I was not going any further – I was going to sleep under that cover till Friday morning.

On the Friday afternoon, for the first time, I slept at the village headman's place. The rain that day had forced me to run for cover to the nearest house. It is an African tradition to welcome anyone running from the rain; even fierce dogs make an exception in such cases. One enters the hut or house without being expected to explain or answer questions. There might be vessels strewn around to catch rainwater if the roof was leaking. After the rain, one may leave, but in my case I was advised to go to the headman's place as he insisted that each and every one in need of a place to sleep be referred to him. He explained to me, 'Times have changed. We are not far from the Lesotho border and rustlers and criminals from that side are pestering us. As a result, we reserve for ourselves the right of strangers to wander around our villages.'

To the question of where I was going, I said I was attending my sister's wedding in Lesotho and would be back after two weeks. I felt I didn't have to tell him the truth as that was bound to complicate matters. For the first time in days I slept in a warm bed.

On Saturday morning, after a wash and breakfast, I strolled to Matatiele town. The first thing that struck me was the presence of a bus from Lesotho bringing people to buy goods in Matatiele. On entering the town, I saw a sign showing the direction to Qacha's Nek – my intended destination.

There was no need to delay, so I was on my way towards Lesotho. The road was not tarred. Then it rained. I ran to the nearest shelter, which was a compound for construction workers. The man I found in the first steel hut was standing in the doorway, but he let me in, showing me where to sit. From the beads he was wearing, I could see he was a traditional healer. He had some powder, or something like it, on his palm, which he blew towards the heavens while mumbling some words. The urban legend is that these healers have powers to cause death by lightning. Sometimes, the legend continues, they test each other's powers by sending lightning to kill another. Quite a fatal game they play, if you ask me.

When the thunderstorm was over, he turned to me and said, 'You will reach Lesotho safely tonight.' That shocked me because I hadn't said a word to the man about going to Lesotho. I nodded in disbelief at his psychic powers and left.

The road thence to Lesotho ascended progressively. Those majestic mountains towering high and scratching the sky dwarfed everything around them. It was midday and some Lesotho cars were already returning home.

It was late in the afternoon when I reached the foot of those mountains and the Lesotho bus passed me. I was now about to enter life in another country, and I couldn't help reflecting on my past in South Africa. I had left my dear family behind without notifying them and was looking forward to forming new relationships, new friendships, and being part of the ANC family. This lay beyond the border that I was going to cross that night.

It was the anticipation of being of service to the entire cause of liberation that warmed my heart. I felt a surge of joy and pride in the will that had brought me that far. I was now on the last lap of my journey, but I needed to be extra careful approaching the border because I was not in possession of a passport.

It was now dark, and I was still negotiating the road zigzagging up that mountain. My tired eyes closed and that brought flashbacks: flashbacks of dogs baying for my blood; flashbacks of villages with thatched rondavel doors all facing east – the source of light – with charms on their rooftops to ward off lightning; the deep gorge in Naudé's Nek; my equine friend on the mountain top; and then …

It was as I turned a bend that I felt light on my eyes. It was the light from the border gate some two or three hundred metres ahead of me. I sprang to life – it was now or never! There was a fence around the offices, but I could see where I could circumvent it, provided there was no other obstacle. My best bet was to keep under cover of the darkness further down on my right. When I got there, something told me to turn on my torch. In front of me was a dangerous cliff – one step forward would have been my last move to a certain death. A whiff of cold air struck my face, which made me stiffen and back away feverishly. I tried to calm myself down and summoned all my resourcefulness to help me find my way to the other side.

A dog's bark from the premises of the offices meant that it had spotted me, but it was chained and those on duty must have thought it was barking because of the cold. Then I crawled along the rock-hard surface of the ground until I made it safely into Lesotho – just as the psychic traditional healer had foretold.

On Sunday morning, 2 November 1980, I woke up inside Lesotho. The rocks around me were dripping clean, clear water into the stream below. I descended the rocky mountain, trying to find the road from the border post to lead me to any human settlement.

The way I got into Lesotho was the same desperate and unlawful way many Lesotho citizens reached South Africa. Their reasons were economic while mine were political. For us South Africans, Lesotho provided a refuge from our political woes, while for them South Africa was an answer to their unemployment. That Lesotho was a free country within the boundaries of South Africa illustrated the bizarre nature of a colonised and fragmented Africa – our common home.

I was still thinking in that vein when somewhere on my far right I saw a flag flapping. It loomed above the trees and the building close to it, and I assumed there was a police station there. I had flirted with danger in the past seven days which had brought out the wild and adventurous element in me, but now I felt I deserved a good rest and time to unwind. And what better people to help me achieve this than the police?

It was indeed a police station and the police heard me out as I told my story and my aim of being a political refugee. They said I would get assistance from relevant people the following morning. I slept that night on a bench and that was to be the pattern till I left for Maseru two weeks later.

Qacha's Nek has some bilingual people – adept in both isiXhosa and seSotho – because of their proximity to Transkei. The general dress code is the traditional Basotho blanket, which does not come cheaply, as some are imported from overseas. Houses are built of stone carved to shapes and sizes that produce buildings of superlative beauty.

The people of Lesotho are peace-loving. The crime rate was very low compared to South Africa, and as a result the police station wasn't that busy. Their greatest challenge was cross-border stock theft, which was rampant at that time. They had a special unit dealing effectively with tracking down the culprits – the Lesotho Mounted Police. Other crimes were diamond and marijuana smuggling. Apart from those serious crimes, theft and assault were met with what seemed to me a curious response: if the complainant came to report that so-and-so had attacked them, the police would ask the complainant why they hadn't brought the suspect along. So, from time to time, two people – the complainant with the defendant in tow – would come to the police station for the former to open a case against the latter.

On 15 November I boarded a flight to Maseru in a Cessna from an aerodrome nearby. The reason given for the delay in transporting me to Maseru was that it took days by road through the mountainous country. I was flying for the first time in my life. That's life: one day you are down crawling, then the next you are flying over mountain ranges. Those splendid views of the Mountain Kingdom – as Lesotho is commonly known – from the sky reminded me of the view at Naudé's Nek, only this time I could see maize and wheat fields on the mountain tops. They resembled tablecloths or blanket coverings. Surely, it was extremely arduous for any vehicle to traverse the roads down there.

I arrived at Maseru airport at midday. After getting directions to the police station, I took my time going there as I was admiring my new setting. I spent the night at the police station, but in the morning I was lucky to meet two ANC members who took me to the ANC refugee arrival centre at New Europa, a suburb nearby. I was warmly welcomed and, on that day, 16 November 1980, I joined the ANC.

CHAPTER 11

We called the place we were in 'camp', though it was a normal house with three bedrooms where we slept, as well as a kitchen and a large, open living area where we often held meetings. Not many people were living there as the arrangement was that once one was declared a refugee under the auspices of the UN, one should make space for new arrivals.

The interior of the 'camp' belied the conventional exterior of the house as it resembled a gallery with pictures and posters hanging on all the walls. For the first time, I saw the banned photos of our leaders, like the then president of the ANC and commander-in-chief of MK, Oliver Reginald Tambo, as well as Nelson Mandela, Walter Sisulu and Elias Motsoaledi; the poster of all the Rivonia Trialists; the Freedom Charter; a photo of Solomon Mahlangu who was hanged in 1979. The colours of the ANC – black, green and gold – adorned every available space. There were shelves with books, booklets, pamphlets and journals like the ANC's *Sechaba* and the South African Communist Party's (SACP's) *African Communist* as well as *World Marxist Review*.

This impressive scenario was enough for any new arrival to be inspired to learn more about our struggle. The word 'comrade' preceding everyone's name created a benign atmosphere. When we spontaneously broke into those revolutionary songs I had heard on Radio Freedom back home, I felt spiritually revived and completely at home with my ANC family.

Political discussions were held twice a week and conducted by a visiting 'senior' comrade, or by one friendly resident I came to know as Tito Mboweni. Now, here was a guy who was always happy to help anyone with his favourite things – politics and cooking. Among many things, he taught me how to prepare porridge since, according to the camp chores, each and every one of us had their turn to cook in groups of two. A homebody to some extent, Tito was the embodiment of the camp, with a certain amount of responsibility even though he was relatively new in exile.

On Monday 17 November I embarked on the official process of being declared a refugee because I had not undergone the whole procedure while I was at Qacha's Nek. So, on 1 December 1980, I received the initial sum of R30 from the UN, which was issued by the offices of the Lesotho Department of the Interior. In the ensuing months it would be R20.

It was at the Interior Department offices where my first encounters with MK trained guerrillas took place, but the three who frequented the 'camp' used combat names: Ten-Ten, Walk Tall and Afrika. When outside Lesotho, Afrika had another nom de guerre – Oscar Sizwe – but his real name was Sipho Malcolm Phungulwa. The trio's visits boosted our morale and, merely because of their presence, we felt that we were already close to victory. Their confidence was infectious and impressive. Little did I know at that time how deeply Sipho Phungulwa's fate and mine would later be intertwined. What I did know back then was that he was the personal bodyguard of Chris Hani, the most powerful ANC member in Lesotho.

In January 1981, I settled at Lower Seoli with Bowen Hans, 'Ntakana' May and 'Banana' Thomas, all from Mdantsane, outside East London. It was the insufficient money for rent and groceries that led us to stay together. It was then that Sipho Phungulwa's visits became regular. In actual fact, it was because he was in love with Ntakana's sister, Noxolo May, who had arrived in exile earlier in 1980. By that time Noxolo was heavily pregnant with Sipho's child. She and her friend Momo rented a room not far from us. When she ultimately gave birth to a baby girl, Nomawethu, early in 1981, we all joined in welcoming the new arrival to the world of exile. She was a special gift to us all and had the potential to be the catalyst that might knit the May and Phungulwa families together.

We were not the only ones facing a shortage of money; there were many others like us all around Maseru's locations. We met for our regular political discussions at each other's places and could see for ourselves that lack of food was a common problem. Some would approach the 'senior comrades' for assistance, just to sustain us till the end of the month. It never crossed our minds why the 'senior comrades', unlike us, always had plenty. One of these was Chris Hani. Some untrained comrades like us were accommodated in the house Hani rented. Fortunately for them, they didn't pay rent or buy groceries. They claimed they had come into exile through contacts, unlike us. The UN money they received could be spent any way they liked. We regarded this with humour, told each other that we were not yet trusted, and laughed it off.

Waiting to be transited to Angola for training proved lengthy because of the disadvantage of having to fly over South Africa from Lesotho. There were intervals of six months between groups leaving the country. It was therefore during this time that political awareness was inculcated in us new members. It was imperative that we be conscious of the fact that we were, first and foremost, politicians, then soldiers. This was emphasised and our minds were preoccupied with the notion that we were not like any ordinary soldier who lacked political clarity of the principles, strategy and tactics of his organisation. Ours was a just war against a system that was universally known as a crime against humanity.

Our classes were presided over by a 'senior comrade' or anyone adept in a particular subject. Once a week we had news analysis meetings where current developments in our country and the world were discussed. Our sources were newspapers and radio stations based inside South Africa, hence the need to put things in perspective to ensure that we did not fall victim to the regime's propaganda.

On other days we covered South African history from pre-colonial times up to the wars of resistance; the formation of the

South African Native National Congress in 1912 and its history of initially writing petitions and sending deputations to England, up to the formation of the ANC Youth League (ANCYL) in the 1940s, which injected fervour into the organisation and led to the adoption of the Programme of Action; then the Freedom Charter in 1955; and then the transition to armed struggle, which saw the birth of MK in 1961.

After covering South African history, we reviewed socio-economic formations: the primitive communal system, slavery, feudalism, capitalism and the first stage of communism – socialism. Our political programme also featured Charles Darwin's theory of evolution of humankind. Inevitably, that led most of us to start questioning the biblical theory that Adam and Eve were the first people created by God. Already conditions were conducive for us to be introduced to Marxism-Leninism, the philosophy of the ANC's ally, the SACP.

I feel compelled to put things into perspective here. The Sharpeville massacre occurred on 21 March 1960 when members of the PAC protested against the pass laws by exposing themselves to arrest by deliberately not carrying the passes required only of Africans. It was supposed to be a peaceful protest, and no one could have anticipated that more than 200 people would be killed or injured by a heavy contingent of police on that day. The banning of both the ANC and the PAC that ensued that same year left the two organisations in limbo. The ANC was faced with the serious problem of overthrowing a murderous regime, given that it was founded on non-violent protest. The close ties with the SACP could only lead to seeking help from the Eastern Bloc; initially it was China under Mao Zedong that trained the first MK detachment militarily, but after the Sino-Soviet dispute of 1963, no further training took place there. The ANC then made a move towards the Communist Party of the Soviet Union (CPSU) whose policy was Marxism-Leninism.

Marxist-Leninist philosophy believes that the working class has nothing to lose but its chains. The workers, or the proletariat, are supposed to rule in a revolutionary dictatorship leading to a future classless society, in which all means of production is in the hands of the people. Only then would poverty, homelessness and all the ills we experience under capitalism perish. Everyone would benefit from the labour and the scientific and technological advances of humankind. It must be emphasised, however, that Marxism-Leninism reserved the right for each country to align its uniqueness to the ultimate liberation of its working class. In the South African situation, it was essential to liberate the most oppressed section of the population – the black people – as a step towards the socialist revolution and the workers' dictatorship. It was with this understanding that the SACP and the trade union federation, the South African Congress of Trade Unions (SACTU), aligned themselves with the ANC for it to be at the forefront of the liberation struggle to ensure the realisation of the people's objectives as reflected in the Freedom Charter.

Arming ourselves politically worked well in many ways: we could defend the policies of the ANC and its alliance partners against its detractors, if and when necessary; we would improve our understanding of the organisation; and we became more convinced of the justice of the fight against apartheid using violent means.

In the first instance, we met and argued with our compatriots from other organisations who were critical of the part of the Freedom Charter that said, 'South Africa belongs to all who live in it, black and white.' Their stance was that Africa was for (black) Africans while we countered that our country's status was colonialism of a special type, whereby the colonialist was not in a foreign country, but living side by side with the colonised. In that process of exchange of ideas between ourselves on one side and members of the PAC, the Black Consciousness Movement (BCM) and the Azanian People's Organisation (Azapo) on the other, many left their organisations for the ANC, and vice versa.

In the second instance, we needed to reach a certain level of political clarity so that we could independently chart the way forward without relying on others to show us the way. Little did we know then that there would come a time when our exercising this right meant we could be on the wrong side, because at that time no one expected any foul play from our beloved leaders.

We were so dedicated that one could wake anyone up in the small hours of the night and ask them to recite the preamble of the Freedom Charter backwards, if they so liked, and they would do so with ease. Nothing could shake our conviction in the justice of the fight against apartheid. In retrospect, that conviction in the justness of our cause was vital, given the paradigm shift towards being a revolutionary hailing Marxism-Leninism and communism. It was a time when there was no middle road: it was the era of the Cold War, when the enemy of my enemy was my friend, and the friend of my enemy was my enemy. It was as simple as that and as a result it was imperative always to be seen to be toeing the line.

There were also security issues concerning the local threat to the stability of Lesotho. Ntsu Mokhetle's Basutoland Congress Party (BCP) was involved in sporadic terrorist attacks. It was alleged that the operatives had training and backing from the South African regime. Surrounded on all sides by South Africa, it was wise always to be on the alert – there had been an attempted assassination of Chris Hani by one of Mokhetle's men. What was mind-boggling was that Mokhetle had once been on the side of the progressives such as the ANC, but after the Basutoland National Party (BNP), led by Leabua Jonathan, refused to hand over power after losing the elections, Mokhetle had to flee to South Africa from the persecution that followed. And in South Africa he got the backing of the Boers while the dictator Leabua Jonathan endeared himself to the ANC, which soon took advantage of that and built good relations with the enemy of its former ally.

Funny how things can turn on their head in politics!

CHAPTER 12

In January 1981, after seeing others receive letters from home at the Christian Council in town, I decided to write home and tell my family of my whereabouts.

I told my parents that they should not worry about me as I was well; that I had joined the ANC and was soon to leave for another country; and that I loved them, but most importantly they should burn the letter and tell no one I had written. They replied and said they were relieved. After I had left without notifying them, they had gone to the police to report me missing, but after two days the police had come and ransacked my outside room and taken all my drawings, sketchbooks and books and never returned them. My parents thus did not pursue their search for me for fear of possible reprisals from the police.

In that letter, Mother enclosed two R20 notes. She added that she hoped I had not left South Africa out of anger over her sending me to that psychiatric hospital, saying she had had to do it to protect me; in other words, she had known that I wasn't insane.

I was overjoyed that my family and I had communicated. I shared that money with the three comrades I was staying with.

Around March that year, two batches of comrades left Lesotho for school and military training in Tanzania and Angola respectively. We who were left behind had to soldier on for another six months or so. By that time, we had been joined by two Botha brothers and Simphiwe 'Tekere' Joka. These three and a fourth comrade were frustrated by having to remain behind. They said they regretted crossing to Lesotho and wished they had decided to go to Swaziland instead. They even went to Chris Hani with their plan of leaving for Swaziland, which Hani warned them against, although without raising any red flags. They insisted and left.

When we were settled in our new place at Qoaling location, we came up with a plan. We four – Hans, May, Thomas and I – decided that at the paypoint at the end of the month we would impersonate the four who had left and receive their money, as it would be there for the taking. We only had to get there early and start by collecting their money and then return later in the day for the money that was rightfully ours.

It worked like a wonder and we kept it as our secret, though we were ready to share the money with others. Things were so hard that we couldn't be exclusive. Some comrades' applications for political asylum were rejected by a certain Mr Mokhele at the Interior Department. He just took an arbitrary dislike to an individual and that person's future in Lesotho hung in the balance. Mokhele was not averse to humiliating a wannabe refugee in front of our senior comrades on pay day by saying to that person, 'Are you still here in Lesotho? I don't want to see your face around here! Hear me!' What was concerning was that there would be no response from our senior comrades intervening on behalf of the beleaguered comrade. It was a grim situation because the comrade in question would not be able to go and stay at the 'camp' because Mokhele's house was next door. That meant we would take them in with us and share whatever we had.

We not only asked for food from our senior comrades, but we also discovered that the Christian Council was of great help financially, though in a form of issuing a loan. So we went there for a loan using an assumed name and never paid back the money.

One day a certain Mrs Hashe arrived in Lesotho from Sipho Phungulwa's hometown of Port Elizabeth. She was a famous activist in political and civil circles. She had come to visit her 'children', as she regarded all of us, though she had one of her own who was with us in Maseru.

Now Mrs Hashe became this concerned parent when she heard

that Noxolo was feeling 'stuck' because of the baby, as she had intended to further her studies at Solomon Mahlangu Freedom College (SOMAFCO) in Tanzania in March that year. After some deliberation, Mrs Hashe, Noxolo and Sipho came to a decision to resolve the situation: Mrs Hashe was to return to Port Elizabeth with baby Nomawethu and hand her to Sipho's family. Indeed, Nomawethu was smuggled successfully into the country, and life went on. Noxolo left for SOMAFCO; Sipho was assured that the baby was with his family, and everyone was happy.

The cycle continued of each refugee receiving R20, pooling it together for rent and groceries, and inevitably approaching other people for help in the last half of the month. One day, some comrades had approached senior comrade Thozamile Botha, who was one of the regular benefactors during such crises. Apparently, Botha had been to the ANC headquarters in Lusaka around March 1981 and had been given around one million rand for the Lesotho region; in other words, for all of us. He had then referred the comrades to Hani for help.

To him it seemed as simple a solution as that, but for those comrades it was a giant step. They decided to call us all to a meeting where they told us what Botha had told them. It was such sensitive information that we had to tread carefully lest we be mistaken for insinuating that Hani was discriminating against one section in favour of another. Ultimately, a delegation was chosen to meet Hani, but before it could even take place, Hani got wind of the developments. That same day we were hunted down.

I had left soon after the meeting for our place in Qoaling, but unfortunately May and Thomas had remained behind. (Hans was elsewhere.) Unaware of any imminent threat, I was snuggled in bed reading the SACP journal, *The African Communist*, when I heard a knock on the door. It was cold that early evening and I did not leave the bed, only saying, 'Come in.' Two men I had never seen before entered the room and came towards me. Above me was a portrait of Steve Biko, which I had made at the request of a fellow comrade. Looking at the portrait, these men asked me if I had anything to do with the BCM or PAC to which I answered, 'No, but there are people I know from home who are in the PAC and BCM.'

They then went outside where they had a tête-à-tête – or were there more people out there? I still lay motionless in bed. They then re-entered with Thomas and May following them. All they said was, 'They will tell you what befell them for trying to be smart.' Then they left.

When I saw their swollen faces, I jumped out of bed, but I was utterly shocked when they showed me their backs and behinds full of welts. I was both furious and terrified – who commits such savagery towards another comrade? They related how they were rounded up after I had left, bundled into a waiting Kombi and taken to a cemetery not far away. That was where the beatings took place. Those who beat them were obviously trained cadres, but they were unknown to them.

I did not feel like hearing much of that sad story, and even less like reading more of that journal. I was disheartened that there was absolutely nothing I could do about the situation. I looked at the portrait of Biko and decided to take it down. As it was, I did not see any threat from the BCM. To my understanding, the BCM argued mainly for black people to be proud of themselves; to liberate themselves mentally from the shackles of inferiority and start doing things for themselves. This, and the historic mission of the ANC to liberate the black people, did not seem contradictory. But it was safer to toe the line than antagonise those in authority.

Nobody really knows what they did to Thozamile Botha, but what I know is that no one ever again went to ask for assistance of any kind from him or any other senior comrade.

CHAPTER 13

What followed was a period of tension and uncertainty about whether there would be any further backlash. Around May 1981 I was approached by two members of SACTU who had seen my sketchbook where I had cartoons depicting the conditions of slavery under which our people worked in South Africa. The apartheid regime was planning to celebrate twenty years of independence from Britain since the declaration of the Republic, and I had a cartoon showing PW Botha et al cutting cake on a stage while the impoverished black majority were crying for food. Those cartoons made SACTU members see that there was something special about me. It is heart-warming when people find out there's more to me than just my nice big eyes. In that first meeting they suggested that I join SACTU as I knew the basic conditions of the capitalist system. I was convinced when one said, 'This ANC-led struggle is just a bourgeois democratic revolution whereby workers' rights are not at all guaranteed. We need people like you who will push the struggle to the next level, which is wresting power from the capitalists. It will only be then that we can talk of economic freedom.'

Wow! Now who would counter such eloquence? There and then, I was going to give all of myself to the noble and ultimate cause of revolution after having recognised that black people's plight had been dictated by the ruling capitalist class since the discovery of diamonds and gold in South Africa. I felt privileged to be recruited to SACTU since it was obvious that I was only one step away from being recruited to the SACP. At the time nobody just volunteered to join SACTU and the SACP. One was recruited because of certain qualities and a certain level of political understanding that they had identified.

What followed was a series of discussions that I had to incorporate within the ANC discussions. We were about seven recruits being instructed in the beautiful, though bloody, history of trade unionism and how SACTU came about in 1955. Among those in the SACTU meetings were Vusi Pikoli, Sizwe Kondile, Thozi Majola and Phaki Ximiya. Then Marxist-Leninist philosophy was included in our lectures. What was evident was that we were lauding the CPSU for paving the way forward for the proletariat. One SACTU comrade said: 'If you want to know how strong a communist party is, look at its relationship with the CPSU.' It was clear we had a clean bill of health regarding our ever-convivial relationship with the CPSU. Yes, there was a thin line between a radical communist party and a not-so-radical communist party even within the communist countries.

What exacerbated the previously mentioned tension was the disappearance of Kondile with Chris Hani's car. He had been kept busy most of the time with the demanding job of being a driver for the ANC. The impact of his disappearance was unbelievable: the emphasis on our safety and security could not be overstated. That there were enemy agents among us was a main concern and it was used against us to justify our leaders' suspicions towards some of us. (Decades later it was revealed to the Truth and Reconciliation Commission (TRC) that Sizwe Kondile had actually been abducted and brutally murdered by the South African security forces.)

A few months later, it was a great relief to hear of positive developments: we were at last to be leaving Lesotho. Mokhele from the Interior Department had to make a nuisance of himself, if only for the last time. We were to sign some papers permitting us to leave for 'furthering our studies at Solomon Mahlangu Freedom College'. Of course, that was untrue – we were off to Angola for military training, but we could not declare that openly, although the Lesotho government knew. I remember Mokhele dropping his pen on the document he had to sign, stretching back in his chair, looking me straight in the eye and saying, 'So, you want to kill the Boers?' I pretended I didn't know what he was on about and said, 'Sir, I'm intending to further my …'

'Hey! Stop! Stop right there! Do you think I'm a fool?' He stood up and paced up and down his office. 'I'm warning you,' he said, 'just like I'm warning every one of you: never take our hospitality for granted because you'll remember it someday when you are in Angola, Tanzania or Russia. We know where you are going.' Then he sat down and signed the document. I had been standing all the time and not offered a seat – that's 'hospitality', Mokhele style.

Leaving Lesotho on Friday, 4 September 1981, was a great relief for most of us. Even though I didn't know the exact conditions in wherever we were headed for, the fact that I was getting closer to my dream of military training was an overwhelming feeling. There were a lot of things I no longer needed to worry about. To some extent I felt that things were bound to be better anywhere else than in Lesotho.

As the plane left Maseru behind and we were flying over South African territory, I assured myself that there was hope for my country once the ANC came to power. The Freedom Charter, although heralding a bourgeois democracy, would bring previously unheard-of radical change to my nation. The migratory labour system would end, and workers would no longer stay in filthy hostels. The houses built by the ANC would be better and bigger than the 'matchboxes' built by the apartheid system. Education would be of world standard. The economic wealth of the country would be evenly distributed, and the minerals would no longer be processed overseas and sold back to us at exorbitant prices.

These were some of the promises the ANC was supposed to keep. Coupled with the workers' demands as espoused by SACTU and SACP, they plainly meant we were headed for a grand victory over poverty, dispossession of land and exploitation. We were not to be like other countries in the world where there was neo-colonialism – when people attained mere political power while the former colonisers still enjoyed economic dominance and exerted political pressure to toe a line set by the ruling party or government.

Oh yes! Our ANC was wise enough not to fall into that trap and betray the people. Well, those were my thoughts as the plane hovered over South Africa. It felt as though it was suspended there forever, and I couldn't wait for it to land in Mozambique en route to Angola.

PART THREE
MILITARY TRAINING AND THE EASTERN FRONT

1984 FAPLA Raid on MK Camp.

CHAPTER 14

Fortunately, we didn't stay long in Mozambique. Some among us were going to Morogoro in Tanzania to further their studies at SOMAFCO, while we were headed for Angola for military training.

It is worth noting here that there was a certain Evergreen Mabaso (MK name) who was doing a splendid job in the Matola residence where we stayed. He was encouraging those going to SOMAFCO to change their minds and join MK, and he was succeeding. Many who had left earlier than us had dropped their initial plans and opted to join MK. Evergreen would be surrounded by all and sundry as he related captivating stories of life in the army. He had been in the then Rhodesia fighting alongside the Zimbabwe People's Revolutionary Army (ZIPRA) forces of the Zimbabwe African People's Union (ZAPU) just before Zimbabwe won its independence in 1980. Wishing to be part of the liberation forces at a time when it mattered was what won everyone over.

The residence in Matola had been the target of a military raid by a South African army commando on 30 June 1981, and fifteen people had died. It was no wonder that everyone appreciated the need to be extra cautious and serious about observing security measures. Besides, for the first time in our lives, we were living according to a strict routine: waking up at a certain time, exercising, making our beds, washing, eating breakfast and cleaning the yard.

After fixing our passports and using combat names – mine was Chauke Mange – we boarded a Mozambique Airlines plane to Lusaka where we were to connect with a flight to Angola. We had all settled in our seats, when ANC President OR Tambo came in with his entourage. Wow! This was beginning to look like a fairy tale! How excited we recruits were! Once we landed in Lusaka, we could not wait to shake his hand. He was also happy for us in our ambition to join and serve in the revolution. But he remained in Lusaka.

The Angolan Airlines plane finally arrived and it was not long before we were in Luanda where we slept in a transit camp called Viana, just outside the city. Viana served as both arrival and departure point between the camps, and for those either going to or returning from abroad. It also had its own routine by which we had to abide, just as in Matola, though this time we would jog in the big open space around the camp. This type of jogging was called toyi-toyi. It was introduced to MK by our comrades who had been with the ZIPRA forces. For us recruits the whole experience was fascinating and a welcome change.

In Viana Camp there were people one could not miss. First up was someone I assume must have been the youngest ANC member in the region. Her name was Puna – Comrade Dimakatso's sweet little daughter of around three years old. She was everyone's darling as she unfailingly took her position next to anyone addressing us, making an announcement from the top of the stairs while flashing us a smile.

Next up were the members of the Amandla Cultural Ensemble – sometimes called Kunjundu. This ensemble played an important role in promoting our struggle for democracy in South Africa during its world tours, while also canvassing for material and financial support for the ANC.

Also in that camp was the ANC National Commissar, Andrew Masondo. When every other leader was deployed in Lusaka or, better still, in London, Europe and elsewhere, Masondo was comfortable staying in the camps. His visibility and presence around the camp could be interpreted as him being accessible to us, though he could be unsettling and overbearing at times when he ambushed us with questions related to the Freedom Charter, or when dispensing his Marxist philosophical wisdom. Now, to anyone this was a man to look up to as his title of National Commissar of the ANC suggested – he was entrusted with the noble task of projecting and protecting the ANC. One thing for sure was that he was an academic noted for his speciality in mathematics – which he had taught at the University of Fort Hare – and also for having been a prisoner on Robben Island, where he served thirteen years.

Now that he was with new recruits like us, it was only natural to pay attention to every word he said. Being a sociable person himself, it was not difficult to achieve this end, more especially given his antics like sprinting 100 metres faster than most of us. Such traits endeared him to many younger female comrades who could not resist his friendly disposition.

His favourite statements were:
- When we send some of you to engage the enemy, they come back saying they did not see the target.
- Telling the truth at the wrong time and place, to the wrong people, does not constitute the truth.
- Support the ANC, whether it is right or wrong.
- I was a bit forward and ill-disciplined on Robben Island, so that Nelson Mandela gave me a hot clap.

I told myself that in due time all those utterances would make sense to me.

After two weeks at Viana we were transferred to a camp in Camalundi, in the Malanje province. The camp's name was Hoji-ya-Henda – a folk hero and guerrilla of the People's Armed Forces of Liberation of Angola (FAPLA) who was killed during the struggle for the liberation of Angola. The camp had formal structures and had previously been used by Cuban soldiers.

There was a detachment of trainees that was midway through its course. Some of them were those who had left us in Lesotho in March. It was interesting to find that those who had left for Swaziland to catch up with this training group were not there and nobody knew of their whereabouts.

We commenced our general course on 17 December 1981, just

a day after we had celebrated the formation of MK. Some of us were feeling a bit groggy after the previous night's drinks. Anyway, we made it on that day, and the next, and so on ... Then the camp came down with a malaria epidemic. The course had to be suspended as most people were affected; we even had two fatalities.

I was one of the few who were not affected. Then it was decided that we were to move camp and open a new one in Caculama, also in the Malanje province. It had been a ZIPRA camp before the ZAPU forces returned to Zimbabwe. Whether it was part of MK's long-term plans to go to Caculama or whether it was due to the epidemic, I do not know. What I do know is that when they asked for volunteers to be the vanguard in opening the place, I was one of those who offered their services.

In February 1982 our group of fewer than fifteen set out for Caculama. The road – or rut, to be exact – from the main road from Caculama town to Quela was still distinct, despite not having been used for a long time.

On arrival at the deserted camp we pitched our tents some 100 metres from the nearby stream. Because I wasn't yet fully trained, I was armed only when I was at the guard post at night. The first thing that struck me was that we had set ourselves up for something way beyond us. The place was spooky, footpaths were overgrown, there was hardly a patch not covered by grass, and the once used dwellings were full of creepers, which gave them a dark and haunted look.

After reconnoitring the place and marking our territory, we decided to limit ourselves to the space around our tents. There wasn't much to do during the daytime, but come night time when all was dark, animals became too active for our liking. Maybe it was the human scent in the air that was disturbing them.

On sentry duty at night there were sightings, movements and sounds all around me – sightings of crouching hyenas encroaching on our area, and a rabbit dancing towards the campfire. In this situation one just froze in one position and listened to the potpourri of sounds. I felt like the conductor of a cacophonous orchestra:

the sound of the swarm of mosquitoes like violins out of tune, the herd of buffaloes marching towards the stream while bellowing and blowing their tubas to the accompaniment of the frog choir croaking in the background; my heart thumping in an irregular rhythm and the applause of a troop of baboons far away ... It was just too ghastly to think this was what to expect every night. In retrospect, it was a once-in-a-lifetime privilege.

We had been there for about eight days when we were joined by the rest of the camp, other than those who were about to complete their training. Our training was obviously suspended as we had to make the wilderness habitable. We had to dig our own defence line and make our dugout dwellings, which took time. In the meantime, those on guard duty at night could not help shooting at the slightest movement in the dark, claiming, 'I've never seen such a big baboon in my life!'

Those shootings would lead to a rude awakening of the whole camp, with everyone running to the armoury to get armed and then rushing to the defence line, only to be told 'a baboon' had been sighted by one of the guards. Some nights this happened twice, after which the administration decided that not having a dead animal to produce as evidence would be punishable. Voilà! There were no more shootings to disturb our sleep. Maybe the earlier shootings had been enough to send the animals packing for safer havens, far from humans.

When we had rehabilitated the area and resumed our training, I fell ill with malaria for the first time. It happened when I was about to assume guard duty. I suddenly felt very hot when the weather was relatively cool. I was advised to go to the clinic and excused from guard duty. I had an early night and felt better in the morning, but was nevertheless included among the people with malaria and taken to Malanje Hospital. I thought it was unnecessary, but our clinic staff weren't taking any chances – I hadn't yet recovered.

Indeed, just as I entered the reception at the hospital, I started shaking uncontrollably, my teeth chattering despite the warm weather. I was hospitalised then and there.

After three days in hospital, we were discharged and transferred to our residence in town. Papa Nxele (MK name) was the commander of the residence: a very friendly and kind person who had visited us while we were in hospital. I was still convalescing when I had to return to the camp to continue with my training. At that time, I did not know that Papa would feature again and again in my life.

What I discovered during training was that we who had been in Lesotho did not have a problem with the political curriculum because we had already been through it all. But I must commend the instructors for making the seemingly difficult terminology so easy to use in everyday conversation.

When it came to analysing news and political developments worldwide, we were, of course, biased towards the anti-imperialist, pro-Soviet school of thought. To us, nothing good could come from the capitalist/imperialist bloc except misery and more exploitation of the working class, resulting in the poor getting poorer while the rich got richer. It was, and still is, the limitation of capitalism in addressing social drawbacks that renders it inextricably vulnerable to those purporting to be fighting for the betterment of the human race. Capitalism is at the root of self-enrichment and might use tribalism, narrow nationalism, racism and classism as pillars from which to draw its strength and support, while in essence it serves the individual. That was why we were drawn to the internationalist doctrine of Marxism-Leninism. We from South Africa had seen enough and experienced much humiliation, deprivation, dehumanisation and dispossession as black people, but with the advent of communism on the horizon, we were confident that the destruction of capitalism was inevitable.

There are times when I look back at that time of my life in the ANC and MK as the best ever, but also as its climax because of the power bestowed on every member to voice criticism openly, without fear of reprisals. It was understood that those who loved the organisation would love it enough to tell it when it was wrong, though of course it was not a carte blanche ticket to be anarchic or destructive in one's criticism.

But unfortunately, out of the blue, we were told that the meetings where criticism was expressed had to end. No explanations were given – we just had to accept the declaration as it was, but a certain amount of unease and uncertainty found its way into each of us. We had moved to an era when our wings were clipped, and the disgruntlement was not hard to detect in the majority of the rank and file. What was evident was that the abolition of criticism was contra-democracy.

Of course, in the military there is no democracy – it is a top-down system in which orders are executed without question. Now, those criticism meetings did not question fundamental military norms but were meant to augment the participation in and contribution towards the struggle expected from every member. It was in keeping with what we had been made to believe from the outset: that we were first and foremost politicians.

It became clear that life before that – more especially when we were at Hoji-ya-Henda – had been ideal. Apart from the existence of criticism meetings, there had been an overarching camaraderie founded on the understanding that we were all patriots to be treated on an equal footing with those in the leadership. We ate from the same menu as the camp command, the gap between rank and file and leadership was nominal (the then general secretary of the SACP, Moses Mabhida, mingled with us without qualms) and the security department guys were not menacing. But now the opposite materialised. The administration had the best food and uniforms. The leadership was to be glorified as though they were infallible. And members of the security department now became so estranged from us it was downright unnerving. One felt like a disposable appendage in the whole equation.

CHAPTER 15

If truth be told, these obnoxious and retrogressive developments were harmful to the movement. It was a downward spiral to the detriment of the robust relations among us.

First was the case of Castro (MK name) who was humiliated by having his beard shaved and beaten on suspicion of being an enemy agent. We had known him back in Lesotho as a sculptor and now it was said he was to be taken to a place called Camp 32, 'where enemy agents are rehabilitated'. Some, in undertones, called this Camp Number Four – a name derived from a notorious Johannesburg jail during apartheid times known as The Fort (now Constitution Hill). And from that were derived Spanish, Portuguese and Russian names for the word 'four' i.e. – Quadro, Quatro and Chitiri respectively. Because of the horror stories associated with the place, some even called it Buchenwald.

Another case that followed was that of Brett (or Brat), with the same accusations that were directed at Castro. He, too, was in the group from Lesotho. He was sent to Quatro.

Last was the incarceration of Kofifi (MK name), also a trainee. He had hit his wife, like us a trainee, for cheating on him with another comrade who was a logistics officer. Kofifi was sent to Quatro.

Just as we were about to finish training, Simphiwe Joka, Botha, Boyce, Lux and other comrades from the Swaziland group arrived at Caculama with a group of new trainees. They were wary of talking openly about their unsanctioned journey from Lesotho to Swaziland. It had seemingly gone well until they were taken across the border to Mozambique. There, instead of being taken to

Angola as they had expected, their lives were turned upside down. Leaving Lesotho despite Chris Hani's advice not to do so showed gross indiscipline and nobody knew who they might have contacted on the way from Lesotho to Swaziland. They were treated as enemy spies and taken to a camp in Nampula province in northern Mozambique.

The Nampula camp was deep in the jungle and infested with wildlife. The occupants were MK members who had demanded to fight inside South Africa rather than be returned to Angola. In short, the camp was a prison to punish those who were regarded as dissident or defiant. We could see from their body language that Joka et al were spiritually broken. What they had seen and gone through was traumatic and shocking.

It was then that I remembered that even in Hoji-ya-Henda camp there had been something disturbing and out of place, though we had overlooked it at the time. It was seeing four comrades being treated like pariahs for having been caught in possession of marijuana. They were under guard around the clock; were woken earlier than everyone else to do the toyi-toyi; they ate alone and were not allowed to communicate with anyone. It was bizarre having us go about our business as normally as possible while our comrades were suffering right in front of us.

These worrying developments in parallel with the struggle as a whole meant that each of us had to develop self-protective tactics. These included what we were told every soldier should do: impress the leadership, from the immediate commander to the ANC President and MK Commander-in-Chief, OR Tambo. In that way our life in the army would continue without mishap. We were told that the end justifies the means to attain it, and we had to understand that these things happened in a revolution.

At first glance, this did not seem problematic, even though the actual implementation might not be easy for some, while others might exaggerate in impressing the leadership. As it happened, the latter's over-zealousness tended to make the former look stubborn and thus they became potential prey.

Going with the flow seemed the safest policy as we rounded up our training.

After the commanders' course, our training was completed in August 1982. I was shortlisted in a group that was to go to the Soviet Union for training in the use of a special weapon. Among the sixteen to attend the course were members from other camps who had trained in the June 16 Detachment. But then there was a change of plan – the Russians were coming!

The course was to train us in the use of an anti-air gun called Strela-2M. It's a ground-to-air, portable, heat-seeking missile meant to down any aircraft within a certain altitude. We were to be trained at a camp near the town of Caxito. That camp was for the final preparations of MK combatants meant to be infiltrated into South Africa.

It was a privilege, believe me, to be in that camp and what made us in the group feel special was that we had our secret, out-of-bounds camp within that secret camp. We were told never to tell anyone what we were doing.

We were partially autonomous, though logistically dependent on the main camp. I was made an assistant medico to administer medication to any in our group who fell ill from malaria, or had aches and pains; if those didn't abate, the patient would be admitted to the main camp and attended to by the medico there.

We had up our tents and impromptu kitchen and followed a daily routine. We even started a small vegetable garden. Within two weeks we had turned a wild place around. When the Russian instructor and his interpreter finally arrived, we were very willing and ready.

The course went ahead unhindered, but one could not ignore the alluring sound of the Russian language. It is so expressive and interesting that I developed a certain love for it. We had been used to Russian commands in our march-and-drill introduced by those who had been trained in the USSR. But being face to face with the owners of the language broadened my horizons.

The instructor was a serious type while the interpreter was the opposite. What was intriguing was the way the interpretation of a very long statement would be summed up in one or two sentences. Even the instructor would be amazed by this and ask, '*Chto onu poni mayut?*' (Do they understand?), to which the interpreter would say, '*Da, oni ponimayut ... tra la la.*'

After we had finished the course and revised it, it was time to say '*Davzudanya, tovarichi*' (goodbye, comrades) to our instructor and interpreter. We were now raring to put our training to good use. By that, I mean being deployed inside South Africa as guerrillas to create more problems for the regime, as was the general expectation of everyone in that camp.

We were taken aback when one day the National Commissar, Andrew Masondo, came to our camp. What was surprising was that he was there to stay.

When we were in Viana on our way to Caxito we had become aware of a certain interesting development. In his own interests, Masondo had formed a group of around a dozen armed young men to be his security detail. They were called AmaPionheiro – Pioneers – and they would be found wherever he was. At first, nothing sinister or noxious could be attached to this issue although it seemed unnecessary – that is, until it was clear that we, the general members, were their primary concern.

When Masondo settled in Caxito with his AmaPionheiro, it was not obvious whether or not he had fallen out of favour with the people in and around Luanda. His presence in Caxito was neither productive nor essential for his position as National Commissar. Caxito was completely different from any other camp; we were obsessed with the task of infiltrating South Africa. Most occupants of the camp had been responsible for the MK attacks there. We knew them not only by name, but were personally close to them. Every time they departed to the front, we knew that sooner or later we would hear that a military operation had been carried out. The only snag was that it was the same operatives who were sent each time; I likened Caxito to Hollywood, with them being the stars and the rest of us the extras.

Being in Caxito meant already belonging to an underground

machinery, and it was not long before we discovered that ours was Joe Slovo's. One bright day, Slovo strode solo into our base wearing camouflage uniform. Funnily enough, he had left behind and out of sight whoever he was with. He had only a pistol for self-defence. Well, that is how secret our base was, not even Masondo set foot there.

Joe Slovo's machinery, among others, was held in high esteem. Its reconnaissance and assaults on military targets were precise. There was concern among those infiltrated that it was always wise to be extra cautious when entering the country. Word doing the rounds was that some of our cadres were killed by the South African security forces upon entering the country, not because of negligence or ill-discipline on their side, but because of information leaked to the enemy by our guys in the frontline states – Botswana, Lesotho, Swaziland and Mozambique. The circumstances in which they died or were apprehended pointed in that direction. How does one explain an ambush of insurgents at just the right time and place? Those who took a different route to the one they were told to take tended to avoid being ambushed, but would not evade being called to order when they returned to Angolan camps, where they were branded as ill-disciplined and chided for 'not having seen the target'.

Those who were captured by the South Africa's counter-insurgency units would be taken to Vlakplaas just outside Pretoria and tortured until, under duress, they turned into askaris – former liberation movement combatants – who were then used to track down and kill their former comrades. Being an askari meant, on the one hand, not being trusted by the people at Vlakplaas and, on the other hand, being an enemy of the Revolution. For our people in the frontline states, it meant the possibility of being prime targets of the South African state, as it had obtained sensitive information about our residences and personnel. The forces of the apartheid state were notorious for conducting cross-border raids to countries harbouring us. The South African Defence Force (SADF) had raided Matola suburb in Maputo, Mozambique, in 1981; Maseru in Lesotho, on 9 December 1982, killing 42 people; and carried out an attack in Maputo killing six people on 23 May 1983. They were unstoppable! Obviously the South African government wanted to keep the rising liberation tide as far from the country as possible.

So, with us entering the fray with our anti-aircraft gun, and with Joe Slovo as our machinery commander, chances were that air strikes could be curtailed and the guerrillas' worst foe – the helicopter – would be totally incapacitated.

For a while there was a lull and no one knew what was to follow after the course. So what happened next took us all by surprise. One afternoon in September 1983 we were told to evacuate our camp at Caxito. We had to leave by nightfall, taking everything with us. We managed to put every tent, every item of machinery – I mean *everything* – into the trucks, but were to leave our weapons at the main camp. On arrival in Luanda, the rest of the machinery of our anti-air gun unit was handed to the Angolan military arsenal. We were then taken to Viana Camp just outside the capital.

The camp was abuzz, as all around there was talk that we were going to the Eastern Front in Angola to assist in fighting UNITA[2] rebels – Luta Contra Banditos (LCB). They were a threat to our camps in Malanje province, we were told.

This news was received with enthusiasm as most of us yearned for action and a change from the monotonous routines within the camps. We couldn't wait to show what calibre of soldiers we were, and of course they said this was just a three-month exercise and then we would be deployed inside our own country. So this was to be practical preparation for an onslaught on South Africa in the foreseeable future: just what the people inside our country were waiting for.

---

2 The National Union for the Total Independence (UNITA) had been engaged in a civil war with the ruling Popular Movement for the Liberation of Angola, or MPLA, after Angola gained its independence from Portugal in 1975.

CHAPTER 16

We were armed and without delay we embarked on the journey to Malanje. For my unit from Caxito things couldn't have changed faster. We were woken from a siesta at fifteen hours that day and then at twenty-three hours we left for a battlefield – it was absolutely surreal. We had to overcome tiredness and adjust to the pressing matter at hand – which was war.

We arrived the following day at a place outside Malanje town that was called FAPLA-Mkhonto, since it was where our forces were to merge with the FAPLA forces. There were also People's Liberation Army of Namibia (PLAN) soldiers from the South West Africa People's Organisation (Swapo) in the camp who were preparing to go to Namibia as it would soon be the rainy season, which they made use of for attacking the South African armed forces occupying what was then South West Africa (SWA). These were soldiers who had experienced combat. En route to SWA they had to avoid engagement with UNITA rebels in the south of Angola. They told us how UNITA operated and what to do and what to avoid. They were an inspirational bunch and we were eager to get as much experience as possible. What better way to attain that end than to throw ourselves heart and soul into the war against UNITA right then!

After a day at that base we were transported to the town of Cacuso, where the ad hoc headquarters of the Eastern Front was based. A tobacco warehouse had been turned into barracks to house the MK soldiers. It turned out that all MK camps in Angola had sent personnel to that front. The only exception was the Caculama camp, where training was still under way.

It was while meeting those I had last seen during training and back in Lesotho that I came across Skhumbuzo (MK name). I had stayed with him in Lesotho late in 1981. He and five others from Mdantsane in the Eastern Cape had been totally dependent on us, having not yet been officially accepted by the Lesotho government. Skhumbuzo now told a group of us of the hypocrisy of the ANC leadership and that he could foresee a time when we MK comrades would be killing each other. Because Skhumbuzo was so loud and outspoken, I felt we should hear him out, but somewhere else, where there were not so many people. One of our group took us to a local house where they sold moonshine. I had never tasted that illicit stuff till that day. We were hoping it would calm Skhumbuzo down so we could change the subject. We even spent most of the time singing, just to distract him.

What Skhumbuzo told us was hard to believe. To us, the ANC leadership was impeccable, but Skhumbuzo was totally disillusioned with the whole 'so-called struggle'. He said people like him didn't live long in the ANC – they were either killed or taken to Quatro, and his mind was made up; he didn't see any reason to live much longer.

Later that day we returned to the barracks hoping Skhumbuzo would put everything behind him, if only for our sake. After roll call, I retired to my sleeping bag and was asleep in no time, although there was still movement inside the barracks.

It wasn't long before I was rudely awoken by gunfire. Of course, I thought we were under attack, so I instinctively grabbed my AK-47 and cartridges and bolted for the door and out to the defence line. Naturally I expected the enemy to come from the exterior, so along with others like me who had just woken up, we trained our guns on the surroundings of the barracks.

Skhumbuzo appeared from the door of the barracks behind us, staggering and looking injured. While trying to figure out what was happening, we heard gunfire from the direction of the railway station, which was also guarded by us. We heard a voice shouting repeatedly in Zulu, 'I have shot him!' Totally confused, we stayed in our positions waiting for orders.

Our commander emerged from the offices opposite our barracks and ordered us to leave our positions and assemble for a roll call. It was found that the man shot at the railway station was unfortunately one of us who had been mistaken for a UNITA bandit.

What I was later made to believe was that Skhumbuzo had not gone to sleep after we returned to the barracks but kept muttering about wanting to kill himself. It was said that he was trying to shoot himself but had only managed to graze his cheek with the bullet. That was the sound that woke us, followed by him firing into the air. Thinking he was shooting at us, one or more of our comrades then fired at him. He was shot in the midriff and his firearm jammed after being hit by a bullet. This was according to those who had been awake.

What everyone discerned from the incident was that Skhumbuzo desperately wanted to end his life but couldn't, and so he needed someone else to end it for him during his shooting spree. Unfortunately (if I may be permitted to use the word), he did not die instantly.

Skhumbuzo was taken off to an office and we all went back to sleep. The following morning I was summoned to the office where I found the rest of the group who had been with Skhumbuzo the previous day. Apparently some had come forward with names of the people he had been seen with. The eight of us were told to hand in our weapons and, in addition, I was told to hand in my medical kit. Apart from Skhumbuzo, who remained in the office, we were taken to a small caravan in a neighbouring yard and locked inside.

On the evening of the second day, we had to face a military tribunal at the headquarters in Cacuso. We were called inside one at a time while the rest were under guard outside in the cold.

Chris Hani was present. After looking at each of us, he said: 'You have disappointed me because you are all here in Angola via Lesotho.' We said nothing to him, but tried to convince the tribunal that Skhumbuzo did whatever he did of his own volition. But we had drunk that illicit moonshine with him in an attempt to dissuade him from his suicidal intentions, and for that we were in the wrong.

We were marched back to the barracks the following morning. The whole detachment was gathered there; Skhumbuzo standing half bent over in front of everyone when we entered. He was a sorry sight to behold. Seemingly, he had not received any professional medical help since the incident. The commanding staff were lined up along the wall behind Skhumbuzo and ourselves.

Chris Hani took to the floor to address the entire gathering. He wasted no time in giving the verdict.

He said: 'The verdict of the tribunal is that Skhumbuzo is to face a firing squad, and I endorsed it.' He paused and turned to look at us, saying, 'As for you, you'll face hard labour for a month.'

Skhumbuzo was led to his fate, but I sensed relief in his body language – if there could possibly be such a thing. We heard later that Skhumbuzo had been executed that same day at Caculama training camp.

As for us, we were woken up every day and were at beck and call of any work that needed strength, like loading and off-loading trucks. We even had to dig a ten-by-seven metre dugout behind the commanders' offices. Our lives were turned upside down and I was ashamed of what I had become. Although I could not really blame them for punishing us, I could not see myself ignoring Skhumbuzo on that day when we had reunited after two years. I had thought that his problem was something he could overcome, and we would have good times later on – not this! It was grim that his thoughtless behaviour had led to his death and, for us, the loss of a comrade.

We were into the second week of our punishment when a convoy carrying our logistics on its way back from Malanje town was ambushed by UNITA rebels. One comrade, Caroline, was killed in that attack. The ambushers were ordinary people from the villages who had vanished into a nearby forest with their loot.

Some of the survivors of the attack reached Cacuso on foot. Every one of us was livid about the attack and the death of Caroline. UNITA bandits had to pay dearly for what they had done! This was a reminder to all and sundry that there really was an enemy out there and we could not stand by and await another strike. Our command decided that an onslaught had to be launched to cleanse the villages of UNITA.

The only good news was that our punishment was remitted; we were given back our weapons and were among those who were to take part in the military operation to redeem our pride. For the sake of Caroline, we were ready to lay down our lives!

Groups from Cacuso, Kilande and Musafo sections, along with the People's Defence Organisation (ODP) composed of Angolans – a paramilitary unit we were fighting alongside – all assembled at Musafo, which was our departure point. Hani was there to give us encouragement for our mission, though he remained behind at the command post.

Our battalion set out alternating from a skirmish formation when in open spaces, and then to column formation when encountering bushes and forests. This was foreign territory and what lay ahead was anyone's guess.

Yes, we were in hot pursuit of those who had had the guts to provoke us. Like a hornets' nest that has been tampered with, we were out to show our deadliness when messed with. Surprise attack was on our minds, so instead of going for the village closest to the ambush spot, we were to start at the farthest village of Mutalukala and rake the area backwards to Kamatetele, the village nearest the place of ambush.

Circumventing those villages took us the whole day. By nightfall we were on the banks of the Cuanza River (incidentally, this is the name the Angolan currency is derived from). On the other side of the river was the province of Cuanza Sul, which was suspected of harbouring UNITA bases. We were only hundreds of metres from the outlying Mutalukala village when we decided to rest and get ready for a pre-dawn raid.

As planned, we progressed towards the unsuspecting villagers. Our reconnaissance group had been excellent so far, and it led us to a small settlement of around fifteen small dwellings. I was in the group that was to encircle the village – no one was to leave or enter the village. Some of us were facing the direction of the houses while others faced the opposite direction – quite a nerve-racking situation where one's safety depended on the vigilance of others. But after a night's rest everyone was up to the task.

Those who were to raid the villagers were in position – each dwelling was encircled. We heard only one loud combination of screams and shouts and knew that there was no way back – we had initiated our move and had to be consistent.

All the villagers, except for the very elderly, were forced to assemble in the central clearing, with men and women on different sides. Those fluent in Portuguese started interrogating them, while others ransacked the entire village. Some of the loot from the ambush was recovered and this angered us even more. The interrogation turned violent. The assault on the menfolk was upped and became vicious, bordering on cruelty. Fine, we had reasons to be incensed, but it was blind, unbridled rage.

The villagers, on the other hand, displayed composure – it was as if this was the fulfilment of what they had expected, and it only made them more convinced of whatever they had perhaps been told.

By midday we had not had any confessions and then the frustration set in. The assaults turned to torture. One tough-looking guy in particular looked unfazed by the whole exercise. It was easy to tell he was a diehard UNITA rebel. He never so much as emitted one sound throughout all the beatings and torture.

The decision made by our commanders was that we should proceed to the next village, Hunga. We took the better half of the village with us as prisoners – the youth, all the menfolk and some women – leaving behind a few to look after the aged. We now had the task of guarding about 30 people as we headed to Hunga.

On the way the commissar of the village, who was of small build, showed signs of weakness while walking and gasped for breath from time to time. He had been heavily beaten and tortured and, given his frail build, it must have been too much for him. There and then he collapsed and died.

We had to bury him there. There were no shovels, but with our bayonets we carved a shallow grave out of the ground, not far from the road, placed him in it and piled a little soil and a lot of stones on top of him. Deep down we knew that this was not his eternal grave – the villagers would come and exhume his corpse and bury him decently somewhere, if the hyenas and vultures did not beat them to it. I could not help thinking that as an MPLA political commissar, he had inevitably received rough treatment, and probably worse torture, from UNITA forcing him to collaborate with them. And now this!

The villagers eyed us as we buried their fellow resident. One broke out into the national anthem. I've never heard any more touching rendition of an anthem since then – it was straight from the heart and a fitting goodbye to one of their own.

We entered the village of Hunga and to our amazement found it had been evacuated. How did a village four times bigger than Mutalukala have so few people? It then transpired that while we were at the previous village, two young boys had been spotted approaching the village but on seeing what was happening, they had run back to Hunga to alert the villagers.

The few villagers left in Hunga pretended they knew nothing. We had run out of food supplies and the village had absolutely nothing to offer us. Mango, banana and papaya trees were clean of any fruit, and no goats were in sight. Surely, they had taken everything and hidden it away so that we should not have anything.

We were left, as they say, with pie on our faces. We spent the night with nothing in our bellies, like snakes in hibernation, until the following morning when two goats were brought to us. The prisoners chose not to eat. It seemed they had worse problems than food.

Our next village was Kamatetele, which we reached before sunset the same day. We put all the men into one small flat on the periphery of the village. The plan was to transfer them to another house in the interior of the village in case of an attack by UNITA acting on information to rescue them, so they would find the place empty.

I was one of those inside the flat guarding the prisoners. The transfer to the house seemed to be going well as each prisoner had his hands tied behind his back. They were in a sitting position and we were, we supposed, at an advantage by being in a standing position. We had had a long day and were looking forward to an early rest and it was promising to be just that.

Out of the twenty-something men in the flat, there would from time to time be a request to go outside and pee. Okay, we allowed them to do so, but those of us guarding them outside complained because they had to draw out the guys' penises and hold them while they peed. This to them was outrageous. No wonder those prisoners came back inside wailing from the beatings they received outside.

But only God in high heaven knew why they were pestering us to go out and pee as you, my reader, will soon find out.

When we were left with only two prisoners and I was leading them out we heard gunshots. I pointed my gun at the remaining two. My colleague found out that their hands were not tied – all along they had been loosening each other's ties and those asking to pee were actually gathering information about what was happening outside. The gunshots were fired at the two I had released earlier to be escorted to the house; they too were no longer in handcuffs and they had run in opposite directions. The one who ran into the bush was shot dead on the spot. The other had run to the interior of the village and miraculously out the other side, unscathed. The remaining two had to face the consequences of messing with us.

At the same time, on the following day in Kamatetele village, a platoon was dispatched to a nearby village that we had somehow overlooked. The mission was to search for our stolen possessions. I was in that chosen platoon.

When we found the village, it was obvious why we had overlooked it: it was situated on a slope. As we descended towards the settlement, I had a feeling it would be a successful mission if we co-ordinated our actions. When we were nearer to the dwellings, we decided to split up.

In one house we found a woman aged around thirty. She looked unconcerned when she saw us entering; I wouldn't have been surprised if she had seen us coming all the way as there had been no cover for us to spring a surprise.

She let us in, and we told her of our purpose – the search for our goods. We were doing exactly that when we found a photo of Jonas Savimbi, the UNITA leader, under the blankets and a lot of paper money. On the wall hung an old picture of the first and late president of Angola, Agostinho Neto. We looked at each other in surprise. One of us wanted to take her with us because of the Savimbi picture, but the rest of us had empathy for her: she had been caught between two forces. When she saw that we were letting her off the hook, she offered us all her money, which we declined. It was enough that she had not had what we were looking for and we had no business making life tougher for her by taking her life savings. Besides, had we taken the money and shared it among us, it could have been construed as accepting a bribe.

We MK guys actually did not have any need for money, as everything was provided for us. So taking the woman's money would cause trouble for us and I, for one, was not going to land myself in trouble again so soon ... or so I hoped.

We returned to our awaiting battalion at Kamatetele with good news – the small village was clean of any suspects.

It was the fifth day since we had left Cacuso and only our commanders were privy to whatever information had been gathered concerning UNITA's activities. What happened next was the arrival of the trucks to take us back to Cacuso, as we had run out of food supplies four days earlier and were dependent on whatever could be foraged – fruit on private property, or stored nuts and sugar cane. Now was our opportunity to return to normal life back in our barracks.

Back in Cacuso, we put our hope in our intelligence unit to do the rest because we had brought with us the bunch of prisoners from Mutalukala. Believe it or not, a few days later we saw our former prisoners walking freely in the streets of Cacuso, even the suspect who we were confident was a member of UNITA.

It was at that time that a certain FAPLA captain made his appearance among us on a daily basis. We had to adjust to a new way of life: the Angolans had their officer among our command.

But had the Angolans not given us that latitude to go the whole hog on our own? Come to think of it, the Angolans actually did not need our help from the start – the Cubans and the Soviet forces, because of their internationalism, had been ready to die for Angola from the day they set foot on Angolan soil. They were better positioned to defend as a conventional unit, rather than we guerrillas, in trying to ward off rebels who were also using guerrilla tactics. The truth was we were ill-equipped for whatever we had set out to do.

FAPLA's recruitment of young peasant boys was proceeding at a rapid pace during that time. We were not responsible for their training, but we were concerned about their readiness to fight alongside us. After just a few days we were prepared to take on UNITA. This time it was going to be a daring mission of crossing the Cuanza River into Cuanza Sul province – enemy territory. Our eagerness remained. We felt we really needed to uproot UNITA from their bases.

Trucks transported us to a designated location closer to the river crossing point via a small town called Pungandonga. We crossed the river as the sun was setting and by nightfall we were on the other side. Our comrade, Post, had made it his responsibility to ferry us across using a dinghy. Although there were others, he was the main man when it came to that business.

We began our march before dawn on the following day by combing the area. At midday we reached a tributary that joined the Cuanza River. Because of the great number of us crossing, we had to be cautious and patient. The exercise was precarious; one slip on those stones could be fatal if one didn't know how to swim.

Eventually we were across, drying up and about to rest ourselves along the riverbanks when we heard a volley of gunfire from the other side of the river – exactly where we were intending to cross. Instinctively, we grabbed our weapons and ran deeper into the unknown. We were disorganised and our commander could not do anything about it as it was a matter of getting as far away as possible from the source of the gunfire.

It seemed that whoever was shooting had achieved their objective, which was to rattle us. Had they so decided, they could have inflicted fatalities on us while we were tentatively crossing the river. Ascending a hill towards the cover of trees, we heard gunfire from the adjacent side, but could not see those shooting at us. Naturally, we fired back in the direction the gunfire was coming from. This exchange of gunfire did not last long when we discovered that we and our reconnaissance unit were shooting at each other.

Reasonably, the whole mission had to be aborted as, given the circumstances, there was no way we could proceed with our plan. Our urgent concern was to avoid fatalities and to ensure a safe return to our base.

We had returned to our temporary base in the Malanje province when it was decided we should again go across the river. It meant we were not returning to Cacuso but were to be brought all the logistics we needed, and then resume our mission. This time we covered a longer distance than during the previous operation. We were ready for any engagement, but there was no sign of activity or of any bases belonging to UNITA, and so we returned to Cacuso. The whole mission had taken almost a week.

The war against UNITA had reached the point where we could not take our foot off the pedal and lose momentum. So a grand mission was hatched. For the first time, it was to include artillery.

As it was obvious that Mutalukala village was the closest on this side of the province to the UNITA bases, we were to launch the attack with artillery pieces from between the village and the river. On reaching the village we were shocked to find that the place was deserted. All those villagers we had taken prisoner, and who were subsequently released, were gone or had been abducted by UNITA, judging from the fact that an old blind couple had been left alone to die of hunger and thirst. Our medical team had to attend to them immediately.

Given the situation, we became more aware than ever before of the kind of enemy we were fighting: a ruthless and callous bunch who thrived on tyranny and mayhem.

Upon arriving at the river, the vanguard, including Chris Hani, was the first to cross using dinghies. They were already in enemy territory when six UNITA rebels appeared, moving towards them. Because they were under cover, our comrades were not seen by the six rebels. They decided to let them pass by, thus averting an engagement. The UNITA rebels proceeded towards the river and when they saw our forces were crossing the river towards their territory, they opened fire at the dinghies.

An exchange of gunfire between the six rebels and those of us still on the water followed. The artillery battery launched a barrage into the perceived UNITA bases and missiles flew over the two warring parties in rapid succession. The UNITA group found itself sandwiched between the vanguard led by Chris Hani and those advancing in the water. The firepower was too overwhelming for them to withstand; they fled in disarray, disappearing into the forest. It was not confirmed whether or not they had suffered injuries or fatalities.

The mission had to be abandoned, but we returned to Cacuso with our heads held high. However, Chris Hani's pride in us gave us more confidence. In an address to the entire detachment he said, 'We now already have heroes of our own,' citing those he was with and those who had been shooting from awkward positions in the dinghies.

CHAPTER 17

Although our morale was high, there was a worrying concern about the behaviour of our Angolan co-fighters in FAPLA. They started to show signs of dissatisfaction with the whole issue of our 'fighting their war' and were averse to our willingness to 'kill Angolans' – meaning UNITA. They were afraid of UNITA's retaliation in their various villages and feared for their own and their families' lives. For instance, our patrollers found them at the guard post, pretending to be asleep while their weapons were metres away from them. This was, as they later confessed, to save themselves from UNITA. If UNITA found them, they would simply take their weapons and ammunition and spare their lives.

When disciplinary action was taken against such conduct, it led to some deserting with arms and ammunition. These young men found themselves in a war that hindered them from continuing to live their simple village life – a life torpedoed by recent occurrences in their once peaceful province.

For example, there was a day when we were securing a passenger train travelling from Cacuso, where we were stationed, to the provincial capital, Malanje, and back. We were doing this because the area was in the so-called war zone. Our task was to be visible from time to time as we moved from coach to coach. We even had the right to search anyone or their luggage at random.

We hadn't been travelling for more than an hour when a rumour began doing the rounds that UNITA had beheaded everyone in one of the villages ahead of us and had taken it over. Some of the panicking passengers looked to us to provide them with protection, but the rest were convinced that our presence in Angola was the main cause of their problems.

As we were a small number compared to the masses on the train, we felt overwhelmed by the situation. What made things worse was the train driver making regular stops at awkward places – places where UNITA could attack with the advantage of the terrain or cover on their side. However, the driver would only say the reason for stopping was a mechanical problem. Once he said the engine had run out of water, and the poor peasants had to leave the train to go and fetch water some distance away. Then the train moved for a few minutes before it stopped again. The problem this time? Too much water.

What should have taken six hours at most for us to reach our destination took forever. We spent the night at Matete village, which was not even halfway. While some provided security for the hapless passengers, others thought it best to inform the local village commissariat of the general atmosphere and find out if they knew anything about UNITA beheading a whole village.

The village commissar was a well-informed and astute gentleman. He told us unequivocally that there had been no such incident. We sat on his veranda while he continued to tell us that UNITA was using panic-mongering as a tactic to create paranoia among the people. It was misleading people with untrue information to cripple the masses' thinking capacity, so that they could capitalise on it. He even said the MPLA was contemplating criminalising panic-mongering and the sentence would be death by firing squad.

That committed commissar even went to allay the fears of the passengers at the station. He lamented the lack of political conviction in his people, despite the education the MPLA was giving them.

On the following day we resumed our journey to and from Malanje without any incident or unnecessary stops. That chaotic journey had depleted our mental and physical strength to an extraordinary degree. It was what you got when you combined tension, confusion, frenzy and pandemonium all at the same time.

Given these unfortunate circumstances, the arrival of OR Tambo at our Cacuso barracks promised to bring a new direction to our overall struggle. A little earlier, army commander Joe Modise had been at Cacuso accompanied by well-armed Soviet comrades in full combat uniform.

Now, Joe Modise was not a man of many words: he could sneak in and out of a camp without addressing his troops. But he would leave the camp with lots of physical tasks to keep it busy for the next three months or so. He held the belief that an idle soldier's mind was a breeding ground for foul play.

On that day, a number of us were ordered to provide security for Joe Modise as he was visiting Caculama training camp and our farm at Cuela all on the same day. In Caculama he checked the defences and left some instructions. Then we proceeded to Cuela, not far away, where our farm was manned by the same staff from Camalundi. It was situated on a plateau as opposed to the town down in the valley. The comrades reported unconfirmed rumours of certain manoeuvres of the enemy in their surroundings.

Two weeks down the line OR Tambo visited us. He came, naturally, with his large entourage. Before he entered the barracks, a roll call was conducted. One commissar, Zenzile, reported that all were present except for two who had deserted, though he did not say they were from the Angolans' ODP. That was an anomaly and we waited with bated breath to hear what Tambo's response would be to such a report.

But what had happened was that by the time Modise reported to Tambo, there was no mention of any desertion. Had desertion been mentioned, it would have had an effect on the main message from the president. No one could blame the president when he uttered the words: 'We should bleed a little for Angola because Angola is bleeding for us.'

Those words sent shock waves through the entire building. We were incredulous about the way things were panning out. We didn't mind dying, but dying in a foreign land and for people who did not appreciate us would not bring our liberation any closer. This was the general feeling of the foot soldier after the president's speech.

In that year, 1983, the SACP quarterly edition of its journal, the *African Communist*, featured an article by Joe Slovo about JB Marks, the veteran leader of the SACP and the ANC. The year was his eightieth anniversary. That article brought to light the problems of democracy facing the organisation prior to the 1969 ANC Morogoro consultative conference. There was something about the article that made our ANC leaders uncomfortable. Early in 1984 that issue became scarce in MK camps and the authorities demanded the recall of those in circulation. That only made us more eager to find out what this article by Joe Slovo had inadvertently exposed.

We had been warned beforehand to beware of those who move from ear to ear whispering things about the ANC, but we did not care at the time. Speaking in undertones and in secret and only to those we trusted, we tried to dissect the article to understand it better.

Then the verdict was that our house was not in order. The Morogoro consultative conference had not come about peacefully – members of the Luthuli Detachment had demanded that the armed struggle be intensified inside the country. The Revolutionary Council was adopted in 1969 at the Morogoro conference, but it had just been abolished by the NEC in 1983. A new body, the Political Military Council (PMC), had been set up.

What we deduced was that, as a people's political organisation, from time to time the ANC needed pressure from the rank and file to avert its downfall brought about by a leadership crisis. The army had always been in the forefront in trying to inject urgency into the question of accelerating the pace and quality of the struggle in all its forms. The people at home were ready to die for the revolution; they were being harassed by the minority government and killed and maimed by Bantustan stooges. The Mass Democratic Movement (MDM) and the trade unions were up in arms, and all they needed was the presence of their last hope – Umkhonto we Sizwe.

We soon heard that we were to join others from Cacuso in another attack on UNITA. However, there was reluctance about going on that mission, and that was when defiance began.

I was one of those who defied participating in any further missions. I had a feeling that sooner or later I would be spilling blood for people who viewed me as an intruder. Besides, I tried to reason that there was the possibility that our positions could be booby-trapped during our absence. Inside the country of my birth, I would lay down my life readily, but there in Angola my political understanding of internationalism, as preached by Marxism-Leninism, was being abused. This time I was taking full responsibility for my life, if that was the last thing I had to do.

Those who acceded to going to fight UNITA were to join a group that had just returned from training in the German Democratic Republic. They were very keen to inflict damage on the UNITA rebels, but news came informing us of a tragic loss of 26 combatants, including some of the Angolans, in what turned out to have been an ambush between Hunga and Mutalukala villages. It had happened in the evening. A drum roll was the signal for the rebels to attack. Our guys were taken by surprise and fled into the bushes and into a hail of bullets.

The mere mention of that ambush sent shivers down my spine because it brought back the memory of burying the frail body of the Mutalukala commissar in a shallow grave and leaving it there to decompose. That same spot had now claimed our comrades' lives ... and I had to deal with that too.

That was the straw that broke the camel's back. Dissatisfaction with the counter-insurgency against UNITA was growing, leading to sporadic shootings into the air that were meant to make our plea to withdraw from the front audible to the ANC leaders. But it was not only that which would satisfy us: as hinted earlier about our responses to Joe Slovo's *African Communist* article, which opened our eyes, our demands now spread to the political problems in our organisation as well.

We had a number of complaints and demands. Above all, we complained about the intransigence of our security department headed by Mzwandile Piliso. We wanted it to be immediately suspended and its activities in its secret Quatro prison camp investigated. Lastly, we demanded the holding of a National Conference. Only when these aforementioned demands were met would we be content that the rear base, Angola, was strong and sound enough for us to embark on an onslaught on South Africa.

All these demands were communicated to the leadership via Chris Hani, Joe Nhlanhla (the then administrative secretary of the NEC) and Lehlohonolo Moloi when they visited us at Cangandala. They had come to order us to stop shooting in the air, but after hearing us out they grasped the fact that we had reached a point of no return. Chris Hani promised to convey our message to President OR Tambo, on whom we all pinned our hopes. They left that day surely feeling we were the ones who were calling the shots.

A few days after their departure, the Eastern Front was closed due to sporadic shootings in the air not only from us in Cangandala, but throughout all camps with MK combatants at the front. We all had the same demand: withdrawing from the front and being sent to fight inside South Africa. The good news was that the ANC leadership appeared to have acceded to that.

We from Cangandala and those from Musafo and Kilande converged at Cacuso, and a few days later the first convoy left for Luanda. I was in that convoy of three trucks of MK combatants armed to the teeth and ready to embark on this historic step of fast forwarding our struggle.

In the town of N'dalathando our truck had an engine problem and it was decided that five of us, including Papa and me, would remain behind with the truck while it was fixed with the help of Angolan army mechanics.

N'dalathando is a large, picturesque town with eye-catching views. We had supper in a restaurant, courtesy of a mutual understanding between the owner and our group. With no place to sleep except in the truck, Papa and I found an army guardhouse nearby where we could spend the night.

Those soldiers welcomed us, and all night long we sang songs of the triumph and sorrow brought about by war. One of those songs was the one we sang together with the Angolans, while returning from missions against UNITA. It was sung in Kimbundu, the local language, by two groups. It goes like this:

1st group: *Ngamkatambunda* (my back is sore)
2nd group: *Ngamkatashinga* (my waist is sore)
1st group: *Ngamkatashinga*
2nd group: *Ngamkatambunda*
1st group: *Malanje*
2nd group: *Malanje ishi yethu* (Malanje is our place)
1st group: *Luanda*
2nd group: *Luanda ishi yethu*

The list of place names included other towns, cities and countries across the whole African continent. The subsequent mutiny was later named Mkatashinga by its detractors.

The following morning we had nothing to eat. One soldier suggested that we approach the Cuban residence up the hill; they might be of help. Papa and I went there and found an old Chinese Cuban who was in charge of the residence. He had an Angolan helper who also doubled as an interpreter. They said the five of us should come for lunch.

When we arrived we found a three-course meal prepared for us. Then in came five or six Cubans, not in full uniform but well-armed. Disbelief was written all over their faces when we were introduced to them as South Africans. They wanted to know how come we were not in South Africa fighting while they were fighting the South African army in the south of Angola. It was an ever-lingering question that we tried to answer by giving them the political rhetoric we had been fed all along about the struggle being 'protracted' and the 'strong rear' narrative. But they didn't buy it at all.

We had not yet succeeded in fixing the truck on the second day when the second and last convoy arrived at N'dalathando. We had no choice but to hop in and leave the truck in the hands of the

Angolans. No one knew what had happened to the first convoy, but what was on everyone's mind was that we were never again returning to the camps in the east of Angola.

It was February 1984. We were approaching Viana Camp outside Luanda in the afternoon when someone started shooting in the air, followed by the rest of us. That volley resulted in the occupants of the camp scurrying for cover, thinking that they were under attack. No one was injured in the process. The camp commander, Pro, demanded that every one of us disarm and surrender our weapons, but we expressed our fear of being victimised if we followed that order.

It then came to our knowledge that the first convoy had been disarmed on arrival without any resistance. Following our refusal, they then demanded their weapons be given back. It was an unprecedented and uncontrollable situation for the camp administration and the security forces, which ended in them fleeing the camp for Luanda. Viana Camp was technically now under us, just as Manor Farm was under the control of the farm animals in George Orwell's *Animal Farm*.

Such an eventuality was not what we had aimed for, but we were not daunted by the responsibility that came with it. It should be kept in mind that we felt we were misunderstood, as though we were trying to topple the leadership – something we totally distanced ourselves from. What we found in Viana was that all personnel who had been staying there before us had been taken to various places around Luanda. The containers outside the camps were empty. We needed to get to MK members in the region and explain ourselves. Some of us who knew Luanda well took the risk of being victimised by ANC security and volunteered to move from place to place, making our stance clear to everyone.

Meanwhile, those of us who remained in Viana decided to form a circular defence around the camp as there was not enough space for all of us in the tents. I shared a bivouac with Veli, with whom I had trained back in Caxito.

CHAPTER 18

Soon people from all corners of the ANC establishments around Luanda joined us in the camp. They had heard negative reports about us and were keen to hear first hand what the conflict was about. When they realised that we hadn't harmed any member of the security personnel, they supported us. That thwarted and frustrated the leadership's hopes of rendering us outcasts in the organisation.

What followed was a marathon of meetings that anybody and everybody was allowed to attend and contribute to. In one of them we were told by Funwell – a resident of Viana before we arrived – that one night when he was officer on duty, he and some security officers found that Solly, who had been incarcerated in a metal container, had suffocated and died.

What the security officers did was take Solly's lifeless body to the outskirts of Luanda and shoot him in the head and then go to the Angolan authorities and report that there were trigger-happy mutineers in Viana who were responsible for his death.

It was a devious plan to set the Angolans against us. We never saw that coming! For starters, we didn't know that there was anyone in the containers. To think that it happened under our watch proved that we had not fathomed the extent to which the wickedness of ANC security could stretch. It was a harrowing story that resulted in revulsion for the security department. It appeared that Solly had been critical of the likes of Joe Modise and Andrew Masondo, the National Commissar of the ANC, which had led to his becoming a prime target of the security department. After suffering from the heavy-handedness of the security apparatus, he had become mentally disturbed. But it was his fearlessness and outspokenness, emboldened by the news of the mutiny on the Eastern Front, that led to his being locked up in the container and deprived of air and water.

The following day we had a visit at Viana from Ntate Dan Mashigo (birth name Graham Morodi, MK regional commander in Angola) and a delegation. After realising that we had a plethora of complaints and demands for the ANC leadership to address, Mashigo and the delegation suggested that we form a committee of ten to present our demands to the ANC NEC. That seemed to make sense and so, after their departure, we had a meeting to draft our demands and collectively elect the Committee of Ten. They were:

1. Zaba Maledza (MK name; real name Ephraim Nkondo), chairman
2. Sidwell Moroka (MK name; real name Omry Makgoale)
3. Jabu Mofolo (MK name; real name Shadrack Lebona Sepamla)
4. Bongani Matwa (MK name; real name Norman Phiri)
5. Kate Mhlongo (MK name; real name Nomfanelo Ntlokwana)
6. Grace Mofokeng (MK name; real name Grace Motaung)
7. Moses Thema (MK name; real name Mbulelo Musi)
8. Sipho Mathebula (MK name; real name Vusi Donald Mndebele)
9. Khotso Morena (MK name; real name Mwezi Twala)
10. Simon Botha (MK name; real name Sindile Solomon Moyikwa)

What had started as resistance to continuing participation on the Eastern Front in the Angolan civil war had now metamorphosed into a political force threatening the political survival of the highest military hierarchy in MK and the ANC. This took the form of our democratic demand for a national conference to review progress in the struggle and for the members of the ANC to democratically elect a new NEC.

The ANC constitution at the time said a national elective conference would be held every four years, but there had been no conference since the Morogoro conference of 1969. Even that conference of 1969 was the result of pressure from the concerned MK rank and file, following MK's participation in the Wankie and Sipolilo campaigns in Zimbabwe in 1967 and the repression of contributors to the Hani Memorandum in Lusaka in 1969.

OR Tambo was made the deputy president of the ANC at the conference but was later made president of the organisation without prior consultation or democratic involvement of ANC members. The reason for his elevation to the presidency in such a manner is often attributed to the secrecy and underground modus operandi of the ANC in exile.

The other crucial demand of the MK troops was for the suspension of the security department – Mbokodo – and the formation of a commission to investigate its activities, more specifically at its notorious prison, Quatro. There was widespread condemnation of the ANC for having its own prison within a sovereign state.

The matter of the lull in military attacks by MK inside South Africa was also high on the agenda. There was a need to infiltrate more soldiers into the country so as to boost the mass action of the democratic movement and the workers' struggle inside the country.

The Committee of Ten, it must be stressed, was very representative of various sectors and institutions of the ANC in the Angolan region. Not all of those who were elected were present at the meeting. Zaba Maledza (MK name), the chairman, was working at the Radio Freedom studios in Luanda. He had been imprisoned in Quatro in 1980 after disagreeing with the military leadership in Swaziland and was released a year later. His impeccable and efficient service in broadcasting made him a formidable force to reckon with. His acceptance of membership of the committee for the common good, while knowing the possible repercussions for himself, was the greatest self-sacrifice one can think of.

Omry Makgoale (MK name: Sidwell Moroka or Mhlongo) had previously been a personal bodyguard of OR Tambo, but because of his 1980 criticism of Mbokodo, he had been taken to Angola, along with others in Zambia. When he was elected to the committee he was MK district commander in Luanda, and he was not present at Viana. He was an astute product of the June 16 uprising in Soweto in 1976 who had been working closely with the likes of Tebello Motapanyane and Tsietsi Mashinini. What led to his election was his readiness to argue for what he was convinced was right.

Jabu Mofolo (MK name) was a member of the Amandla Cultural Ensemble and its political commissar. When he could have stayed off the committee and saved his skin, he put his neck on the block for his beliefs.

Bongani Matwa (MK name) was one of the June 16 Detachment political prototypes – an intelligent yet humble and accessible comrade. In an equitable scenario, which politics seldom is, Bongani could easily have risen to a leadership position.

Kate Mhlongo (MK name) was not elected on the basis of balancing the gender equation, but because of her inspirational nature. Her courage and preparedness to face the consequences were what mattered most.

Grace Mofokeng (MK name) was the other woman who commanded respect and led by example.

Moses Thema (MK name) was political head in Caxito camp who happened to be in Luanda at the time.

Mwezi Twala (real name) was elected because of his honesty and efficiency in articulating his viewpoint.

The only three who had been on the Eastern Front were Simon Botha, Bongani Matwa and Sipho Mathebula. Simon Botha was down to earth and representative of the rank and file, while Sipho Mathebula was a former battalion commander on the Eastern Front.

The composition of the Committee of Ten thus showed not only representative qualities on a wider scale, but also the participation of a large percentage of MK personnel in Angola. We knew that what we had done, however well intentioned for the organisation, was not going to be taken lying down by the leadership of the ANC. And as sure as our expectations had been, the backlash from the leadership proved us right. This was despite our placing placards on the walls of Viana saying 'No To Bloodshed – We Need A Conference'. We were looking for a non-violent, peaceful, democratic conference, which we expected would take place from the words of Regional Commander Mashigo.

On 12 February, at around three in the morning, I retired to the bivouac I shared with Veli. Prior to that, I had been watching games of table tennis in Viana's hall. I found Veli sound asleep and in no time I was asleep too.

I must have been asleep for about 30 minutes when I heard a combat bell ringing in the camp. That meant there was trouble! I then heard a short burst of gunfire and this time I could hear the rumbling sounds of a combination of engines coming our way. I shook Veli for a few seconds (it seemed like a lifetime), only to find that I was shaking his knapsack – he was gone. That told me the bell had been ringing for a while and that Veli thought I hadn't returned yet.

I grabbed my bazooka, the five rockets, the AK-47 and about two hundred rounds of ammunition, and ran for dear life towards the defence line. There I joined Papa, Mbeko, Mahatma and Majoe, all of them armed with AK-47s. To our surprise the 'enemy' didn't come from outside the trenches but was sneaking up behind us in an attempt to encircle the camp. That meant we now had to turn our backs to the parapet and be exposed.

Those engines were armoured personnel carriers (APCs). One of them went straight for my and Veli's bivouac and went right over it, leaving everything in shreds. Had I not been awoken by that bell, I would have been dead meat. I was simultaneously angry and scared. In a short while their encirclement was complete. They might have encircled the camp, but the vehicle in front of us was encircled by the five of us. What they were waiting for was an order to raid the camp, but that order did not come as there appeared to be no one inside the camp.

In the semi-darkness, the five of us in the trench could have sneaked out and stealthily made our way to the bushes some 200 metres away, but the problem was that there were some already there who might mistake us for the 'enemy' and shoot at us. In other words, we were stuck in that trench and our survival hung in the balance.

The wait was becoming long, and the absence of action was becoming tedious. Then the APC driver opened the roof aperture and jumped onto it. It was the same driver who had left my bivouac in tatters. It became apparent that he was likely to spot us as we were only about 20 metres from him. And, indeed, he did!

It must have been the beauty of the place that morning that made him turn around and around, and then ... there we were: five men, guns aimed in front of us, my bazooka aimed at the APC.

He jumped inside the APC and, opening the side door, alerted the others occupants to our presence. His commander came boldly towards us, but the driver restrained him, pointing out that we were armed. The commander then ordered us to get out of the trench or else ... Just then, when we were trying to engage him in dialogue, we saw the APC driver turning the barrel of the APC in our direction. Instead of answering our question as to why they were there, and seeing that we did not intend to surrender, the commander reached for a grenade, pulled the pin and was about to throw it at us when I pulled the trigger of my bazooka. I knew what fatalities would ensue if the grenade landed in our trench.

The sound of the rocket leaving the bazooka was so loud it disturbed him, and the grenade fell only metres from us. The others in the trench also opened fire, but only to scare the Angolans who were now running towards the camp. I had used all my rockets when I realised that the APC was in flames.

With the Angolans running towards the camp, we had the chance to run further away towards the nearby bush. When the Angolans turned and saw us running they opened fire. We were fortunate that all those bullets whizzed past our half-bent bodies as we scrambled for safe cover, and no one was hurt.

Those on the other side of the encirclement became aware of the imminent danger that faced both sides. It was at such a crucial stage in this mini battle that the FAPLA forces knew they would probably all perish, while we, on the other hand, knew we would after all be hunted down and, before nightfall, would perish too.

Something had to be done. So, talks between our Committee of Ten and the Angolans commenced. The national chief of staff of FAPLA, Colonel 'Ndalu' (Antonio dos Santos França, later General), and his crack force – the elite Presidential Guard Battalion 24 – had come to drench our place with blood. Their first shots had killed Babsy, a Quatro guard, as he was jumping over the wall while trying to escape the raid. Compromising on the order to annihilate all of us was not easy for Colonel Ndalu, but reason got the better of him.

The agreement was that when we disarmed, all MK personnel, including the security staff, would follow suit. The Angolans would provide security so that we would not be victimised by the Mbokodo.

Being disarmed left us very vulnerable. Chris Hani arrived, accompanied by two members of the Organisation for African Union's Liberation Committee. He lambasted us and our demands, saying our conduct had been instigated by dissatisfied members, and that the ANC could do without us. Then he called on those still dedicated to the organisation to leave the hall. We all left because we all still regarded ourselves as committed and authentic members of the ANC, even though the organisation had deviated from its own democratic norms.

What happened after three days was treachery by the Angolan government: Mbokodo was armed and entered the camp, securing Joe Modise and Andrew Masondo. They had come to introduce us to the five members of the commission of inquiry mandated by OR Tambo to look into the mutiny. These were James Stuart (chairperson), Tony Mongalo, Aziz Pahad, Sizakele Sigxashe and Mbuyiselo Dywili.

The following day, 16 February 1984, Joe Modise and the security rounded us up and ordered us to gather inside the camp. We took our time, but he didn't mind. He even said, 'You will find me very patient today.' He knew he was ultimately in control.

When everyone had gathered, he read out the names of 30

people, comprising the whole of the Committee of Ten and others who were deemed to be the ringleaders and main protagonists of the mutiny. I was expecting to be named among them for the APC episode, but the name of another MK cadre, Mbeko, was called. What Mbeko had done during the negotiations with the Angolans was to take my bazooka and brag about 'his feat' with the weapon while dragging his feet (this was his signature walk). So, in lieu of me, he was then imprisoned with the Committee of Ten and alleged ringleaders in the maximum state security prison in Luanda. The rest of us were taken to two camps in the north of Angola – Quibaxe and Pango. We were now, all of us, mutineers, at the mercy of Mbokodo, the Grindstone.

I was in the group that was taken to Pango Camp. It was operating on a skeleton staff, as most of its erstwhile inhabitants had been sent to the Eastern Front. Now they were back, but with extra personnel, like me, from the other camps. As a result of our great number, sleeping arrangements were cause for concern and some of us slept on the veranda of a house called Santiago.

After the series of events culminating in the arrests at Viana and our transfer to the north, our daily routine became boring as we had nothing to do ... until the commission of inquiry headed by James Stuart arrived. Ever since Mbeko had been arrested for the destruction of the APC and the death of its driver, I had been very edgy. I knew it would not be long before Mbeko, under duress and torture, admitted the truth – that I was responsible. After we assembled, the commissioners said they had a list of specific people they would like to participate in the work of the commission but that anyone not on the list was welcome to take part too.

When they called out the names, mine was the first. There was a pause before they called the next and, watching their body language, I knew that they knew – the noose was gradually tightening around my neck. That being that, five questions were put forward:

1. What are the causes of the unrest?
2. What role have you played in the mutiny?

3. Why did you want a National Conference?
4. What can you say about the role of the enemy in this?
5. What do you think can be done to improve the state of affairs in the army?

To the amazement of the commissioners, there were many who volunteered to participate. We were all transparent in answering those questions: it was one for all and all for one as we helped each other in drafting the answers. In no uncertain terms, we disputed the notion that the committee had dictated what to demand. The committee who we had elected by name had been representing us and our demands. Of course, this was a surreal moment in the history of the ANC in what was later regarded as its greatest crisis in exile. One principle of elected individual representatives faced its opposite: top-down unelected command.

The issues of that time have continued to be central in South Africa through to today. Those not on our side were exposed. It was now clear who was on which side: the side of the patriots or the side of those hindering the democratisation of our organisation. The irony, though, was that the latter regarded themselves as the actual revolutionaries and, in their view, we were the counter-revolutionaries. Talk of unity of opposites in the struggle! This was a classic example: those who hero-worshipped leaders on the one hand, and on the other those who emphasised the organisation's policies, norms and objectives as values that would take the organisation forward, regardless of who the leader was. Of course, every political person loves it when they enjoy popular support, and might overlook opportunism from those claiming to be supporters ...

Not long after the departure of the commission, we were introduced to what was termed a 'reorientation course'. In other words, we were ordered to believe that the mutiny was somehow an enemy-generated event and we had to abandon our belief in our cause. We were still unarmed, unlike the security and those 'loyal' to the ANC, but we naturally resisted their attempts to disillusion us about our fundamental principles.

The odds were loaded against us and the security officers felt that they had us where they wanted us. Insubordination was going to be punished, so we decided to follow orders, which is the cornerstone of discipline in any military establishment. The camp command then demanded that we return to the camp routine we had followed before going to the Eastern Front.

One of the chores was to fill a water tank for the use of the administration. The path to the stream was steep, so we had to form a human chain relaying the buckets all the way up. Filling that tank took a long time and we had to repeat the exercise every two days. This triumph on the part of the administration catapulted their confidence to new heights. We were apparently being broken and never, they must have thought, were we ever to recover.

Then early one morning, Naledi, a security officer in the camp with whom I had trained in Caculama, came to me and said I was to be sent into South Africa to fight. The snag was that I had to travel through the bush to Quibaxe town where I was to get transport to Luanda.

This sounded very suspect to me. How could I walk unarmed when we knew that rebels from the National Front for the Liberation of Angola (FNLA) had renewed their counter-revolutionary activities around northern areas?[3] I said to Naledi, 'How about arming me so I can defend myself in case of an attack?' He was quick to assure me that there was no need to be afraid as I would be provided security by three 'loyal' comrades.

I stood my ground and said, 'Either I am armed, or I am not taking your offer. Go and give it to someone else. Look around, there are so many of us.' He lost his cool and became desperate, saying, 'You make my work tough for me!'

Now I must say that never in the history of MK had a soldier had to be beseeched to go to the front. It had always been the

---

3 After Angola gained its independence from Portugal in 1975, an armed conflict broke out among three Angolan nationalist movements – the MPLA, UNITA and the FNLA. This became known as the Angolan Civil War (1975–2002). Both UNITA and the FNLA opposed the ruling MPLA government.

opposite – we had gone down on both knees for an opportunity to lay down our lives for liberating our country. At that juncture I was sure my suspicions were well founded. Something was fishy.

When Naledi left, many were curious to know what our disagreement was about. I told them that I was actually the one who had shot at the APC and also about the offer from Naledi. They all saw through his devious lies. Someone even said that it was possible I would have been killed that day had I agreed, while others said I was to be taken to Quatro.

On my side, I felt guilty that Mbeko was imprisoned instead of me. I was ready to face any consequences as long as my imprisonment, or even death, was not veiled by lies about my being sent to the front.

On the following day, Naledi came back and repeated his attempt to sell me the story of going to South Africa to fight and again I objected. But on the third day, while we were having breakfast, one of the 'loyal' comrades came with an announcement that Selby, Sidney and I were to prepare ourselves to be sent to South Africa and that transport was provided, although we would remain unarmed.

On hearing this, those I was with said, 'Don't go! We can organise something!' I remember those words clearly. I remained calm and said, 'I cannot stand this suspense. At least now that you know about my APC narrative, I am ready for any repercussions.' I rose and headed in the direction where the transport was supposed to be waiting.

But they were not going to wait for us. When Sidney, Selby and I were halfway there, we saw a Land Rover V8 coming towards us. It was driven by the son of the MK regional commander in Angola who had instructed us to elect the Committee of Ten to represent us in discussions with the MK command. But because he didn't know us, he passed us, until Naledi, who was at the back of the vehicle, called for him to stop, shouting, 'Stop! Here they are!'

The new arrivals were all armed (except poor Naledi) and ready to use force. However, I was not going to resist or defy any order on that day. The three of us submitted to their demands. The van reversed to Santiago house for us to collect our worldly possessions. Selby and Sidney went for theirs, but I remained at the van. When it had driven over our bivouac at Viana, that APC had smashed everything that Veli and I possessed to smithereens, so I had nothing except a face towel, the toothbrush in my hand and the clothes on my back.

We left in silence while the van weaved its way through the bush at high speed until we reached Quibaxe town. There we were transferred to a truck. How convincing it seemed, because there was no member of the security department aboard the truck as we set off to Luanda.

At the back of my mind I had this belief that they were playing for time before striking. When we reached Luanda, we were taken to Viana Camp. It was back to the usual Viana I knew, though reminders of the recent conflict were evident. Behind the camp was a blown-up Land Rover. I was told the story behind it. Vuyisile Maseko (MK name; Xolile Siphunzi, real name), who had been tracked down after we had been taken to Pango and Quibaxe, had blown it up with an F-1 defensive grenade in the presence of Joe Modise and Chris Hani. Whether he had wished to die in that instant, along with Modise and Hani, was anybody's guess. What we knew was that Hani had demanded that Vuyisile be executed for that act were he to recover, but that Modise had said he should suffer first. He was taken to join others in Luanda state prison, though first he had to be hospitalised due to injuries he had suffered in the explosion.

Another who also went to hospital with injuries was Khotso Morena (MK name; real name, Mwezi Twala). He was rounded up at an MK institution called Plot. Hani and Modise ordered that he be shot for resisting arrest. One bullet penetrated from the back and exited through his stomach, also piercing and damaging one lung. His sin was being a member of the Committee of Ten, and he had been missing when the others were arrested.

The camp commander, Pro, acted normally towards us. There was satisfaction that he was in charge again. On our return to Viana there was no briefing as to when we were going to the 'front'. We joined the rest of the people there and adhered to the camp programme and routine.

On the third day there I intended approaching Pro to ask him to help me with some clothes I had seen in a metal container. I was washing myself that morning behind the wall on the side of the camp when Sash, an old friend from Caxito who was next to me, received a bottle containing something that turned out to be moonshine. Sash had not opened it when, from out of nowhere, a young security guy sprang upon him and demanded the bottle. He went to report to Pro that we were going to drink liquor. Pro called us over to him. I wanted to defend myself by saying I was not involved in the procurement of the thing, but Pro seized me by the collar of my shirt, clenched his fist and uttered these words, 'You think it's that APC you destroyed?!' I expected him to punch me, but he lowered his clenched fist and ordered us to be punished by assisting in the kitchen for three days.

The mention of the word APC and the anger with which it was uttered meant the whole camp now knew I was the culprit. To me, it meant the cover had been lifted – I was not forgiven, by any means.

Working in the kitchen, chopping wood, cleaning pots and fetching water rendered my only clothes even dirtier. I had to be helped with some hand-me-downs from other people to look presentable. It is sad to feel alone, a pariah and an orphan at the same time, but until one says to oneself 'it could have been worse' the world might seem to devour one alive. The gift of having the ability to count one's blessings even when the chips are down can inject life into a hopeless situation. I would say to myself: if Pro felt he had the right to punch me, then what about those already imprisoned? They must be paying a heavy price for trying to democratise the ANC. They must be deeply despondent under the tyranny of Mbokodo's bully boys, renowned for their brutality.

The suspense engulfing me was broken when after a week or so Selby, Sidney and I were briefed thus: we were to be taken to an underground house where we would be prepared for the last time before being infiltrated inside South Africa. Another ruse? Training people inside a house or flat is not only possible but was practised even inside South Africa. Whatever the game was, the three of us went to the underground house.

The place was actually an apartment in the centre of Luanda adjacent to a big cinema built inside a large traffic circle. Those residing there were friendly towards us. They even took us out to the cinema and to an open-air cinema with a view of the sea. Miramar was the name of the place. There was no mention at all of military training; our conversation didn't even touch on the subjects of armed struggle or politics.

Oh yes! And the food was exceptionally good! They ate freshly produced food bought at the shops that catered for foreign diplomats in Angola. It was the best food I had had in years, not the tinned stuff we were used to elsewhere. Live that life and you are living an idyllic existence, reflective of an organisation that cares for its members' well-being – an organisation you would defend, come what may. Unfortunately for the three of us, it was a short-lived cameo. Selby and Sidney were taken away one night. The following morning, 26 April 1984, I was fetched by five security officers. They said I was to be taken to Caxito – the camp I'd been in before going to the Eastern Front.

I hopped into the van and we headed towards Caxito.

However, I ended up in Quatro!

PART FOUR
QUATRO

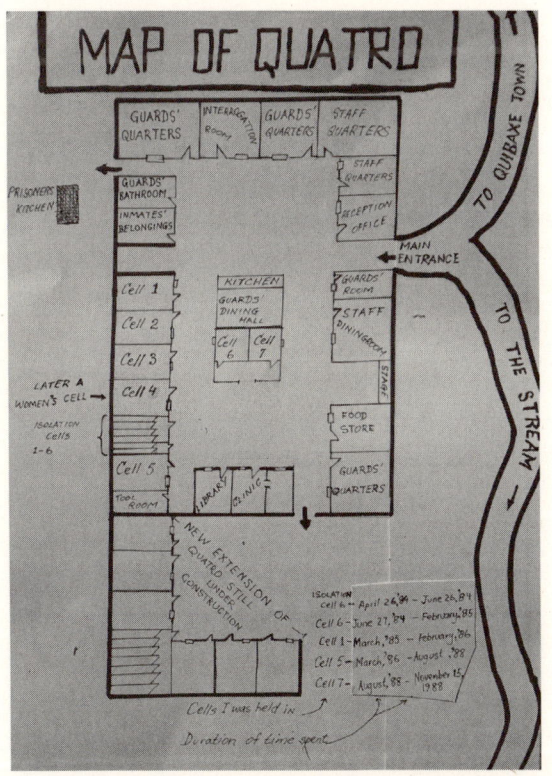

Map of Quatro.

CHAPTER 19

A loud 'Yoh! Yoh! Yoh!' should precede the story about Quatro and may its echo reach everyone and express the anguish that comes to mind on hearing the word.

The narrative of Quatro is like an underground river of tears that is deep and keeps resurfacing from time to time in my life, showing how alive it is. I really suffered there, but what happened on the way there is worth mentioning too.

On leaving the underground house, I was time and again assured by the five security officers that I was really being transported to Caxito. But as we were about to branch off to the camp, there was 'someone' they had to fetch in Pango, some hundreds of kilometres away. It didn't make sense not to drop me in nearby Caxito and then proceed to Pango, and it only confirmed my earlier suspicions.

We hadn't travelled for more than 30 minutes when one of them in the back asked the driver to stop so he could urinate. Then they disembarked one by one until I was the only one left inside the Land Rover.

Suddenly I heard an aggressive voice commanding, 'Get out of the van!' I thought, 'Here it is, the masquerade is over.' I reached for the tailgate and slowly disembarked. The van and I were completely surrounded, their weapons were cocked and pointing at me. I took some time to look up and down and along the sides of the road: it was so straight one could see an approaching vehicle a long way away, and there was a dense forest on both sides of it. It was a perfect place to execute someone and get away with it.

I wasn't thinking of running into the forest. I had made peace with the thought that it was the last day of my life. I lay down as ordered and waited for them to put me out of my misery. Instead of shooting me, one of them tied my hands behind my back, gave me a kick in the ribs and ordered me to get into the van again and to lie on my stomach. They then piled a lot of newspapers on top of me and off we went.

Honestly speaking, I was disappointed. It's not every day that I am as prepared to die as I was that day. I had had this feeling that once I died heaven's gilded gates would be wide open awaiting my arrival because, despite all the wrong things I had done in my life, I was basically a man with good intentions. So when they spared my life, I definitely knew they had a wicked plan worse than death for me. That was Quatro: a place on earth worse than hell.

It was hot that day and the pile of newspapers on top of me made me feel like I was inside a hot oven, dying slowly from lack of air and hyperthermia – a traumatic experience that never seemed to end.

After more than two hours of suffocating, the van came to a stop. I could hear them all leaving the vehicle and talking to people in our South African languages. Then someone ordered me to get out of the van. I managed to shake the newspapers off me; I was wet with sweat from head to toe. As I was trying to lift one leg over the tailgate, one of them sent me reeling back with a mighty punch. He waited for me to rise so as to give me another of his heavy blows. The third time I somehow mustered some strength despite the punches and forced myself out of the van, though landing clumsily with a fall. From there I was kicked and punched all the way to the reception office. By the time I reached it, I had already lost a tooth.

Inside I was ordered to undress and then one of them hit the soles of my feet with a cable, saying that was to make it difficult for me to attempt to escape. A guard with a squint brought me a two-piece, lice-ridden uniform and two oversized sneakers, both for the same foot. He then dragged, punched, slapped and kicked me while hurling insults at me all the way to a single cell. Before locking me in, he said, 'I am a very kind man when I'm out there, but in here I am very, very cruel. It's because of the likes of you! If you want to leave this place all you have to do is knock on the door and we will listen to your story!' Then he slammed the door in my face and left.

I was left standing in the darkness and it took me a while to get accustomed to it. Then I saw what was in the cell: a non-functioning airbed, two blankets and two plastic containers – one with water and the other for me to relieve myself in. There was a small opening that let in some air and a bit of light. I lay on top of the blankets, still reeling from the pain in my battered body. That afternoon the door was opened, and I was given food and told unequivocally to finish it.

The following morning after breakfast I knocked at the door. I told the guard on duty that I would like to see the camp administration. He later returned and took me to the admin. I found all the officers gathered there. I asked them why I was being detained; I didn't deserve to be in a place for enemy agents because I wasn't one.

Instead of answering my question they left the room one by one. In came two guards who pummelled me and then took me back to the cell. They later brought me a pen and paper to write my biography. When I gave it to them they said I should write it again, but this time not on both sides of the paper. After that they said my name in Quatro would be APC. That somehow spelt out the reason I was being held there.

In my biography I tried my utmost to show that it was in self-defence that I had shot at the APC and in the process had saved five lives, despite killing the APC driver and destroying the vehicle. That didn't make any difference. I was to stay there indefinitely without having a fair trial or even knowing whether I would ever leave the place.

A day in Quatro started with an eerie silence broken by the sound of heavy boots crossing the yard, followed by the audible opening of the door of the inmates who cooked for other inmates, to let them go and prepare breakfast. Then all those in single cells had to take out the containers with the excrement, one at a time, and place them in front of the cells. Others from cells with groups of inmates would then take them and dispose of them in a hole 200 metres from the buildings. After that it would be breakfast and, later, time for work.

For those in isolation cells there was nothing to do except expect a regular slap from the bad-tempered guards every time they opened the door to bring the inmate food. On Saturdays there was a general search of all the cells. It was conducted with beatings drowned by singing from all the other cells. This continued for a long time, until the guards had satisfied their sadistic appetites.

In Quatro everyone expected beatings upon beatings. It was a daily dose, keeping the prisoners anxious. As a result, inmates groaned grudgingly all day and moaned mournfully at night ... day in, day out.

There were strict rules we lived by:
- No one was to peep through the openings to see prisoners from another cell. If a group of prisoners was working and another group was to pass them, they would run and hide so as to avoid seeing each other.
- Once in Quatro everyone had a new name, and we were not allowed to use MK names when addressing each other.
- We were to refer to the guards as commander.
- No one was supposed to say they had been beaten – we had to say we had been 'corrected'.
- Prisoners always had to be on the double when moving from point to point within the yard.
- Nothing was too heavy or too difficult for the prisoners. There was a saying that we had no rights at all, except the right to work hard and be beaten. Another was that no prisoner gets tired.
- When a prisoner was ill, he was expected to recover after three days' treatment and resume work duties. Even at the clinic, just behind the door there were a few coffee-tree sticks at the ready to beat the daylights out of anyone suspected of malingering.
- We had to finish the food served to us, no matter the quantity because we 'had accused them of eating alone'. It was not an

unfounded accusation that the leaders – from camp admin to the top echelons – were eating exceptionally better and more nutritious food, compared with us.
- And in Quatro, never complain about anything or try to reason with what you think is right or wrong. You are always wrong! You are subhuman, so better play the part! Or else ...

Just being in Quatro was torture. Relations between prisoners and guards were like those between counter-revolutionaries and revolutionaries – an unhealthy state of affairs. Not only did they regard themselves as revolutionaries, but they were also the privileged elite of the organisation. But who were these people? They had been hand-picked and groomed to believe they were special: the chosen ones who should defend the revolution against enemy agents that were out to destroy the organisation.

They had been to Communist Party schools, mostly in the Soviet Union and East Germany. Almost all of those I knew from Lesotho had been the ones who had stayed at Chris Hani's place. These were people who had tasted only the good side of the ANC, having been the recipients of the ANC's generosity from their first day in exile. They truly thought us mutineers or 'dissidents' were an ungrateful bunch who should suffer for the rest of our lives. According to them, whatever bad treatment we got from them was a huge compromise, because what we really deserved was the 'firing squad'. The ANC's leniency towards us irritated them and they felt we were taking advantage of the situation. What they were longing for were knocks at the door and our confessions attesting to being spies for the Pretoria regime.

What was confusing was the way we so-called mutineers were addressed. The guards referred to us as 'enemy agents'. The officers, however, never called us enemy agents, yet never called us comrades or used the Quatro names but, instead, they called us by our individual MK names. Visiting ANC leaders would call us comrades but ascertained first that they were out of earshot of the guards. In a way it was very unfair to the guards and to us, because the guards were being used to carry out sadistic acts against their compatriots. If they knew that the same leaders who told them about our counter-revolutionary deeds were calling us comrades, I wonder if they would have continued to ill-treat us with such fervour. What they didn't know didn't hurt them, but hurt us the most.

There was something that bothered me more than anything else: the unhesitating readiness of a black person to harm another with such zeal. As far as I remembered, this practice dated back to primary school; then I also remembered Matanzima unleashing brutality on those who opposed him, but it was beyond my comprehension that our ANC could duplicate such barbarity. Now that I was in isolation I could not help trying to understand the implications of the mutiny. Sure, we had rebelled against the war against UNITA and, by doing so, broken the golden rule during the Cold War: an enemy of a friend is my enemy. In the eyes of the socialist fraternity, we were an unruly element deserving to be declared 'enemies'. It was an ideological and political issue but, to our credit, our independent minds revitalised the need to prioritise our own national liberation struggle.

As for the daily beatings – comrade inflicting pain on another comrade – Masondo's narrative of having been slapped by Nelson Mandela 'for being forward and ill-disciplined' seemed to have been the justification or a forewarning of such eventualities. However, it was an unfair comparison when taking the gross human rights abuses into consideration.

I spent two months in isolation after which I joined a group of seven other mutineers who had been arrested on that day in Viana and then transferred from the state prison in Luanda to Quatro. These were:

Bongani Matwa of the Committee of Ten.

Errol Mdanda (MK name; in Quatro, Shorty). He was an effervescent character who I had first met in Lesotho. There was no dull moment with him around. He didn't like conflict wherever he was and restoring peace among those he held dear was his speciality. He was the cell commander.

Tiger in Quatro was Terror (MK name) of the June 16 Detachment who ended up fighting alongside ZIPRA forces in the then Rhodesian liberation war. He was very vocal and indiscreet in his criticism of any unfairness he came across.

Oscar Sizwe (MK name; real name, Sipho Phungulwa). He was renowned for his marksmanship during his training and later became Chris Hani's bodyguard in Lesotho. He had been infiltrated inside the country many times to train numerous comrades, especially in the Transkei.

Vuyisile Maseko (MK name, real name Xolile Siphunzi) was an amicable fellow. He was named F-1 in Quatro after the name of the grenade he exploded in a Land Rover in Viana.

Qotho (MK name; Robe in Quatro) was very friendly and communicative. He had served time on Robben Island before skipping the country in 1980 and staying at Chris Hani's place in Lesotho. His independent mind and rebelliousness didn't help him.

Kentridge (MK name; Pangaman in Quatro) was an enigma. No one knew what his feelings or thoughts were on any subject. He didn't mind just lying on his back and looking at the ceiling all day without uttering a single word to anyone. He later declared that he had an eye problem – so 'will you excuse me from reading any of the communist books?'

For me, meeting these people meant great relief after being alone with nobody to talk to in solitary confinement. In the single cell I had been exercising lightly, so I continued with the routine, only this time restricting myself to the morning session before breakfast. The downside of it was that nobody had washed since arriving in Quatro. When one day we were brought water to wash ourselves, we were sure that we were leaving Quatro, only to find that this was just a new concession in the place.

Besides disposing of our excrement along with that from the isolation cells, there was nothing else we did in that cell. And that was when I became the daily target of a certain guard called Fortune. Every time we ran back from emptying the containers, he would single me out and thrash me with such hatred 'for trying to mess up our good relations with the Angolans'. It came to my attention that the narrative had been twisted, and I was compromised; it was no longer the Angolan army who came to shoot us, thus killing the Quatro guard Babsy, but it was I who had started firing at the APC for no apparent reason. I didn't have the right to argue or defend myself, so I just succumbed to my fate. I knew then that my being brought to Quatro was meant to punish me very severely.

In that cell we had a chance to get books from the camp library. Once a week our cell commissar, Bongani, would assign each of us a political topic for discussion. This happened in each and every cell where there was a group of cellmates. The camp administration also provided us with novels by Russian writers such as Sholokhov, Leo Tolstoy, and Dostoevsky. It was there that I got used to Russia's pre-revolution literature. Classics such as *War and Peace* taught me about the classes and social strata of the time. There was something unique and compelling about this literature: the protagonists were mostly ordinary people caught in a web of wars benefiting none of them.

In October 1984, we were transferred to another cell where we were joined by Omry Makgoale (real name; MK name Sidwell Moroka or Mhlongo, the most senior prisoner in the camp as former MK district commander in Luanda). We were joined also by Sipho Mathebula (MK name; real name Vusi Mndebele), a member of the Committee of Ten and former battalion commander on the Eastern Front) and Samson Lerothodi (MK name; real name David Makhubedu). They had all spent six months in isolation cells at Quatro after having been transferred from the state prison in Luanda.

David Makhubedu had left South Africa in 1975 and joined the PAC in exile, but joined the ANC after returning from military training in Libya. He went to the Party School in Bulgaria and became a commissar in Luanda. He was the one who had alerted the camp by ringing the bell when we were about to be attacked by FAPLA forces. By that act he saved many lives but, ironically, he was sent to Quatro.

The question on everyone's mind was: where was Zaba Maledza

(the MK name of Ephraim Nkondo)? The trio of Omry, Sipho and David, who had joined us, had been brought to Quatro from the Luanda state prison – where they had been tortured by Mbokodo – together with Zaba who had been in an isolation cell next to one of the three. Seemingly, Omry had overheard one of the guards saying, 'This one has killed himself.' Zaba had been to the offices prior to that, but how he had got hold of something to hang himself with was bizarre. Omry had seen him being pulled across Quatro with a rope around his neck.

One can only imagine Zaba's state of mind at the thought of coming to Quatro for the second time – the anticipation of savagery and possible death at the hands of people who see you as an aspirant to a leadership position. Surely it must have been very traumatic for him, but I do not believe the narrative that he killed himself. Our lives and our destiny were in their hands. May Zaba's soul rest in peace.

When Chris Hani and John Motshabi visited Quatro in February 1985 we were naturally expecting good news – being freed was on our minds. Instead, Chris Hani made a mockery of our call for a National Conference when he said that they – the NEC – had decided it was time the ANC held its National consultative conference in June that year, 1985. And no, none of us was to attend the conference. That cast a cloud over the authenticity and validity of the conference. How could our demands be represented if we were all still incarcerated? But the greatest revelation was the fact that our hope in Hani's intervention on our behalf was never to materialise. After the human rights abuse associated with Quatro had been highlighted as one of our main concerns while we were in Viana, he was seemingly content with the arrangement.

Just before the conference, one of us, Terror, was set free after a visit by Mzwandile Piliso, the main architect of Quatro. When the fever of the National consultative conference was gaining momentum, some changes were introduced, such as getting better uniforms and proper boots. Even the food improved with the provision of meat at least once a week. This seemed to indicate that there was uncertainty about the outcome of the conference.

When the conference was over, we were told boastfully that the ANC 'had emerged more united than ever before'. Our camp commander, Pro, bragged that those who were trying to represent our voices were met with an unpopular reaction by representatives from other regions like Zambia and Tanzania. From the look of things, we were back to square one and the security department was enjoying every minute of it.

That year something unexpected happened when two commanders were visiting us. Shorty, our cell commander, had been critically ill with anaemia. He had been beaten at the clinic, accused of faking illness, and had since stopped going for treatment. That only made his condition worse. When they entered our cell we stood to attention, but Shorty took time to stand as he could not maintain his balance. They were livid, saying he was disrespecting them, but Shorty wobbled, collapsed and died in full view of them. That was very painful for all of us because Shorty (may his soul have peace) could have lived had the paramedics heeded his complaints of joint stiffness and varicose veins just after we had been to fetch the 1 000-litre water tank, as a result of which we were flogged mercilessly.

Using us to pull that tank full of water up the steep hill was unnecessary as there was a truck or two in the camp. It was just a pretext to torture us. Of all chores, that tank was the bugbear of every prisoner. Although we prisoners were fetchers of water, we were always thirsty because of the tiny water ration we were allowed. It was the most wicked of tortures to look at the clear water of the stream flowing by and be barred from having even a sip. This was slave labour worse than anything in the gold mines, with the principal purpose of exhausting and dehumanising us.

One would not associate torture and beatings with Christmas. But in Quatro everything was possible. Take Christmas Day of 1985, for example. It was a day when everything seemed to be going well, what with Pro paying us a visit and seeming to be spreading the day's spirit. But soon after we had had our lunch we were told to hop onto a truck and lie in prone position. The truck came to a stop at a clearing full of tree stumps. We had axes and saws with us and were told to fill the truck with firewood.

As we hadn't worked for a long time, and also had not been exposed to the sun, our progress was too slow for the guards' liking. David Makhubedu tried to reason with them, saying we hadn't been getting enough vitamin D while inside the cell. That sparked off a wave of beatings: we were all thrashed and told that was the vitamin D we were in short supply of.

Another one of us, Robe, had said in English: 'Commander, it is the texture of the wood that is hindering our progress.' For that innocent statement we were accused of thinking we were better than them by speaking 'big English'. That earned us another round of beatings, and this time every step we took warranted endless punishment. We had to go down a steep slope and then ascend the hill opposite carrying the logs to the truck parked up on the road behind the hill and then come back for more. It was the longest, most horrifying four hours ever. When we finally made it back to the cell, we were not only exhausted, but had suffered injuries. The skin on our necks and shoulders, where the logs had rested, were chafed, exposing the dermis. After eating in silence and in the darkness, we crawled to our blankets, each moaning unseen. It was still Christmas out there, but to us it had been a nightmare.

At that juncture, there could not have been a better distraction from the stressful situation than art. I was fortunate to have a large box of art materials in our cell. I was the artist in the camp who made banners and posters during the days marked for celebration by the ANC and its allies. Initially I had to do the artwork in a room used for storage, but because there was a possibility of me peeping through the openings and seeing what I wasn't supposed to see, they decided I should work in the cell.

That was like throwing me a lifeline when floods were about to overpower me. I dabbled away with those thick watercolour brushes or splashed the paper with drops of a mixture of colours to see what would come of it. I was trying all means to escape from the cruel world I had found myself in, and that box of goodies was my source of relief.

Unfortunately, when the authorities realised that I had turned the cell into my own studio, it was not acceptable. Any means of self-expression was prohibited in that institution. And when art and I were parted, I remembered I was doubly a prisoner.

CHAPTER 20

The first two female guards, Lindiwe and Sally, arrived in 1986. (Later there came Mpho and Vanessa. Vanessa remained behind when all the others had left.) We supposed that meant there would be an increase in female prisoners. The two took to the job in an amazing fashion, sometimes surpassing their male counterparts in terms of harshness and aggression. Their zeal for their work was excessive. It was evident that they did not want to be undermined because of their gender. They were later joined by another female, though apart from Vanessa they all left and never returned while we were there.

Around that time a new batch of guards were young men from the 'Young Lions' generation of the mid-1980s. From teenage activist to Quatro guard! Our leaders had commented that the ranks of MK were swelling in greater numbers than after the June 16 uprising in 1976. In other words, we of the June 16 generation were now dispensable. What was really happening was that we were being pitted against each other – something that worked wonders for the enemy in Pretoria.

In a reshuffle of prisoners to different cells in 1987, I was put in a cell that was condemned to that most dreaded daily chore – pushing and pulling the monstrous water tank. As though that was not enough, we would also cut logs and bring firewood to the camp on a daily basis. There were eleven of us in the cell, seven of whom were mutineers. Mwezi Twala was the only member of the Committee of Ten. Our cell commander, Stix, had been in Quatro long before we arrived. He had been in the security department before being imprisoned even prior to the mutiny. Of course, we didn't know from the start that we were marked for exceptionally

hard work, but we soon found out. From my previous cell there was Xolile Siphunzi (real name). Others included:
- Mompati – real name Diliza Mthembu. He was embattled during his early years in MK because his father, Abel Patrick Mthembu, was described as a sell-out. His father had been one of the founding members of the MK in 1961. In that year, before the official beginning of MK, he had been sent for military training in China with Raymond Mhlaba, Wilton Mkwayi, Andrew Mlangeni, Joe Gqabi and Nandha Naidoo. He had been arrested and tortured after they had each secretly returned to South Africa and had given evidence for the state in the Rivonia Trial and the trial of the second MK High Command. While Diliza was in exile, his father was shot and killed in South Africa by MK and that was the beginning of Diliza's horrendous experience. He was jailed in Luanda when he was ANC rep in Benguela Province, and then again during the mutiny. It is difficult to understand the emotional, physical and psychological suffering he went through all those years, being in the midst of people who killed his father.
- Callaghan Chama – real name Vusi Shange. His straightforwardness could make some uncomfortable, but his sincerity was what won him true friends who saw his generous side. What you saw was what you got – he was true to himself.
- Eddie (MK name) – real name Amos Maxongo – instilled confidence in those around him with his humour and streetwise personality. His positive attitude was contagious most of the time. He was skilled in tailoring and once sewed uniforms for all the prisoners. No other Quatro prisoner was able to do what Amos did in London in 1991 by telling Nelson Mandela in one-on-one discussion what we had suffered.
- Mbomboshe (MK name) – real name Buthelezi – was a feisty individual renowned for his portrayal of Zulu traditional dance, without being tribalistic. Had his talent been cultivated rather than wasted in Quatro, he could have been one of the finest performers on the world stage.

For the following two weeks we had a problem with bringing the tank to the camp. I remember we would set out as a terrified bunch marching to a revolutionary song about leaving family and country and venturing into foreign lands to fight for liberation.

We would sing that song with feeling and enthusiasm. Birds along the way would have flown away, but whatever birds had been there had long flown away, intending never to return. The peasants in their fields would hear that song from afar and, in anticipation of the imminent wails and cries for help from grown men, would scramble in panic, leaving their hoes and cassava behind and scamper awkwardly towards their village beyond the fields and behind the hill. They could not afford to expose their children to such barbaric experiences. And how would they explain it if their children asked, 'What have they done, Mama and Papa?'

When we reached the stream that flowed silently by, the singing ceased as we had a huge task at hand. However hard we tried, that cruel tank would not budge. Minutes would turn to hours and all that time our energy was fast depleting, giving rise to more beatings being unleashed on us. The beatings, in turn, sapped us further, rendering us weaker and no longer able to push.

After the whole morning session had been spent with no results, the guards would also show signs of exhaustion from punching and clobbering us. Probably they were hungry too, and that left them with no alternative but to take us back to the camp, leaving the tank behind.

We would force ourselves up that hill, a bedraggled bunch of wrecks. And the guards? Proud of themselves for being high-handed. Some day they will learn that by inflicting harm on others we hurt ourselves. I've always had this belief that though we might not be joined at the hip, there is me in you and you in me.

Having suffered for two solid weeks, we decided we could actually manage to bring the tank to the camp. For many years we had heard the chant used by another group that had mastered the task. We had to know the right chant for a certain condition of road; those pulling in the front had to know when to raise or lower or veer to the sides, so as to make the task manageable. We also had to learn how to deal with all the positions of the tank so as to rotate easily while one of us was being 'corrected' by the guards.

When we ultimately worked out our plan to overcome the tank, we were surprised at how working in co-ordination made a difference. In that process we were one with the tank – it was not the foe, but just an object presenting itself as a challenge. We could either succumb to it or tell ourselves that we would be victorious over it.

Oh, how sweet a prize it is to rise above one's ostensible limitations through sheer grit and resolve! With love and not hate, with peace and not aggression, the things we so dearly need do come true. It was a most decent way of saying to the guards: 'You can imprison our physical bodies, but you cannot imprison our boundless spirit.' From that time on, we were not intimidated by the tank or anything else. We called ourselves 'Amaswaiman' – from one of the chants that delivered us. (It was 30 years before I could paint that experience.)

Overcoming the tank did not mean we were out of the woods, but only got us fired up for the next task – procuring firewood. It was mid-morning and by nightfall we would be back at the prison having reached the target for the day: piles of wood for cooking and for boiling water so the personnel could wash. Only then could we say we were done for the day, and rest – only to wake up the next day to the same routine of fetching the tank and bringing the firewood.

Besides the axes and saws when going to cut, saw or chop wood we needed to bring along a burning piece of firewood and make sure it never died out or we would all be in trouble because the guards would not be able to light their cigarettes! The one carrying it would have to pick up kindling along the way and keep blowing into it to keep it burning. It was quite a feverish exercise. Well, the old trick of rubbing two sticks together – and voilà! fire! – still works till today, but no one had a right to make suggestions.

Once we reached the chosen place to chop wood, the guards would take up strategic positions so that we were well surrounded.

We had to keep a certain distance from them and their weapons, or else we might be mistaken for attacking them. Such guardedness from the guards was the main source of tension between them and us. They always entertained the idea that we were desperate to flee or inflict harm on them.

We had somehow to trust each other never to make such a stupid blunder, ever. We had a way of making each of us feel responsible for each step or move we made. Our collective survival depended on the character each individual conveyed: if we were obedient and carried out every order with precision, hopefully we would have a better day with fewer beatings ... or so we thought.

During the days preceding the June 16 commemoration in 1987 the authorities decided we should chop enough firewood to last from June 16 to June 26 – another day celebrated by the ANC, commemorating the launch of the Defiance Campaign in 1952. That meant ten days of firewood. It sounded as if we were headed for a long holiday from going out daily to seek firewood.

The enthusiasm with which we embarked on the mission was very commendable. For three consecutive days we amassed heaps of wood, some of which we left in the wild for later collection.

Things were going well on this Angolan morning when one guard, Mayibuye, ordered me to make a headstand, not on the ground, but high up on the branch of a tree. I guess he must have been eavesdropping and heard someone in the cell asking me to do a headstand. I knew that I was headed for disaster as I climbed the tree. Yet he insisted that I make the stupid headstand. That was when I lost my balance and fell.

In addition to my falling, he came over and beat me till I was dizzy. I was trudging towards the tree stump I had been chopping when everything went blank. When I regained consciousness, I was inside the cell and it was already late afternoon. When I looked around and saw the relief on the faces of my cellmates, I knew they had been on tenterhooks. Maybe they had feared I was going to die that day.

At the clinic they pumped me with drugs to alleviate my cerebral malaria and the epileptic fits I had suffered during my unconsciousness. Of the latter I was told by my cellmates. After falling on the way to chop the tree stump, I had started muttering incomprehensibly and then my body began jerking. My cellmates rushed to my aid and it was obvious that the day's work had to be suspended on my account. I was carried all the way back to the prison clinic where they tried various ways to revive me, but with no luck. Ultimately, the guards returned me to my cell, still unconscious, leaving instructions to alert them of any change for better or worse.

Those drugs helped me, but their side-effects were adverse: I began hallucinating. When awake I would see non-existent beasts in the cell. When I closed my eyes, I would see Robben Island in flames and when asleep, I dreamt I was in outer space with the universe in turmoil – something out of a *Star Wars* movie. This continued day in and day out. I was devastated because during the day I would be left with Diliza Mthembu and Mwezi Twala whose health was also not good. I had become their additional problem, although they welcomed the responsibility. In return I would try to cheer them up with a story of my favourite couple while I was growing up in Mthatha. Brother Felix had been brought up by a single parent and had never known his father. His mother took care of his needs, mostly education. He met and loved a woman who he later married and they both played tennis. In his entire life, brother Felix never had friends – I was the only person who had ever befriended him, until his wife came along. I would go on about the couple till I felt the effects of the drugs and yielded to their lulling effect.

What was always going through my mind as I related the story was a deep-seated fear inside me that I might never live to meet the one who would ever love me, as long as I was inside that hellhole. The one who would be the object of my affection would receive my total loyalty. She would have to be loyal too. We would cook, do the laundry and clean the house together, and if I could afford it, I would have a safety net so that if she ever fell, she would not hurt herself and … and … and …

After two hectic weeks, I could tell that I was well mended. It had been an unprecedented case in Quatro where a patient was allowed to recover without interruption. But the first task assigned to Diliza and me was too tough. We were to cut the grass at the shooting range using two pangas each. The grass was knee-high for 100 metres, more or less. The three guards on duty that day weren't vile at all. I think they saw the task as enough punishment on its own and that any verbal or physical abuse was uncalled for.

That lukewarm atmosphere only made us exert more pressure on ourselves to complete our undertaking in record time. On the following morning, the after-effects of the previous day's work were aches all over the body. We had been inactive for too long and the sudden turnaround affected every muscle. That morning had been our first day back at work. But with the protection of my cellmates, I managed to make it through, taking it a day at a time.

CHAPTER 21

8 August 1987 is a day I will never forget. The day was surreal in the sense that we did not go out to work, and no one was beaten or chided. We had our cell door opened to let in fresh air and our uniforms were changed the day before. Unknown to us was the imminent visit of the president of our beloved organisation, OR Tambo.

It only came to our knowledge when he took one step, then another, into our cell. Among his entourage were the administration officers; the guards remained outside. He seemed composed though he had to take time to acclimatise to the dinginess of the cell, despite it being midday. It was definitely a far cry from his usual haunts of brightly lit and air-conditioned rooms. Pro, the camp commander, introduced us as 'mutineers'. Tambo, in a camouflage uniform and boots, looked closely at each face before shaking each hand in turn. When he was through, he said: 'That was the worst period the organisation has ever been through in its history.'

He said the words with feeling. It was like he was reliving how he had felt at the time. He did not seem to put the blame on us or anyone else; it was as if he had welcomed its inevitability and accepted its aftermath. His attitude towards us must have taken the security officers by surprise, because in us he was not seeing enemies to be thrown into a lion's den, but compatriots who had accidentally done something wrong but for the right reasons.

He didn't say much but left our cell for the next one. Whatever he said there is not to my knowledge, but the sombre mood he left behind in the cell was indicative of the fact that he had not come to free us. The opportunity had not been utilised, so it was evident we were to remain there indefinitely. We had to live with the idea that, although he did not know the extent of how gruesome life there was, and though the place had been overhauled specially for his tour to suit the requirements of a 'rehabilitation centre', he was complicit in our abusive and ongoing detention without a fair trial. It was quite a shocking realisation and set us back as far as our hopes and wishes were concerned.

Maybe the project that came up towards the end of that year had to do with improving our living conditions. It was of immense proportions: we were to construct bigger, more airy cells as an extension alongside the existing ones. We in our doomed cell were to be involved in every step: making bricks from a mixture of gravel and cement and drying them in the sun; digging the trenches for laying the foundation; the actual bricklaying; setting up the shuttering structure for the concrete roof and, lastly, applying the concrete on the shuttering.

It was an undertaking that proceeded in phases without relieving us from hauling the water tank and chopping wood. We had grown a thick skin when it came to the soulless treatment meted out to us, and we protected those who were perennially delicate or recovering from illness.

That being that, it did not mean we no longer felt the strain of being overworked. Taking the obstacles one at a time and encouraging each other through humour helped. Each of us knew that things could be worse if anyone in that cursed cell pulled in the opposite direction.

Throughout those phases of building the extension, there were moments of burnout when, on reaching the cell, one would be looking forward to an early night. Such was the day in 1988 when we had to pour the concrete for the roof shuttering. We had constructed a ramp the previous day and the crushed stone was ready. We had to finish the shuttering on that very day.

It was a very laborious task, repeatedly pushing the wheelbarrows full of concrete up that ramp in the sweltering Angolan heat. Add grumpy guards and harassment to the equation and you have a day in hell. Spare a moment of thought for the frail and sickly Mwezi Twala who was also ordered to work on that day; he had been there when Quatro was built, and now he was not only a prisoner, but was also to be instrumental in its extension.

What I found interesting was that none of us ever commented negatively or positively about the construction of more cells. It was a known fact that we should be wary of whatever we said inside the cells because the guards constantly eavesdropped. If one was saying something that had the potential to indict him, we would all be affected. So, we avoided any sensitive topics. Any new arrival in Quatro had to learn the lesson as early as possible: that to probe, to enquire or be too inquisitive would only land one in a sticky situation.

We were going about our business as usual: the construction, the water tank, the firewood, the beatings, and new arrivals in bad shape from torture – in short there was no sign indicating our release. Then it suddenly happened – 16 November 1988. But unfortunately not all mutineers were released on that day,

We were informed of our release late on 15 November and were gathered, all 26 of us, in one cell. It was not the benevolence of the ANC leadership that brought us our freedom, but the UN Resolution 435 in conjunction with the Chester Crocker Accords. The resolution of the Namibian question, according to the Accord, demanded that the Angolan government had to rid its country of all Cuban, Soviet, Swapo and ANC personnel on the one hand, while South African occupation troops, on the other hand, had to evacuate Namibia so that the people of Namibia could determine their own future through free and fair elections.

There we were, about to be released, when a security officer, camp commissar Griffiths, came into the cell and said that at no stage were we to tell anyone about our stay in Quatro. Once that little secret was out, the person concerned would face a firing squad. We all had to sign that we swore to keep the secret.

At the time I told myself that I wouldn't bother anyone with such a sob story. The world was already full of despair so, on that score, I would be silent, just as all those before me had been silent ... but for how long? How does one get counselling if one does not reveal each and every thing one has experienced? It was an open secret that Quatro was the ANC's version of a Nazi concentration camp, like Buchenwald, or as I later learnt, the Gulag of the Soviet Union.

Had someone asked me before my coming to Quatro if that was possible, I would vehemently have said it was not. But having been there, and having gone through what I had, I knew that even the South African racist regime would be shocked at the degree of mercilessness some blacks can readily inflict on one another. At that time, I felt we had run away from one brutal bully right into the hands of an even worse one – Mbokodo.

Our cellmate Robe would say (in whispered tones) that Robben Island was a holiday resort compared to Quatro. Well, he knew – he had been a prisoner on Robben Island before coming to Quatro. It might seem unfair to compare the two prisons, but it is no exaggeration to say that Mbokodo had mastered the technique of terror. What does one expect if omnipotence, elitism, impunity, secrecy and unaccountability are bestowed on a handful, when the rest are deprived? Complete disdain for the law, humaneness, ethics and morality. Like the birds of Quatro, these qualities were all gone, never to return!

Besides not knowing one's day of release, in Quatro there was a plethora of things we didn't know since we were literally in a blackout about developments in the outside world. If the world was coming to an end, we would have been the last to know. For starters, we didn't know what the findings of the Stuart Commission had been. Had they put the blame on us, or had they exonerated us? What had happened at the Kabwe national consultative conference? Were any of our demands met? It came to my knowledge that the other two comrades with whom I had been to the underground house in Luanda – Selby and Sidney – had been taken that night to join others in the Luanda state prison. Except for those who were taken to Quatro, others were released after a year. To some extent that gave credence to the idea that those remaining in prison were the guilty ones.

We did not know either that Matanzima had been ousted as head of the Transkei and that, after a so-called 'bloodless coup', General Bantu Holomisa had taken over as head of the territory in January 1988. Holomisa was well disposed towards the ANC and other liberation organisations.

Something else we did not know was that there had been a second mutiny in Pango in May 1984 after I had left. It was the worst tragedy to befall the ANC as it resulted in a major loss of life, on both the side of the mutineers and the so-called ANC faithful. Seven were later sentenced to death by firing squad. Ironically, three of the seven were among the 'heroes', who had crossed with Hani into enemy territory, but this time he was the one who endorsed their death by execution. Their remains are in a mass grave in Pango. Those who survived were tortured and thrashed while naked. That was until the head of the ANC Women's League at the time – Gertrude Shope – brought the torture and further plans of execution to an abrupt end. Eight mutineers were brought to join us in Quatro, though the authorities made sure that we did not mix with them. Others were to serve various punishments in Pango. And so the era of taking up arms to fight for a democratic ANC ended.

That second mutiny can only be blamed on the harshness of the behaviour towards the unarmed former mutineers. The mutineers' fatal decision to seize weapons and overrun the camp was not the wisest, but it was born from the desperation of their daily depressing and deteriorating relations with the administration. This was coupled with the accelerated, vengeful heavy-handedness of Mbokodo. Its victims saw no other option; the two sides had reached a boiling point and a collision course was inevitable.

As for the Stuart Commission findings, everything was kept under wraps not only for us mutineers, but for the public at large. This was the result of the division in the NEC as to whether or not to reveal the ANC's human rights violations. The majority was against hanging its dirty laundry in public for all to view. The findings took nine years to reach the public domain, finally being released in 1993 after the exiles' return to South Africa, along with the findings of the Motsuenyane Commission of Inquiry appointed by Nelson Mandela to investigate those human rights abuses.

The Kabwe conference had not heeded our demands in calling for the suspension of the security department, Mbokodo, and the investigation of its activities, especially at Quatro. After the conference, things were almost the same as before, except for the sacking of Andrew Masondo from the NEC and the inclusion, for the first time, of all racial groups in the NEC.

Andrew Masondo's sacking from the NEC was not unexpected, but we felt he was being sacrificed to authenticate the Kabwe conference. Our expectations were of a shake-up of the NEC on a grander scale, involving sacking of Mzwai Piliso, the chief architect of Quatro, and Joe Modise. These three were directly involved in ordering deliberate imprisonment, torture and eventual death of numerous people suspected of being ill-disciplined or being enemy agents. Mzwai Piliso only got a slap on the wrist by losing his position as head of security to Sizakele Sigxashe – one of the Stuart commissioners. Piliso became head of the department of manpower. Joe Modise retained his position as Commander of MK.

The story of Masondo's moral degeneration is quite an intriguing one. For the man with academic achievements anyone would envy and having been exposed to men of integrity on Robben Island – the likes of the Rivonia Trialists – it is difficult to fathom his shift to malice. Was it in retaliation for years spent in jail, or the result of the paranoia in Angola fostered by prevailing tensions since the so-called attempted coup by Nito Alves on 27 May 1977, which resulted in thousands of innocents being killed by the MPLA regime? Whatever the reason might have been, it was still unacceptable!

One last piece of news kept secret was that the war against the counter-revolutionary UNITA and FNLA had resumed, though this time in the northern region where Quatro, Pango and Quibaxe were situated. UNITA insurgents were working with the FNLA because the latter enjoyed popular support in the area, unlike the south of Angola where UNITA had its support base. Even mercenaries plied their expertise in the war.

Words from one security officer at Quatro – that we should be glad we were held prisoner while people were dying out there – had not made sense to us. It was in the war against the UNITA rebels that our MK combatants lost many lives. They were young and had been duped into believing that they were heroes for sacrificing their lives, and that they understood the dynamics of our 'long and protracted struggle' better than we did. To them we were cowards who had chickened out.

Needless to say, it was regrettable that their unquestioning obedience led to their untimely end. It was at a time in our struggle when those in MK had to identify with the powers that be. The changes brought about by the Crocker Accords, could not have come at a better time for us and for all MK personnel who were in that war.

It was the time of our release. All those in Quatro who were not released with us were taken to Uganda as that country provided the ANC with training-camp facilities – and a prison for those brought over from Quatro, and elsewhere. Of course, we did not know that at the time, just as we did not know our fate. It is true that we are not absolutely free until we – and not someone else – determine our own fate.

PART FIVE
EAST AFRICA

OR Tambo in Quatro.

CHAPTER 22

Leaving Quatro was a celebration on its own. It was like being promoted from subhuman to being human again. We were all eagerly looking forward to being out there to mingle in a free world and stake our claim to our rights as citizens: to live long enough and die naturally.

Yes, it mattered not where they were taking us, as long as we were leaving that place of suffering. We would be fine; it was a second bite at life – a vacation the doctor recommended.

On that morning we were dressed in the uniform of all MK general combatants as we boarded a truck. For the last time we had to lie face down all the way until the truck was far distant from the prison. After that we were able to sit.

Two vans escorted us, one in front and the other at the rear. The weather that morning had signs of imminent rain: the atmosphere was humid, and the skies were overcast. We gulped the sweetness of the fresh air as we sped towards Luanda, chatting unstoppably.

There was not a single trace of fear of the guards, unlike inside Quatro – they were there to secure our destination against any likely attack from rebels. Funnily enough, they did not call us by our Quatro names. They had to learn our MK names – things had changed big time! It was time to bridge the gap between us, though tentatively. That boded well for when we came to checkpoints manned by the Angolan police: we were one unit with no misunderstanding among us.

We arrived in Luanda in the afternoon and were taken to a newly opened warehouse. We were not allowed to leave the place and seemingly no other MK members were allowed in. Probably no one knew about our release or our whereabouts, except those in the security department.

There was nothing in particular for us to do there except wake up, wash and eat. This went on for more than a week. Because we were emaciated on our arrival, some of us gained so much weight that Mwezi Twala joked cynically that it was a 'fattening-up process' so that when people met us they would not be shocked. Another remark was 'they were starving us to death, now they are killing us with food'. Many interesting philosophies abounded.

What brought us hope of a better future was when we had a medical check-up and were brought brand-new clothes: shoes, shirts, trousers – you name it. And we all got two pairs of everything. That stimulated discussion about individual plans outside of army life. Somewhere out there life was waiting for us.

When we ultimately left the warehouse, we were taken to the airport where we caught a flight to Lusaka. On arrival there we stayed in the airport lobby the whole day. When it was dark, we were smuggled to a house where we were given supper. We thought we were going to stay in Lusaka, and just as we were getting comfortable and ready to sleep, we were told we were to board a bus to Tanzania. At three in the morning!

When we passed the town of Kabwe we only exchanged glances – no comments. Besides the Tanzam railway, which from time to time was visible, there was not much on the journey to write home about. That railway is historic as it connected landlocked Zambia to the seaport of Dar es Salaam. The Chinese had sponsored it, but unfortunately it ended up not being utilised.

We arrived at the Tanzanian border at night and had to wait until morning to cross over because the customs office was closed. The next day was another long day on the road till at last we got to Morogoro. What struck us was the great difference between rural Zambia and its Tanzanian counterpart. The latter was well developed agriculturally, thanks to the Ujamaa programme introduced by Mzee Julius Nyerere.

From Morogoro we were driven to Dakawa. But first, though, before we could meet the people of Dakawa, we were to be debriefed at a place called Ruth First Reception Centre, or Eighteen. This was the ANC security department's place. It said something that it was named after someone who had been assassinated by the apartheid regime and would have loathed any association with Mbokodo. We were not surprised when we were told we had to abide by the promise not to tell anyone about our experiences in Quatro and afterwards. They also wanted to know if we still felt the mutiny was justified. Of course we were convinced that our demands and proposals were justified. Somehow we held a unanimous view, although we were interviewed as individuals.

For us it would have been disingenuous to suggest the opposite. It would not have been reflective of our true selves. Sometimes there's a point of no return, and honesty to oneself is best rather than complicating things in a web that might entangle everyone involved.

Relations between security personnel and the general membership at Dakawa were sour. The atmosphere was gloomy despite cosmetic changes. Attempts to change people's perception of the security department had failed, despite Mzwai Piliso having been replaced as head of Mbokodo by Fort Hare graduate Sizakele Sigxashe, since the department's personnel was unchanged. In fact, Mbokodo had consolidated itself after the mutiny and permeated all structures, which could lead only to low morale and disillusionment.

Dakawa was a centre where demobilised MK combatants from all detachments were stationed. There were family units and singles at V4 village. We from Quatro initially pitched our tents and had our own kitchen. That setting, close to V4, was sheltered by trees and so pleasing to the eye that one Bernard named it Hawaii. And Hawaii stood out alone as a vibey place because of the positive attitudes of its inhabitants, despite everything.

That positivity was soon to inspire the neighbouring V4. The welcome we got was warm, but it got warmer as time went on because of our willingness to revive Dakawa's almost defunct political structures: the Zonal Political Committee (ZPC), the Zonal Youth Committee (ZYC) and the Regional Political Committee (RPC). These structures had been democratically elected by members but were finding it difficult to sustain themselves without support from the leadership, more especially from the headquarters in Lusaka.

The local administration was fully operational because it was apolitical. Despite that, nothing could uplift the people from the doldrums. The housing project had stalled because of a lack of enthusiasm and involvement. People pitched up at work, loitered, got something to eat and dismissed themselves. Some would go to neighbouring Mabhana and Magole villages and spend the rest of the day imbibing alcohol.

With our never-say-die attitude, the need to involve ourselves in all matters concerning us, be they political, cultural or on the labour front, became a paramount necessity. We wholeheartedly engaged ourselves in all areas.

When the administration saw that we were trying to reverse the pattern we had found to be prevalent, it tried by all means to come aboard. What inspired us about the project was that houses were to be built for all of us in V4. They were of brick and mortar, unlike the tents of Hawaii or the wooden structures of V4. Bar the fact that we were no longer to be active in the unfolding struggle for the liberation of South Africa, it was the improvement in the quality of life that attracted us. Besides, it would be in keeping with the clause in the Freedom Charter that says, 'There shall be houses and security.' If we could contribute practically towards the realisation of that dream, then so be it.

Also, with some of us having had experience in building from our work at Quatro, it came naturally for us to choose construction work. We were nurturing a skill and at the same time getting paid. It was something new for us to get pocket money while getting free supplies of food and clothing. For someone who had been in Quatro, it was an amazing opportunity that we could not let go by.

Some of us decided to go the academic route. SOMFACO in

Mazimbu was the stepping stone to achieving higher education locally or abroad. Surely everything seemed to be coming up roses. But that was what things looked like superficially, because when we dug deeper we discovered the rot.

Despite the warm welcome and kind words from ANC secretary-general Alfred Nzo that we should be emulated for our keenness in political matters and that we should be integrated into the community and be eligible to vote and be voted for, the reality was that when we took the first step of resuscitating the political structures, the results did not sit well with the leadership.

Out of the nine members of the ZYC who were elected by all the ANC exiles at Dakawa, including ourselves, five were former Quatro inmates, including three members of the Committee of Ten. That was a problem for the ANC leadership, which was further compounded by the election of ex-mutineers to the Cultural Committee and the Works Committee. But it was not easy for the leadership to forcefully put an end to a democratic process, lest they risked being accused of going back on the words of Alfred Nzo.

A seminar held at Dakawa on 24 and 25 April 1989 was meant to review progress achieved and to consider new projects. On the agenda was also the establishment of an autonomous administration for Dakawa. We had a meeting at which the ANC community of Dakawa accepted the views and proposals that had been agreed to at an earlier youth meeting. Yet our ZYC was then barred from attending as a participant. After challenging that absurd decision, Dakawa ZYC was allowed to send one delegate. The chairperson, Sidwell Moroka (real name Omry Makgoale), was to represent us.

That third seminar at Dakawa had heads of departments from ANC headquarters – though with Piliso no longer heading the security department but that of development of manpower (DMD), and Thomas Nkobi, the national treasurer. The main bone of contention was between the youth of Dakawa calling for elected bodies instead of appointments from headquarters. Now that was a heavy contest – pitting Makgoale against Piliso was like a grudge fight between two pugilists. Knowing Makgoale's uncompromising stance on principle, I can only imagine that any attempt by Piliso to discredit him would have been met with facts and reason. The results were in favour of our ZYC's recommendations.

When a delegation of the ANC youth was due to attend the World Youth Festival in Pyongyang, North Korea, a telex was sent to Tanzania from Lusaka cancelling the names of four delegates who happened to be ex-mutineers. No explanation was given. Democracy was being trampled on and weakened across the whole of the ANC. The headquarters in Lusaka then ludicrously claimed it was not responsible for the telex. From discussions between the Dakawa ZYC and Jackie Selebi, the chairman of the National Youth Secretariat, all fingers pointed in the direction of the security department. All ANC structures in Tanzania were dismayed by this development.

At that time I was also working as an artist at Dakawa Textile Printing and we had worked overtime to produce prints relevant to the theme of world peace. I had personally added caricatures and watercolour paintings to those to be exhibited there. No one knows the fate of all that hard work – did it even reach its intended destination?

Besides working at construction and textile printing, I was also the art director of our *Dakawa News and Views* – a news bulletin on a board mounted on the premises of our community hall. It was the brainchild of Bandile Ketelo. My job was to furnish the bulletin with a political cartoon or artwork by me or any local artist. It had to be relevant, and not obscene or of low standard.

When boxing and soccer sports codes were opened up, I joined the former. There were about ten of us who were seriously attending the gym. At one time we challenged the famous Simba Sporting Club in Dar es Salaam, but returned from Dar es Salaam without having fought. They later made up for it by coming to Mazimbu.

I fought in the middleweight division. A Simba middleweight boxer, accompanied by his trainer, came over and checked out our knuckles. The other middleweight boxer in our team was Zamuxolo Tshona, also an ex-mutineer. The Simba boxer decided to fight me because Tshona was just muscle and no fat, while I was more on the fatter than fitter side. Well, I'm used to this; I found long, long ago that actually nobody fears me.

When I went to that fight, I had one thing in mind – not to lose, no matter what. I would be doing it for the club. It was fortunate to get a fight, as they could be few and far between. Training hard and getting no fights can be frustrating for boxers.

I jumped into the ring with some confidence. It was to be through body language, flair and mobility that I intended to convince the judges that I deserved to win. But the more I upped my work rate, the more my opponent upped his. After the first round, my corner officials jumped up and splashed my face with water while I was still approaching them. They muttered only these words: 'You are doing good!' Good of them to spare me the unnecessary lecture that seconds are wont to give their boxers. The first three minutes of that round seemed never to end. In the second round, the crowd was calling for action, action, action. I jumped from the chair as though it had suddenly turned into a hot plate. I was baying for the poor guy's blood as the throngs of people demanded nothing less. I had a reach advantage, so I used jabs, thus avoiding an in-fight. I had to pace my energy carefully for the last round as I found out that my opponent was a tough guy.

I mustered all my strength as I stepped forward for the last round's 'shake your hands' routine. Then we were at each other like sworn enemies. I remember ducking a blow, but misreading it. I paid dearly for that mistake – he got me just above my temple and I wobbled. Yes, he got me nice and clean. I was counted because I had slipped and touched the canvas with my glove.

Now, dear reader, the referee was a comrade who knew me by name from way back in Lesotho. As he was wiping my gloves against his jersey, he said, 'Luthando, go for the stomach!' and then, 'Box!' Of course the Tanzanian boxer was in the neutral corner and did not hear what he said. Besides, the referee said it in my Xhosa language.

This time I put everything into it. He was going for the head, thus giving me a chance to have a dig at his unprotected solar plexus with a flurry of blows. I could hear him gasp for breath and I wasn't stopping. He flopped to the canvas and the referee pointed me to the neutral corner before counting him. He beat the count, but seconds later the gong went and it was time for the judges to show how they had scored the fight.

The decision took forever. At such times a boxer should not sit down but move around the ring to show that there's still strength in him: punching the air and waving at the crowd because – believe me – the judges took all that into consideration.

After a long time, the decision was a draw: two judges gave the fight to each of us with equal points while the third gave it a draw. I was happy that I hadn't lost. We shook hands and hugged to show our sporting spirit and left the ring. I can't tell what transpired in the last bout of the night as I was in the changing room very, very exhausted.

I never got another chance to be billed for a fight, but I continued training. The last boxing competition was held in our backyard in Dakawa. We were fighting the same Simba Sporting Club. We had all kinds of sports during the day but the evening was reserved for boxing. I will never forget the bout when one of our fighters, who I had never seen at the gym, took to the ring. I was the timekeeper that evening. Our boxer went for the kill from the first second of the fight. It was clear he wanted to end the fight inside the first round with a knockout. His opponent could only block without a chance of retaliating. It was amazing that he survived the first round without falling from that avalanche of blows.

Now I had just rung the bell for the mandatory 50-second break after which a whistle is blown for the seconds to exit the ring, when our boxer turned to me and, through the rope, shouted at me that I was foolish to ring the bell when he was about to finish off the fight. The other boxer was being pampered and listening to advice while ours was brushing the seconds away, just to have a go at me. I only managed to say, 'Okay, okay.' Then I found myself instinctively hitting the gong for the second round without checking whether or not the minute had elapsed.

He rose from his seat to continue where he had left off. I leaned back to one of our guys, Mbeko, and asked, 'Who is this?' The answer was: 'It is Doctor. Doctor, the guard back in Quatro.' So, Doctor thought he could mess with me here just as he did in Quatro? I became livid with rage. If only the Simba boxer could turn this fight around – I was hoping and praying, especially since Doctor's strength was ebbing fast and his opponent was gaining the upper hand.

One blow caught Doctor and sent him staggering across the ring, but the referee did not stop the fight. I wasn't looking at the stopwatch now but was fixated with the fight, which was turning out to be my prayer answered. That Simba boxer was clinical as he took his time sapping his opponent. The referee momentarily looked my way, maybe suggesting that it was time to end the round. Well, he wasn't the one who had been insulted just minutes before and would he please let a man savour the moment!

Yes, I was wrong, but flashes of Doctor clobbering me back in Quatro got the better of me. And who did he think he was, to have his way with the likes of us for the rest of his life? In retrospect, I am aware of the amount of trauma and anger that had welled up inside me, and was not released. It imprisons and limits one's outlook and can only destroy a person and those around him.

Well, Doctor lost on a knockout; a very sorry end to someone used to being the giver, and not the receiver, of punches.

When I look back at that time, I feel convinced that had fate given us a break, we could have turned the whole of Tanzania into a boxing-loving nation. With the excited spectators gathered there, the spectacle of boxing was finding fertile ground to grow. But fate had different plans for us ex-mutineers.

CHAPTER 23

There had been many positive developments on the labour front. We had accelerated our construction output. After that third Dakawa seminar we had attained our autonomy at administrative level. Old man Dennis, who had always been the head of administration, pulled out all the stops when it came to providing us with essential support, which facilitated our work and spurred us on.

Within a short time, we had finished building three houses with the help of a local construction company that specialised in roofing and other final touch-ups. Because this was a private company, their workers were fairly remunerated since the funders, the Norwegians, had pumped a lot of money into it. Little did we know that we, too, were to be rewarded on a par with the private company. We had been paid 600 shillings every month for our time at Dakawa and now we found that we were to get a living wage. We were overwhelmed with joy and disbelief. To think we had been paid a pittance all along! Of course, the others were still receiving the lousy 600 shillings a month.

All of a sudden, I realised that there would be a bright future for me. After a long day at work, then an early evening at the Textile Printing Workshop, I would retire to my single bed and dream. Not of a fancy house on the hill with a view of the sea and a fleet of cars with personal number plates. No! I would dream of a warm home: warm not only from the sun's rays through the window or from the heat of the fireplace, but warm because of the mutual love, trust and care my future wife and I would so much value. This wishful thinking would continue every night till sleep overcame me.

Yes, I would have achieved that if I had saved a lot of money, and if the security department had not got wind of what was taking place. Suffice to say, that was the first and the last time we received that living wage. A series of events had led to a collision course for ex-mutineers and the security department. We could not co-exist peacefully and none of us was relenting. It didn't matter how much we exercised democratic tendencies to supersede their autocratic tendencies, we were always on the losing side. The power wielded by the security department over the political department was tantamount to an internal coup. With all the political empowerment that we ostensibly had, we were just lambs in the way of a dangerous marauding pack of wild dogs.

The news bulletin also proved to be a thorn in the side of Mbokodo. Some articles were critical of certain practices that went against the very founding principles of our organisation. It is highly significant that this was happening in Tanzania against the backdrop of the changes in the Soviet Union brought to the fore by the Mikhail Gorbachev administration. Gorbachev's *glasnost* (openness) and *perestroika* (socio-economic transformation) ushered in a new era compared with the jackboot legacy left by Joseph Stalin. This drastic shift was not palatable to some of the old guard who were used to the archaic modus operandi, which benefited them.

It seemed we were having a similar situation in the ANC: some were resistant to the change that was disturbing the comfort zone of top-down power that suited them. This was sharply displayed in September 1989 when Omry Makgoale and Mwezi Twala were elected by ANC members at Dakawa as chairperson and organising secretary respectively of the RPC – the highest political body of the ANC in the country. The election was attended by the Rivonia Trialist Rusty Bernstein, who wrote very warmly to Nelson Mandela about Omry the following year.

On 16 September 1989, however, Andrew Masondo, Graham Morodi (the then ANC chief rep in Tanzania) and Willy Williams (David Motshweni, then head of Mbokodo at 'The Farm') together with security personnel, refused to allow the democratic results of the election to prevail. Morodi said the results needed the approval of the NEC.

On 18 September Omry Makgoale received a letter barring the newly elected RPC from taking office, the reason being that the response from Lusaka was still pending.

On 5 October the RPC was dissolved by Morodi with the blessing of the ANC secretary-general, Alfred Nzo. The reasons advanced were that there had been violations of procedures and nominees had not been screened prior to the election. This meant that the ANC security department had an overriding power to annul any democratically elected structure if it disapproved of those elected by the ANC membership.

A new body was appointed from ANC headquarters. It was called the Interim RPC, but we regarded it as a 'dummy structure'. It didn't last because the youth of Dakawa wouldn't have it. It was an open onslaught on democracy, and we were out there to defend democracy.

On 24 December 1989 – Christmas Eve! – Chris Hani and Stanley Mabizela, as representatives of the NEC, called the community of Dakawa to a meeting. Mabizela said ex-mutineers were not allowed to take office in ANC structures. In addition to that, he appealed for the support of the community for the Interim RPC.

Speaker after speaker denounced the NEC decision. The arguments were that the NEC was acting undemocratically by reaching such a decision without consulting the general membership; that the cause of the mutiny had never been openly discussed by the general membership; and that there was still torture of detainees by security members. This was a reference to what had happened to Dipulelo, who headed the *Dakawa News and Views*. He was accused of subversion, having reported – accurately – that OR Tambo had suffered a stroke. He was detained, and none other than Doctor – the boxer/Mbokodo member – tortured him at the Ruth First Detention Centre. We had not seen Dipulelo for some time and when he appeared, he had lost weight and looked subdued. It was at that meeting that we heard what had befallen him.

When it was apparent that the majority of those present at the meeting disagreed with the announcement, Chris Hani stood up and had to shout to be heard. He pounded on the table with his fist as he announced that the decision was unchallengeable, as it was an order from the NEC. The meeting descended into chaos, when members of the security department wanted to arrest anyone who wanted to raise a view. Also there was the Tanzanian Field Force Unit (FFU), which the locals sarcastically called *Fanya Fujo Uwone*, roughly translated as 'Dare do any nonsense, you will see!' in the KiSwahili language.

The meeting ended on a bad note, and we all returned home feeling incapacitated and worthless. This had not happened in the army where orders are not discussed; this was supposed to be a microcosm of a democratic society for the future free and liberated South Africa, yet self-expression was non-existent. A democratic election was being overruled. The question was: when will the people govern?

The last nail in our coffin was on 28 December when a list of names was circulated officially banning nine members of different committees. All on the list were ex-mutineers. How fast things were changing! We had been out of that notorious prison for little more than a year, but now the signs were there for all to see that further incarceration and possibly killings were imminent. A sequel to Quatro was too ghastly to contemplate.

The following evening we ex-mutineers met secretly on the outskirts of Dakawa. We analysed the situation and decided that if we remained in Dakawa we would ultimately all die and none of us would be able to tell our story to our people back home. Like a rip-current, fate had reclaimed us and thrown us back into the deep open sea of the vast exile wilderness – to survive or die.

Our sin had been to rejuvenate the erstwhile dull Dakawa, introducing cultural events and sport participation, turning the dumping place for disillusioned MK cadres into a vivacious hub attracting young and old, and resuscitating political participation among the membership. It was unbelievable and horrifying.

Yes, we were going to escape from Dakawa; that was the most sensible thing to do. It had come to that sad decision in a dark hour in Dakawa.

Leaving the ANC was analogous to a partner leaving an abusive and toxic relationship after having tried all avenues to salvage it. But either we took responsibility for our future and fled, or we succumbed to being victims out of fear of being left in the cold, without the ANC support system to sustain us.

On 30 December 1989 it was announced that the administration had decided to thank all of us who had worked on the construction site at V4. We were to be sponsored for a trip to Dar es Salaam and would spend the New Year having a barbecue at Bagamoyo Beach, next to the historical East African slave trade port. On top of that we were given 1 000 shillings each. Talk of Lady Luck smiling in our direction! This happened when we had yet to come up with a plan as to how we would leave Dakawa, and the money would be handy when we were on our own.

On 31 December 1989 – the eve of change in South Africa – we received the promised money, boarded the bus and left for Dar es Salaam. We were sworn to secrecy never to divulge our intentions, which were to give them the slip at the first available chance. That chance availed itself when we stopped at the ANC offices in downtown Dar es Salaam.

No one noticed as we made our way to the buses going to various destinations. We took a bus to Magomeni, where we checked into a guesthouse.

There were eleven of us former mutineers and three women who were romantically involved with three of us. Each had with her their three-year-old child. The real names of our group were:
- Bandile Ketelo, who had been a commissar in Caculama training camp. He and others had left the camp to join us mutineers in Viana. He had also been detained in Luanda state security prison and later in Quatro. He had been instrumental in the forming of *Dakawa News and Views* and was one of those barred from going to the World Youth Conference in

Pyongyang although he had made it there due to a mistaken identity.
- Zamuxolo Tshona had also been detained in Luanda state prison and in Quatro. He had been very active in the boxing club at Dakawa.
- Luvo Mbengo was also a former Quatro detainee, having been handed over to ANC security by the Soviets when he and others had gone to seek help at their base after escaping during the second mutiny in Pango.
- Ronnie Masango was incarcerated by ANC security in Angola and Tanzania and had been severely tortured for his beliefs in democratic norms.
- Selinah Mlangeni was a June 16 Detachment member and was with us on account of carrying the child of Amos Maxongo.
- Nontyatyambo Yokuqala Mzimela had been one of the first female guards at Quatro. She had moved to Dakawa after giving birth to a daughter. She and Diliza Mthembu were in love and by that time she was also pregnant with their child.
- Patricia Patheka Sodo was Vusi Shange's girlfriend.

Finally, there were David Makhubedu, Mwezi Twala, Sipho Phungulwa and me. Omry Makgoale was not with us, due to his pending move to Germany to study.

On 2 January 1990, we approached the office of the United Nations High Commissioner for Refugees (UNHCR) in Dar es Salaam, where we laid bare our harrowing story. We needed protection, as well as financial and educational assistance, if possible. After hearing us out, the officials told us they could not help us while we were still members of the ANC.

That led us to the door of the ANC residence in our vicinity in Magomeni. A date for an appointment was set. When we met with the relevant persons, we each had to state the reason for leaving the ANC. We said ours was an unenviable position in which our safety within the organisation was compromised.

Even though our reasons were understandable, it was again the story of the abusive partner who promises to change his ways when the abused party threatens to leave. And when the abused says, 'Look, let's not make this harder than it is ...', then there's no convincing the abuser otherwise. It is clear the abused party is ready for the challenge of being on their own.

Our fundamental source of confidence in taking that gigantic step lay in the political situation at home in South Africa, given the rapid pace of change unfolding within the country. On that score, the pros seemed to outweigh the cons. But we needed the immediate protection of the UNHCR, without which we would be diving from a plane without a parachute.

Resigning was thus forced on us. It was not a good feeling. It was admitting defeat to forces we knew did not have the people's interest at heart. That was why we continued collectively to draft a document outlining the path the ANC had taken that had led to it losing its democratic ways and morals, degenerating into an organisation where a few powerful individuals abused their power and thus derailed the course of the struggle.

We also highlighted the causes of the mutiny and its aftermath, and how we ended up resigning. Our document had originated in Dakawa, with contributions from Omry Makgoale and Norman Phiri (MK name: Bongani Matwa). The aim was for it to reach the internal leadership, as it was clear that relations between ourselves and the exile leadership were deteriorating progressively. This was the collectively authored memoir that was ultimately published in London in July 1990 from an early draft as 'A miscarriage of democracy: The ANC security department in the 1984 mutiny in Umkhonto we Sizwe' in a banned exile magazine, *Searchlight South Africa*, under the names of Bandile Ketelo, Amos Maxongo, Zamuxolo Tshona, Ronnie Masango and Luvo Mbengo. It was the first verifiable, first-hand report of the origins of the mutiny, the cruelty at Quatro and the destruction of democratic elections in the ANC in Tanzania. It has never been challenged and is cited in all relevant academic studies.

After coming under UNHCR jurisdiction, we were able to get

financial assistance on a weekly basis. The sum of money was not enough to provide us with shelter and food, so we had to cut down on a lot of things, such as three meals a day, as well as unnecessary moving as a group when visiting embassies to seek further assistance such as scholarships and finance. We soon realised that help in these matters would not be forthcoming in the near future.

While we were busy with these day-to-day challenges, we heard that Walter Sisulu, the former Rivonia Trial accused and Robben Island prisoner, was coming to Tanzania, along with others who had been released by the apartheid government. We thought this an opportune time to communicate our document to the internal leaders. With the help of some sympathetic comrades, we sent the document, intending it to reach Sisulu. But even prior to them setting foot on Tanzanian soil, some of us were rounded up when there was a sweep on the guesthouse by the Tanzanian police. Luvo, Ronnie, David and I were not there and so escaped arrest. The three women and their children were spared.

David and I were leaving the Malawian consulate downtown when we heard of the arrests. We alerted Luvo and Ronnie about the negative developments. We had to lie low, change guesthouse every day and try to evade arrest in places as far from Magomeni as possible.

Our visit to the Malawian consulate had been an attempt to solicit a passage back home in conjunction with the South African embassy. We were divided as far as this idea was concerned: some were convinced it was premature to trust the South African regime, while others had lost faith in the African countries helping people who were no longer members of either PAC, Azapo or ANC. There had been evidential proof of this. One comrade had run away from Tanzania hoping to find refuge in Kenya, but was handed over to Tanzanian authorities, who in turn had handed him to ANC security, and he ended up in Quatro.

We argued that with the ANC and MK now unbanned, and with Nelson Mandela and all the Rivonia Trialists free inside the country, there was no way the apartheid government was going to free the big fish and then go for small fish like us.

The Malawian consulate, on the other hand, found itself on unfamiliar terrain, judging by its lack of zeal in helping us. It was to be expected, because Malawi under President Hastings Banda operated outside the parameters of other southern African countries, except South Africa. Enjoying diplomatic relations with apartheid South Africa had isolated Malawi from other countries that recognised liberation movements like ANC, PAC and Azapo as the authentic representatives of an alternative democratic government in South Africa. Malawians who opposed Banda were either in jail or in exile. It was therefore the first time that Malawi had to deal with political refugees seeking asylum and they took our story with a spade full of salt. Why were ANC troops opting to come to Malawi, of all countries in southern Africa? Maybe the officials' main concern was that this might be a ploy to attack the country by those who were baying for Banda's blood. Or maybe it was the fact of so many people trying to enter their country. One will never know what was going through their minds.

After five days, including two days of hunger strike, the Tanzanian police released our comrades, but not without a warning: 'Nelson Mandela will visit our country soon and we will have to detain you again.' That was bad news indeed. It made the rest of us move from Magomeni and sojourn in different places. Things were getting tougher for us. We even approached the PAC office in Dar es Salaam, asking for help on a humanitarian basis. They offered us unconditional assistance of food for two weeks, after which they said that that was as far as they could go, since they themselves were operating on a small budget. We were grateful, nonetheless.

Things deteriorated when the Tanzanian authorities told us we had only one week to remain in the Dar es Salaam precinct. According to them, anyone who did not belong to either ANC, Azapo or PAC would be moved to a remote place called Kigwa in a rural part of Tanzania, where we would be given cooking utensils and tools or machetes to chop down trees and make charcoal to generate money, or cultivate the land and become farmers.

It was unpleasant news since we were not used to rural life. It is worth noting here that this was a ploy by the authorities to discourage members of liberation movements from leaving their respective organisations. It led to many PAC members joining the ANC and vice versa, just to avoid being taken to Kigwa.

For instance, in the office where we were to receive our last stipend, we met David Makhubedu's younger brother Derrick. He had been sent to Kigwa after leaving the PAC and was intending to join the ANC after the hard time in Kigwa. He was, of course, astounded when he heard our side of the story, but we respected each other's choices and wished each other good luck.

After receiving that last stipend, which was double the usual amount, we decided it was now or never. Going to Kigwa was out of the question. The question was, where to from Tanzania? One group, including Ketelo, Maxongo, Tshona, Masango, Mbengo and others, chose Kenya, but I was with those who decided to go to Malawi even though the consulate had not yet given us the green light. I was with Mwezi Twala, Sipho Phungulwa, Diliza Mthembu, Vusi Shange, David Makhubedu and Nontyatyambo Mzimela (with her daughter Lazola) and Patheka Sodo (with her son Lonwabo). In that way, we would be off the radar of ANC security and the Tanzanian police.

CHAPTER 24

Parting with the group that would later go the Kenyan route was difficult and not pleasant for either group. Kenya seemed to appeal to the others, but don't all destinations of refuge seem attractive until you get there? There were shining examples of betrayal of trust by both these African countries, and by the UNHCR. Many refuge seekers had either been shot on sight while trying to enter such countries, or deported. The UNHCR either turned a blind eye or played dead. To some extent, it seemed morally right for these countries to roll over at the whim of the ANC whether it was right or wrong, and the ANC capitalised on that.

Malawi would be different if one considered that it was a country that was more aligned to apartheid South Africa than to the liberation movements and estranged from the rest of the continent. It was for that particular reason that we had been engaging with the country's consulate in Dar es Salaam. It was a time when the political situation in South Africa was fluid and moving towards a peacefully negotiated solution. One thing our group was sure of was our political clarity: talks about talks had long been doing the rounds, and with the unbanning and release of Robben Island leaders there was no going back as far as those talks were concerned.

The armed takeover of the country by MK was never going to happen, as it had never effectively taken off from the start. The Pretoria regime and the liberation movements, especially the ANC, knew that. The sad part is that it was not due to incompetence or lack of expertise on the side of the liberation movements, but the combination of many factors: on the one hand, the regime's obvious infiltration and turning of the ANC leadership to discourage an armed conflict; and, on the other hand, the internal divisions in MK. There had been concerted efforts by the leaders to alienate each detachment from the others. The Luthuli Detachment, for example, formed in the 1960s, perceived the June 16 Detachment as political upstarts; while after the mutiny the subsequent detachments were told lies about it.

With such a polarised guerrilla army, it was inconceivable to topple the South African regime militarily. Returning home with bad memories of life in exile could not be helped, but it was better than dying in unnecessary wars in our host countries – wars that did not advance our own struggle. It was 'enough is enough' for some of us, although maybe not for those who were still comfortable with their positions in exile.

Information about how to get to Malawi and how to survive there had been given to us by Malawians residing in Dar es Salaam. They were either students or political refugees escaping their country's repression of opposition. Two of them would accompany us and tell us where to disembark from the bus. They would also provide other advice.

It was on a Saturday afternoon at the end of February that we boarded a bus bound for the southernmost parts of Tanzania. Those buses, 'dala-dalas' according to locals, would be overloaded with passengers inside and luggage on the roof carriers. However, after shaking them up and down when rushing over potholes or tossing them sideways at every curve, there would miraculously be ample room for everyone. Apparently, the driver had been speeding with that intention in mind, because he dropped the speed as we cruised all the way.

We sat in twos and apart from each other to avoid identification as a group travelling together. The only people who knew us were those two Malawians. By midnight we reached Iringa and by midday on Sunday we were in Mbeya. That was where the Malawians told us the exact stop to disembark.

When we got to that specific bus stop, we were the only ones to alight from the bus. The road was just as they had said: there was a bridge ahead, and then a village nestled among gigantic trees, then down a little path there would be the Songwe River separating the two countries.

As it was Sunday late afternoon, there was no traffic except for cars speeding past us in opposite directions. We walked in twos, leaving a gap between us. We had passed the village and were on the way towards the river when we were approached by two teenage boys who offered to help us if we wanted to cross the river. We had been told to look out for those boys, as we would need their expertise. We were now together as a group and we told them their help would be highly appreciated. They led us to a certain spot on the banks of the river and said we should follow them in single file with our parcels and bags on our heads, while the children sat on their mothers' shoulders as we waded through the river. The current was strong, and it was getting dark. At certain points the water was shoulder high, but for the children nothing could have been more fun.

We reached the Malawian side of the border without incident. After giving the two boys all the money we had – which was a generous gesture – they offered to take us to the safest route over the mountains and through forests to avoid Malawian police. They thought we were smugglers. When we declined and asked the way to the nearest village, they told us and then quickly vanished from sight. It was as if they thought we were crazy to want to go to a village in Malawi, and they wanted nothing further to do with us.

We presented ourselves to the first household in the village. Those from nearby houses came closer to listen. They were all dressed formally, with spotless white shirts and ties for men of all ages. They first demanded to search our bags. When they were satisfied, they referred us to the village headman who listened to our story after having made sure that we had nothing dangerous with us. He took us to a satellite police station some 100 or so metres from the village. There was the same searching routine.

I had realised that the sight of a condom brought a look of utter disgust to the faces of the people of Malawi. It disturbed them to the extent they did not have the inclination to search further. I therefore decided to put condoms among the top clothes in my bag before we got to the police station. The expression on the face of the police officer turned to revulsion and he stopped searching. Another police officer was going through a photo album with women in bathing costumes on a beach. When he saw the scantily dressed women he dropped it immediately. A further police officer came across a book by the then Soviet Union leader, Mikhail Gorbachev, with his picture on the cover. He looked at the face on the cover, and without reading a word he exclaimed, 'Ah! PW Botha!' He had mistaken Gorbachev for PW Botha! I was beside myself – had they never heard of Gorbachev in that part of the world?

When the search was over, we were not told what to expect next. It was now already night and the mosquitoes were harassing us in the semi-dark police station. So far, no one had commented on what was in store for us. At around twelve midnight, a van came to take us to the nearest town, Karonga, where we spent the rest of the night on the police station benches. In the morning, we were supposed to write our biographies and be randomly interviewed. Towards midday we were again bundled into a van and, with all our belongings, booked into Karonga prison. Shoelaces and belts were removed, and a thorough body search was conducted on all of us. Then we were ushered into our respective male and female sections of the jail.

It was a small dilapidated prison with leaking waterpipes. There was menacing barbed wire right above us, covering the whole yard. It was such a depressing environment and I could not bear to think of what lay ahead for us. I just found myself a place to lie down and went to sleep. After a while, I was awoken and told it was lunchtime – some soup and beans, all half cooked. Whether we were hungry or not, we had promised each other to co-operate with the authorities in the country. After lunch, we were told that we were being released but this time we were taken to Mzuzu police station in central Malawi, and later to a prison.

The whole exercise of taking us to prison was partly because the country did not have a budget to cater for any eventuality when there might be political refugees like us. It also boded well for them from a security point of view. Malawi, under His Excellency, the Life President Ngwazi Dr Hastings Kamuzu Banda, was an authoritarian state. The people were in fear of him because he had detained and killed thousands of people who dared oppose him or show dissent. He was a dictator who enforced allegiance by all means, at all times.

Every household was supposed to hang his picture on top of every other family picture. All women were expected to wear a cloth with his picture on it if they danced at any event he attended. The pro-government newspapers were supposed to have a daily headline story about the president. Women, even tourists, had to wear clothes covering their knees in public. There was a measuring tape to measure the centimetres of exposed flesh from the knee up – the more centimetres, the more time in confinement. Trousers for women were taboo. Every inhabitant of Malawi had to wash and be presentable and clean, and Sunday was special. At the airport, there were police with scissors to deal with men with long hair, and no dreadlocks were allowed.

Our Malawian friends in Tanzania had made us aware of all these rules and regulations. Malawi, to the outside world, seemed a peaceful country whose inhabitants were content with Banda's rule. It was more like a swan perceived by an onlooker to be gliding effortlessly across a lake while in fact, concealed by the water, its feet were labouring excessively.

Before being taken to Mzuzu Prison, we were told at the police station that two of our colleagues – Luvo Mbengo and Ronnie Masango – had, earlier than us, sneaked into Malawi. But unlike us, they decided to continue towards Lilongwe, the capital. They had been apprehended on the way and deported back to Tanzania. That was a shock to us, because they had not shown any interest in going to Malawi. Our visiting the Malawi consulate in Tanzania had worked well for us, as the authorities there confirmed our visits to their office over a period of three weeks.

Mzuzu Prison was bigger and we men had a cell to ourselves. The women and children were in a separate section. The main problem we had, besides mosquitoes at night, was that of food. We were served stiff porridge with beans daily at twelve midday and that was it. We would eat half the dish and save the rest for supper. For something better to do, we started writing a document similar to the one we had sent to Walter Sisulu while in Dar es Salaam. By writing it, we aimed at informing the internal ANC leadership of the troubles we had encountered in exile. Our assumption was that once we reached home as free people, we would have a chance to meet the leaders and present our case. It would be a step towards redeeming ourselves and an attempt at returning to the fold of our beloved ANC.

After two weeks in that prison, we were visited by the South African ambassador, along with two Home Affairs Department officials. Their mission was to ascertain whether we were genuine South African citizens. Again, we had to write our biographies. For the first time in weeks, we were all together and the two children were excited to see us. Also, for a change, we were outside the prison premises and naturally we were in no hurry to return. When we were asked if we had any problems, we said we hoped they would hasten our return home as we were virtually being treated as prisoners. We could tell they were convinced we were South Africans.

Most people in that prison were being held indefinitely for petty crimes, but there were others who were there for dubious reasons. One old man was taken prisoner during a raid on his house, and his rubies and diamonds were taken despite him having a licence to deal in precious stones. A man claimed he was held because during a raid at his home the police found a picture of his grandfather, which happened to be so big that it dwarfed that of the president alongside it. There was a teenage boy confined on suspicion of following in his dad's footsteps by being critical of the Malawian government. It was such a sad thing to see the future of a brilliant mind fizzling out in front of his own eyes. Then what about the man who had spent two years there, not knowing his fate? He was born in South Africa to a Malawian father and a South African mother. His father had died in the mines, and his mother failed to get him the necessary documents to become a naturalised South African. When he was arrested in South Africa as an illegal immigrant, he was deported to Malawi, but the Malawian authorities also rejected him and did not even bother to find his family. He had hoped to settle in Malawi once and for all, having once visited it with his father when he was younger, but was to end up in that prison hoping that one day he might be free. Yes, freedom ... nothing beats freedom!

Two weeks after the Home Affairs officials had left, three South African security officers arrived. They said they wanted to find out whether we had been involved in any armed attack inside South Africa. We had to write other biographies. None of us had been on such a mission. Even Sipho Phungulwa, although he had infiltrated the country, had only trained people in underground work, and mostly in the Transkei territory. The security officers left, returning two weeks later to take our photos and ask what we expected on arrival back home, and what we would be doing.

They said they would return. We told them it was tough in the prison and we were apprehensive about them dragging their feet. Another two weeks passed, and then one day we were transferred to the biggest prison in Malawi – Lilongwe Prison. In one cell, there were 60 people, then 80 the next day and 100 on the third day. The cell boss kept the blankets to himself, but he made an exception for us.

At night, we had to sleep facing towards one side in order to accommodate everyone. If you went to the toilet, you should not be shocked not to find your space when you returned. The meagre amounts of food were awful. We had by now finished our document and, for something worthwhile to do, I embarked on shaving the prisoners' heads with a razor for free. I would do that for the whole day and every day until one morning we were taken from the prison straight to the airport to board a plane bound for South Africa. That was on 24 April 1990.

PART SIX
RETURN TO SOUTH AFRICA

Christmas '85 in Quatro.

CHAPTER 25

There we were, on the way home. It felt as if a trip around the world was coming to its logical end. In no time, I would be reunited with my family. The struggle for liberation was on its last lap too.

The plane landed at what was then Jan Smuts Airport and who did we meet alighting from another plane? Struggle veterans Walter Sisulu, his wife Albertina, Govan Mbeki and Wilton Mkwayi converged with our group at the entrance. We were excited to meet them and were eagerly looking forward to a conversation with them when the security people who had been to Malawi to interview us arrived. We had only managed to collect our bags when they indicated we should get into two cars parked around the corner. That cut short our brief encounter with the former Robben Islanders and Mrs Sisulu. We were not briefed about our destination. Certainly we did not expect anything so untoward as landing up in detention in remote Barkly West, north of Kimberley, under the Internal Security Act.

On the following day, 25 April, the security officers brought us the *Star* and *Sowetan* newspapers. They said, 'Now read what your leaders say about you! Ha! Ha! Ha!' On reading the newspapers we found nothing remotely funny. Apparently, there had been journalists awaiting our arrival at the airport to interview us, but not seeing us and instead seeing the Sisulus et al, had asked them about us and Sisulu had said we would probably be 'debriefed' by the security police.

The Star continued: 'Mr Sisulu said he believed the group was being held for protection from other hostile groups by agreement between the state and the dissidents.' It added that 'a spokesman for the Minister of Law and Order said the group was merely being held for questioning.'

Under the headline 'Returning ANC exiles detained', *The Sowetan*, stated: 'Commenting on the arrests, Sisulu suggested they were merely a cover-up for the State's obligation to protect the dissidents who were allegedly tortured by Umkhonto we Sizwe as South African Government spies who had infiltrated the ANC.'

At that time, we did not know that *The Star* had published an article on 16 April under the headline 'ANC admits torturing members' – the first article in South Africa to 'highlight the plight of seven former MK members who quit MK in Tanzania and fled to Nairobi'. (The earliest report had been in the *Sunday Correspondent* in London, on 8 April.) *The Star* continued: 'Mr Nelson Mandela had admitted that ANC had tortured dissident members to extract information.' On the following day, *The Star*'s headlines were 'ANC man justifies torture of mutineers' and added, 'A top-ranking member of the African National Congress, Mr Steve Tshwete, has justified the torture of former members of the organisation saying they had been South African agents or mutineers.' He said: 'No army can play with mutineers. We had to suppress the mutiny with all the force at our disposal, just as any army would do when faced with a mutiny.'

The fact is that Nelson Mandela and Steve Tshwete were not in Angola during the mutiny, which can only mean that they were briefed by the ANC security department. Mbokodo was fighting our reformist and democratic ways with all it had. Moreover, this was now continuing ....

With Sisulu's inference that we were actually enemy agents giving information to our masters, we felt our lives were in danger. We had hoped he would give us support, as he had been handed our collective document in Tanzania. Therefore, we had to deduce that he, too, had accepted the ANC security department's opinion of us.

During our detention in Barkly West we were asked in detail

about our biographical accounts. They were trying to establish whether or not we could be trusted. They produced photos of MK members I identified as having been taken in Lesotho at our 'camp' in New Europa by our MK people. I could not understand how they came to be in the hands of the South African security police.

What became obvious was that the apartheid security police had already secured information about all the people in those photograph albums, either from their agents in the ANC and MK, or extracted by torture from MK members arrested while on a mission inside the country. That was when I realised that MK had long been a subject of interest to the South African government. It had pulled out all stops to infiltrate its agents and turn leaders with influence and power to supply it with information to influence the course and pace of the struggle. We had thought we were wild and free, yet the opposite was true: we were like fish in a small pond whose numbers were closely watched and whose culling was predestined in Pretoria.

After they had satisfied themselves that we were not a danger to the regime, they released us on 15 May. The following day the Reverend Evangel Malamb of Soshanguve, Pretoria, facilitated a press conference for us in Johannesburg. We were itching to put the record straight that we were not against the ANC, but against those individuals who were derailing the struggle and were responsible for the repression of those who wanted to bring the organisation back onto the right track.

That press conference was attended by reporters from both South Africa and abroad. Some were hostile towards us, accusing us of being askaris. The reason our detractors accused us was to discredit us and our attempt to democratise the ANC. Reverend Malamb was not spared; he was cross-questioned for his alleged association with the South African government, but he stood his ground and defended himself.

Our aim was not to destroy the ANC but, on the contrary, to make it face its demons. Going to the media had been initiated by ANC leader Walter Sisulu, leaving us with no option but to go the same route. Reverend Malamb had responded to our call for clerics like Reverend Frank Chikane to intervene, but they had failed us. Reverend Malamb put his neck on the block for us to impart our message – a message that would benefit the whole nation, the ANC included. Had the interests of the nation been prioritised at that stage, there would have been no friction between us and the internal leadership.

The main concern for our critics was our call for the formation of a commission of inquiry into the abuse of power and atrocities perpetrated by the ANC security department against its own members. We did not mind if that commission also looked into similar atrocities by the apartheid regime. That development left the ANC leadership squirming and led to more scurrilous accusations against us. At a press conference, the ANC Chief of Intelligence, Jacob Zuma, lambasted our group and all other ANC prisoners for 'participating in assassinations and spying'. He went on to claim that we were 'people with instructions to sow discord within our forces and to aid a situation of uncertainty, even with specific instructions to organise mutiny'.

Zuma did not tell the nation that in our group was a former Quatro guard who had never been involved in the mutiny. She had joined us of her own volition, because she was in love with one of the mutineers. Surely the leaders did not mention her because the story of our being askaris would then not hold water. Later, in a statement to the *Sunday Times*, she apologised for ill-treating prisoners at Quatro and especially Olivia Forsyth, who had been detained there after confessing to being a double agent.

Another factor was that we never had any shady deal with the South African government, as the public knew of our return. Thirdly, we were not against the ANC. Fourthly, it was well and good for the big fish of the organisation to shake hands with the killers of the people, as we witnessed during the ANC and South African government talks on 4 May at the presidential residence, Groote Schuur, which resulted in the signing of the Groote Schuur Minute. We small fish, by contrast, would be vilified. It was unfair that they could slander us now that the ANC and MK were unbanned and great leaders like Walter Sisulu and Nelson Mandela were roaming free, enjoying protection from the same 'enemy'.

What was most worrying at the time was the lack of support we had expected to receive from public organisations aligned to human rights. Lack of moral support made our load heavier. There were to be serious consequences.

CHAPTER 26

At Reverend Malamb's place, we were visited by the families of those among us who were from the Pretoria, Witwatersrand and Vaal (PWV) region. Only Sipho Phungulwa, Nontyatyambo Mzimela, Phatheka Sodo and I had families far away. Therefore, when the rest reunited with their families, they took us with them. It was logical that Phatheka and Nontyatyambo would go to the families of their loved ones in Zola and Dube, respectively. I went with Mwezi Twala to his home in Small Farms, Evaton.

Mwezi's wife was renting a place nearby, so he decided to stay with her there. I did not stay long with his family. It was time for me to go home. I met Sipho at a Johannesburg taxi rank to catch taxis home – him to Port Elizabeth and me to Mthatha. We had seen the other people's families: it was time now for us to see our own families and get on with our lives.

We decided to start by going to PE. However, there were no taxis going straight there – their route ended in King William's Town. Judging from the time we had to board the taxi it would reach King William's Town very early in the morning. I thought that rather than wait in King William's Town for a taxi to PE, we should get off in Queenstown in the evening, see my family there, and then proceed the following day to Port Elizabeth. Things went as planned. I promised my family in Queenstown that I would be back soon and we left for Port Elizabeth, arriving there in the afternoon.

What came to our knowledge as soon as we arrived in PE was that Sipho's child Nomawethu, who had been born in Maseru, Lesotho, had never been taken to the Phungulwa family by Mrs

Hashe! We made the Hashe family in KwaZakhele one of our first calls as a matter of urgency.

We disembarked from a taxi some 20 metres or so from the house when I spotted a young girl who so resembled Sipho that I was certain it was Nomawethu. Pointing at her, I said to Sipho, 'There is Nomawethu.' But when we called out, 'Nomawethu!' she just looked at us, seemingly not seeing any need to respond to two strangers who had surely mistaken her for someone else.

All right, we let her proceed and then went to the house. Fortunately, Mrs Hashe was there. As expected, she had been following developments in the news regarding our return to the country, so she wasted no time in getting straight to the point. When she and Nomawethu arrived in South Africa and she explained the child's presence to the authorities, the Special Branch began keeping a close eye on her, waiting for any slip on her side in relation to her story of her grandchild born in Lesotho. Since then she'd had to play the part by registering the child as a Hashe. What had seemed simple – taking the child to the Phungulwas – was then practically impossible. The bond between the two had grown as years went by. In other words, after ten years Nomawethu had to learn that she was not a Hashe and 'would we be patient, as she was young, so she could understand and adjust?' Mrs Hashe had grown accustomed to the child and vice versa from the word go. It was going to be a near impossibility for her to let the child go easily, however willing she might have been. The situation had become emotional, and all parties involved wanted a win-win agreement. The child was introduced to us and told the truth, but that she would remain with the Hashe family as long as she wished – from the look of things, forever. Then the topic turned naturally to politics.

While in Port Elizabeth, Sipho and I decided to get ourselves documents. In town was the Home Affairs Department for Sipho to get his ID, and for me, the Transkeian consulate office to help me with an ID and passport. Since Sipho had had a South African pass before skipping the country, it was easy for him to apply for a renewal and temporary one was issued. I had to settle with the fact that I was a Transkeian citizen. It was awkward to accept the status quo, especially for me, but there was no other way to reach Mthatha to see my family.

As usual, the Home Affairs offices were chock-a-block from early morning, and it took almost all day before Sipho was through, while in my case it did not take more than an hour because few people needed Transkeian services. It seemed to me that nothing had changed after all the years in exile, but I was sure that with the unbanning of the ANC, SACP and PAC the transitional period was afoot. To be alive at such a critical juncture in the history of the country and seeing the democratic processes unfold was what every forward-looking person was hoping and longing for.

On the first weekend in Port Elizabeth, at the insistence of Sipho's aunt Elizabeth 'Keya Phungulwa', we had a formal meeting with local ANC leaders from Zwide Township. Sipho's cousin Mandisa accompanied us there, and took minutes of the meeting. We told them what had happened in exile; what had led to the mutiny and later to Quatro, and why, and under what circumstances, we had returned home.

By the time we were halfway through our story, the house was filled with young people and one could tell that they were overwhelmed with disbelief. To everyone's surprise, the house owner, who was chairing the meeting, said what we were saying concurred with what they had already heard. We welcomed that information. It was now up to the Mthatha ANC structure to accept our story on the last leg of our long journey. We hoped it would be successful, given that Sipho had been an MK operative in the area.

But before that, it was time I took Sipho to see my extended family in New Brighton. He was bewildered to find that the elderly woman we found there, Nombuyiselo, was actually my cousin. It had been a similar case in Queenstown with cousin Thenjiwe, who could pass as a mother to me. Their children were almost all my peers; this is a family tree that never fails to confound me, being the youngest of a generation that spanned four decades.

In our busy schedules we made sure that we also visited Luvo

'Valdez' Mbengo's mother at Zwide near The Square. She was overjoyed at the news that her son was alive in spite of everything.

However, what is Port Elizabeth without a jolly good time? It is not called The Friendly City for nothing; these are the friendliest folks one could ever come across no matter where one travels. They have the right formula for transforming a sombre mood into an unforgettable celebration. What happened was an impromptu lunch organised by Keya to welcome us. Among those present at short notice were cousin Nombuyiselo, Sipho's mother Lilian, his uncle, and Valdez's mother. It was supposed to be a low-key event, but it ended up as a full-blown party with neighbours joining in. That is Port Elizabeth at its best!

In a matter of days we left for Mthatha on a high note, hoping for another happy experience. Reaching Mthatha on the afternoon of 5 June, I felt as if I had completed one long journey around the world, and had learnt more than I had set out to. My whole family was still going strong, and the years that had passed had changed nothing much in their lives. My sister was out of work and raising a six-year-old girl, Nomaxabiso. Her two older daughters, Nondyebo and Nomvula, were in Malelane and Port Shepstone respectively, and another, Brenda, was a private doctor's receptionist in town. My father was taking care of a fully furnished house in town whose owner had numerous such unoccupied properties. Talk of the anomalies of life: while there are people without houses, there are houses without people.

The warm welcome from my family showed just how much they had missed me and had been looking forward to the day when I would be back. Actually, my arrival was not a big surprise. Besides them having seen us on television, while in Dar es Salaam I had met a comrade's mother who had come all the way from Mthatha to see her child. I had written a letter to my parents on the spot, promising them that I would be home soon. I'd asked the woman to post it in Mthatha, and they had indeed received it.

A few changes to the old home I once knew were plain to see. The mulberry tree had to go as it had grown to a grotesque size;

the kitchen garden and the chicken-run had provided space for the building of an extra room. But what survived was the painting, *The Aragonese Dancer: The Fandango* and the rambling rose – those two interior and exterior trademark memories. I immediately felt home.

Within two days father had slaughtered a sheep in a gratitude for our safe return. I was spared questions about my immediate plans, though I somehow picked up a feeling that here were people who would do anything for me to ensure I never wandered far from them again. Indeed, having no plan at all meant I was to remain in Mthatha as close to the family as possible. The most important next step, though, was for Sipho and me to meet ANC local leaders, tell our story, and later for Sipho to go back home. We would take it from there.

On 11 June, my sister accompanied us to make an appointment with the relevant people of the ANC. Sipho immediately recognised some people he had trained underground. One was Kaizer Mbethe, who made the appointment for 13 June at 2 pm.

That Wednesday, 13 June, we were in the ANC office before 2 pm. Kaizer Mbethe told us that the persons we were supposed to meet had not arrived and asked us to wait a bit longer. By 3 pm they had still not arrived, and we realised the meeting would have to be rescheduled for another day.

Just then, a young man hurried in and went straight to Kaizer. He had his back to us while Kaizer was facing our direction. After a few mumbled words, the young man turned and looked at us. It was obvious they were talking about us. That was when I had a chance to see his face. I was later to learn that his name was Mfanelo Matshaya.

He left the office in as much of a hurry as he had entered. Sipho and I decided we could not wait any longer, so we told Kaizer we were leaving but he insisted that he had just received a message saying that those we were to meet would be there at 6 pm. We said we could not wait until then and left the office.

Outside the office was a beige Peugeot 404 with a driver whose name I later learnt was Ndibulele Ndzamela. He was looking at us so intently that we could not help wondering what the matter was, but we continued to the taxi rank and boarded a taxi to my family's location.

When we got out at a street opposite my home we saw the Peugeot right behind the taxi. Matshaya got out the back and came towards us saying, 'Comrades, there's something we need to …' He did not finish the sentence but produced a Scorpion pistol and shot Sipho who was standing between us. In that brief moment, I knew the shot would be followed by others, which would end Sipho's life. I did the only thing I could do … I turned and fled. I managed to escape unscathed, jumping over the walls of several houses and constantly changing direction.

I came out of hiding when it was getting dark and headed to the Ngangelizwe police station to open a case of murder. I'd had more than ample time to reflect on the tragic end of Sipho, whose life was dedicated to the struggle for freedom. His words from exile in Dakawa, 'The ANC taught us to elect leaders of our own choice …' were well articulated and will forever ring true. They reflected the general feeling of the majority of those who attended that meeting in Dakawa. That could have been the real reason for Mbokodo to end his life. Though we were aware of their impact, we naively assumed that Sipho's words were an innocent and simple statement, hardly imagining there might be severe repercussions. But it had likely been intended as a double assassination.

At the police station, I went to lengths to explain how it all came about – that the culprit and victim were both ANC members and that the one had killed the other. I was still there when my sister arrived to open a case too. She confirmed that Sipho had passed away on the way to hospital. The police officers who drove us home said people from the Murder and Robbery Squad would ask me to show them the crime scene.

I told myself that the passing of Sipho would not be the end of the values he lived and died for. I had to dig deep inside myself to find strength to deal with the trauma of having to live with the incident forever etched in my memory. My life was not mine alone any more. The future I had had in mind was not going to happen. I had witnessed the unexpected. After the dreadful stories of people being killed in exile, the reality of this happening now, inside South Africa, after the release of Nelson Mandela, was shocking. It continued the pattern of an army that never engaged its enemy in a decent battle but found it not difficult to eliminate one of its own.

For everyone killed in this way the hopes and dreams of the victim's family are shattered. The victim's contribution – be it material or otherwise – is usurped, and those who survive are no less dead either. Waking up to an empty space where the victim used to lie; seeing their favourite things or hearing the songs they used to dance to ... it is so hurtful for any of us to lose someone close and dear. It is even worse when that person dies in front of us, as happened with Sipho and as happened with Shorty in Quatro.

They remain special in my life. I couldn't save them, but I can save their reputation and redeem their worth by writing this book.

CHAPTER 27

As promised, the Murder and Robbery Squad came to my home shortly after Sipho's murder and took me to visit the crime scene. There were a few spent cartridges from the weapon. I gave them the details they needed. They left, saying they would come back to me if they needed more information.

Then there was my unenviable responsibility of breaking the news first hand to Sipho's family in Port Elizabeth. Of course they were shocked; his cousin had already secured a job for Sipho for when he returned from Mthatha. The Phungulwa family was so gracious and magnanimous despite the painful tidings, to the extent that they said I was not safe in Mthatha and that they would welcome me as family.

I stayed in Mthatha for a week. I had informed my friends in present-day Gauteng of the death of Sipho. The news reached the media and caused a frenzy that made me feel the urgency to leave Mthatha – to leave home. Transkei had turned into a death trap for me as the police seemed to have done nothing in that period of seven days. All the information pointed to the involvement of the ANC office, but there seemed to be a lackadaisical approach on the part of the police, so much so that I feared for my life. I was the survivor who could point out the culprits, therefore I was most probably the man to silence next. Mine was not to lick my wounds in peace. My work was cut out for me: I had to reunite with the others as soon as possible.

The day I left for Johannesburg I told my sister that I would not tell my mother of my plans to leave and asked her to tell her later that evening before she went to bed. I could not bear to tell her that I was leaving her again. After almost ten years apart, we had not been together for no more than three weeks. My father could take it, I assumed, but it was going to be tough for both my mother and me to see the last of each other.

Fortunately, when I got to the taxi rank in town, I found the last taxi to Johannesburg. It was odd to leave home in a so-called homeland and flee to a supposedly hostile South Africa under the apartheid government. It was more like going into exile, because I did not see the Transkei police jeopardising their now good relations with the ANC over one Sipho Phungulwa. Transkei under Bantu Holomisa was prone to roll over and let the ANC have its way. It was an African country's shortcomings, and Holomisa would not be immune from it.

Actually, it transpired that Nelson Mandela had been to his home in Qunu in Transkei on 26 April 1990. *City Press* of 29 April 1990 reported that many MK cadres had recently been 'released from Transkeian jails by the military council'. Nelson Mandela's visit to the territory pushed them into the front line as bodyguards for the ANC deputy president. It went on: 'MK cadres Mfanelo Matshaya and Phumlani Khubukeli were unexpectedly freed shortly after the hunger strike by political prisoners at Umtata Prison.' That showed how near impossible it was to expect justice.

On arriving at his home in Small Farms, Mwezi Twala was harassed and threatened by ANC comrades because of his comments at our press conference. It was to be expected, when one took into consideration the earlier words of Walter Sisulu and Jacob Zuma. Sipho's death had been the product of such libel, whether purposefully or unwittingly. They were irresponsible statements from people who wielded power and influence in the public domain.

In an unrelenting and unrepentant mode, our group rolled with the punches. Stronger than before, we were not hesitant in believing that Chris Hani, who was in the Transkei at the time, had a decisive hand in the murder. Having been Hani's bodyguard in Lesotho, Sipho died because he knew too much and could have jeopardised Hani's standing in the public eye. Anyone in a lower position than Hani could not have ordered Sipho's death. If Hani had not said we should be marked men, Sipho would not have been killed.

When interviewed by Cliff Saunders of the South African Broadcasting Corporation (SABC), Hani avoided the question of his involvement in Sipho's murder but ranted about us being killers acting on behalf of the South African state. Unknown to Hani, Cliff Saunders had interviewed Twala and me earlier next door to where he was interviewing Hani. He asked Hani if he would mind us joining the interview, but he objected vehemently. There was bound to be prevarication about Sipho's murder, because of the lies that had been told about us. People still in exile were fed fabrications that Sipho and I had raided the ANC offices and that Sipho had died when MK cadres inside retaliated. Another version was that I, too, had died there.

These lies corresponded with the original lie that we were askaris. The point is that askaris did not go to ANC offices unarmed to let bygones be bygones, as we had done. Lie after lie ultimately created a complicated maze of misinformation. Had justice for the murder not been delayed and subsequently denied, those false statements would have been unravelled – something that would eventually have blown a highly esteemed person's cover.

Given our wish for intensification of the campaign for the release of prisoners in ANC prisons and an independent commission of inquiry into the ANC's human rights abuses and atrocities in exile, we formed an organisation in Johannesburg called Returned Exiles Coordinating Committee (RECOC). We still had the group in Kenya in mind and were concerned about their well-being. We would not rest until they were back in the country. RECOC was formed to strive for their safe return and the organisation hoped for a helping hand from anyone with a similar interest. We needed assistance in all spheres, as we did not have office space or funds to rent space or the logistical requirements an organisation needs.

Reverend Malamb was a distance away as we were based in

Johannesburg and he was in Pretoria, but by going to the media, we did not ease the pressure on the ANC. We felt the need to keep up the momentum as our survival depended on it. It was a gargantuan challenge, but fighting was the only way; we had seen how easily a person's life could be taken.

At that time, among many organisations and individuals with which we made acquaintance, one political organisation stood out. It was called the Federal Independent Democratic Alliance (FIDA), and was led by John Gogotya. FIDA consisted mainly of black mayors in urban areas, mostly in the PWV region. Since they were community based, it was assumed that they would be the ones driving for change in their various locations. By invitation from the organisation, where we were given a chance to expatiate on our public statement, we were told we could use the facilities in their Braamfontein office. We accepted this joyfully – any assistance was important, especially when it was unconditional.

We respected FIDA's political standpoint as long as it strengthened our multiparty democracy. Given the volatile conditions prevailing in the country at the time, FIDA's centrist position could attract moderate sentiment from all racial backgrounds. So many people longed for a political home outside the ANC because of its alliance with the SACP, and FIDA fancied its chances of wooing support from people on the periphery.

Yet, as is the wont with emerging small parties, experience and the time needed for them to become known might work against them. It was at such times that they would invest in personalities already known in the political scenario. FIDA was no exception. Though they helped us unconditionally, they harboured hope that we would eventually become members. When it became clear that we were resisting joining, we were not to have a lasting relationship. We had to think on our feet, and fast. At that time there was money available for returning exiles. It was not much, but we needed it. The problem was that it was being received by those who had been returned by the ANC, not by we who had returned through our own efforts.

One day we went to Khotso House – headquarters of the South African Council of Churches (SACC) – to see the Reverend Frank Chikane, because that was where the money was being distributed. We had earlier solicited his intervention on our behalf, but he had not come back to us. On this day, we were there to highlight our entitlement to financial assistance. Reverend Chikane heard us out and was prepared to make a concession – we were to receive the money even though we did not have the documentation that was a precondition. He even said he had met with the ANC leadership and it had concluded that we were not 'dissidents'. That was good news! Though we would have wished for it to be in the public space, we knew that would be asking too much as the balance of forces at that time was a different matter altogether.

It was during those monthly pay days that we would meet those who had been with us in exile and heard their versions of what had transpired during 'our raid of the ANC offices in Mthatha and how Sipho and I had been gunned down'. Well, they had to believe that I was still alive.

Not long after our arrival home, Luvo Mbengo and Ronnie Masango arrived back in the country from Kenya. We organised a press conference in Johannesburg. Their arrival gave us hope that Red Cross International was going to bring the rest of the group home. When the duo's account of the events leading to the mutiny corroborated ours, and they reiterated the call for an independent commission of inquiry into the human rights abuses and atrocities perpetrated by the ANC on its own members, our cause got the attention it deserved.

Every word they uttered was invaluable at that crucial and decisive time, and tipped the scales in our favour. It was that additional voice defying all odds that we could not do without. By contrast, in a silent world where the voice of light is subdued, we are doomed to darkness.

Next came news that the rest of the group in Kenya were returning. Red Cross International informed us of the date, the time and the number of the flight. We organised journalists from several media houses and we descended on the airport on that specific day. Before that we had had telephone contact with them. We were trying to embolden them so that they should not be cowed, since we had laid a good foundation and their support was crucial. They had responded affirmatively and, as they appeared from Customs, we could not be blamed for expecting fireworks.

But, alas! They disregarded the journalists approaching them with questions and did not even acknowledge us as they passed by like somnambulists. Then we realised they were following Moss Chikane – Transvaal secretary of the United Democratic Front and national co-ordinator of the ANC team responsible for the return of ANC members from exile – who told the media that the press conference they were looking forward to would be held at ANC headquarters, Shell House.

We did not see that one coming. Everybody was scrambling into their various modes of transport and heading towards the city centre. Mwezi Twala managed to get a lift, but Vusi Shange, David Makhubedu, Phatheka Sodo and I had to rush to nearby Isando railway station to board a train, as that was the only way we could reach Johannesburg. Even then, because of the distance, it took us almost two hours to get to Shell House.

The hall was full, and we could not find seats. The press statement was being read by Bandile Ketelo. We felt, there was no way, even though accompanied by Moss Chikane all the way from Kenya, that anyone who had shared our experience would not state the fact that grave human rights contraventions and undemocratic malpractices had taken place in exile. That announcement would matter the most. Instead, we were saddened that we could not even have access to our Quatro comrades, and vice versa. We could tell that something had gone wrong.

It soon became known that Tokyo Sexwale – subsequently premier of Gauteng and Minister of Human Settlements – had visited them in Kenya prior to their return, and asked them to rejoin the ANC. He even admitted that Sipho had been killed by MK members 'although not ordered by the leadership'. In other words, it was fatal to be regarded as an ANC or MK defector in South Africa.

The group had in fact not rejoined the ANC, but the underlying threat to their lives must have had an impact, which resulted in them shunning us. It was very sad to leave Khotso House without a conversation with them or to have any prospect of seeing them again.

The matter of rejoining the ANC could not be taken at face value. To a certain extent it would imply invalidating our criticism of the organisation, or that there was no need for a change in leadership ethics. Either way, it would mean reneging on our initial position with the possibility that our wings would be clipped again once we were back in the fold. Eventually, the cause that our fallen comrades had laid down their lives for would fizzle out. That would imply dire results for the ANC as an unquestioned autocracy, though it was encouraging that the Kenyan group had not agreed to rejoin.

Actually, there had been an abortive meeting between us 'dissidents' and ANC veterans that had taken place some months earlier, just after I had arrived in Johannesburg from Mthatha. It had been organised by Tokyo Sexwale, and we met at Tata Walter Sisulu's house in Orlando West, Soweto.

Those who could make it there were David Makhubedu, Vusi Shange, Phatheka Sodo and myself. It was our opportunity to be heard. Early that evening we were taken by Tokyo to the Sisulu house, where we found Tata Wilton Mkwayi, Tata Alfred Nzo, Tata Raymond Mhlaba and of course Tata Sisulu waiting for us. Mama Albertina Sisulu and other members of the family were busy preparing a meal, presumably supper, in the kitchen.

The ambience was welcoming and cordial. We were well settled and about to commence the meeting when the whole of Soweto went dark – power blackout! At the time, there were few places in Soweto that had backup power sources like generators and the Sisulu household was not one of them. All of a sudden there was a scramble for matches and candles which, apparently, were not readily available.

In the semi-darkness, Tata Mkwayi reminded us that we should never forget our humble backgrounds of using paraffin stoves and battery-powered radios and lamps, and how essential they still were. I remember how that sparked a light conversation and everyone had something to say. In short, somehow we were not treated like outsiders, but like everyone else in the ANC fold.

It was close to Christmas. For the first time after ten years in exile when Christmas never mattered much to me – and we had suffered that appalling Christmas chopping wood in 1985 – it struck a sad note not being able to be with my family. However, I could make the best of the opportunities I had; I could reach out and embrace the love and kindness of the Shange family in Zola, or the Makhubedu family in Meadowlands, or the Malamb family in Soshanguve, or stay with the Twala family ... I was spoilt for choice. As it was, I spent Christmas 1990 with the Shange family in Zola.

Amid the warmth and cheerfulness, I could not help wondering how Sipho's family and mine were faring. Were they despondent and not taking part in the festivities around them? Were they overly worried about my safety? If so, what could I do to allay their anxieties and fears? The distance between us made me feel the need to be part of them more than ever, but in my heart of hearts, I wished them the best the day could offer. All this occupied my mind until I decided to take part in the festivities. Something deep down told me I deserved a break, and to have fun without being ashamed of it.

CHAPTER 28

Early in 1991, I was at Mwezi's home in Gauteng and happened to be in the right place at the right time: Radio Metro was interviewing General Bantu Holomisa, the head of Transkei from December 1987, when the radio host asked him if there was any 'cover-up' on the side of the Transkeian police concerning Sipho's murder. Holomisa seemed upset by the question and was quick to answer, maybe off the cuff, that 'with the help of the Boers' I could go to the Transkei for an identity parade. The way he put it was that I had to get the commissioner of police in South Africa to ask the commissioner of police in Transkei to protect me in order to take me to the identity parade. Oh, how proudly Transkeian he sounded! However, I had no choice but to oblige.

Imagine the excessive administrative work and time I spent on that. But if I had not been listening to that radio station – how would I have got the message? At least there was hope for a way forward. I wrote a letter to the Ministry of Police and asked to be escorted by the South African police, as I wanted justice to take its course.

After many moons, I received a reply that the two commissioners of police had agreed I could be escorted to and from Mthatha. Soon after that I was contacted by the Vanderbijlpark Murder and Robbery Unit and told that I would be escorted to Mthatha. On the specified morning in October I went to the offices as instructed and we left for Mthatha. Because it was a long journey, we slept on the way and reached the Transkei Murder and Robbery Unit offices the following morning.

I positively identified Matshaya and Ndzamela in the identity parade and we left Mthatha a few hours later. While there, I asked for contact details of the detective handling the case and kept phoning him for updates. The two, Matshaya and Ndzamela, were later arrested and appeared in court.

In the court appearance, it transpired that there were two additional accomplices – Aga Tiya and Phumlani Khubukeli – who were in a different car that was following the Peugeot. What still puzzles me is how they were indicted in connection with the case; I had never included them in my statement to the police. If they gave themselves up voluntarily then (and excuse me if I am wrong) maybe they had seen a chance to be counted among the MK 'heroes' for killing 'an enemy agent'. I cannot, for the life of me, understand any motive other than that. The two had known me before I left for exile. Phumlani's brother was my friend while I was growing up. When we mutineers were in Viana after quitting the Eastern Front, Phumlani and others had joined us after deserting the Caculama training camp. I can understand proving one's allegiance to the leadership at that time of suppression of dissent and also reciprocating the release from prison brought about by Mandela, but someone giving himself up to be prosecuted for Sipho's death is astounding. I still cannot understand it.

Given bail of R100 each, they were out indefinitely on a charge of culpable homicide. Bail of R100 on one side of this system of justice; a charge of homicide – not even murder – on the other. I was never contacted or told the court date or any further court dates. In addition, I was not allowed to mention the case because it was 'sub judice'.

When I phoned Nceba, the detective responsible for the case, to be updated about developments, he could not restrain himself from expressing his frustration. To put an end to my calls, he said that the case involved politicians in high places, thus making it difficult for him to make any progress. He never said who those politicians were, and I did not enquire any further.

It was a pity that the case had to come to such an unceremonious end. Justice was the casualty, with a man who had dedicated his life to his chosen noble profession of apprehending killers finding himself incapacitated by an abrupt intervention by powerful, influential politicians.

Living in a country with the world's focus on it – with all eyes on Nelson Mandela – that albatross around the ANC's neck could not be forgotten without due probe. Consequently, in 1991 the Skweyiya Commission of Inquiry was instituted by the ANC NEC under the formal title 'Commission of Inquiry into complaints by former ANC prisoners and detainees'. It was composed of Advocate Thembisile Louis Skweyiya, Miss Bridget Mabandla and Advocate Gilbert Marcus. The hearings were not open to the public – something to its discredit, considering also that the commissioners were all themselves ANC members.

Another factor that detracted from its credibility was the limitation of the terms of reference: evidence was not to include cases where there were murders or disappearances. The commission was found wanting and our frustration was justified. Nevertheless, several of us went to testify. On the day of my testimony, Mzwandile Piliso, the chief architect of Quatro, was there looking more down-spirited than any of his victims. He had with him a big leather bag bulging with documents and I wondered whether they contained information dating back even to the 1960s. Piliso cast a lonely figure, with no bodyguard in sight.

The calls for an independent commission of inquiry were met when the Douglas Commission was set up by a pro-capitalist organisation in Washington called International Freedom Foundation (IFF). It gathered information in the form of sworn statements from witnesses that portrayed a grim picture of life experiences in the ANC in exile. When I attended the commission for my testimony, I found that many victims from as far away as KwaZulu-Natal had heeded the call to testify. ANC leader Chris Hani also gave evidence. The commission even used the article 'A miscarriage of democracy' by the Kenyan group that had been published in July 1990 in the banned exile magazine edited in London, *Searchlight South Africa*. This was a version of the same document we had collectively drawn up in Dakawa and Dar es Salaam, and which had been presented in Tanzania to Walter Sisulu.

By this time, Makhubedu, Shange and I had thought long and hard about our future. It was clear we could not go on depending on handouts forever. We had to come up with a sustainable plan to ensure our financial independence.

Having been active in construction work in Dakawa, we found it an appealing idea to continue it here at home. There was undoubtedly a great need for housing in the country as more and more shacks were popping up everywhere around urban areas. People needed decent houses that provided security and privacy, as enshrined in the Freedom Charter. We of the ANC had been critical of the four-roomed houses provided by the apartheid system because of their size. We had even called them 'matchboxes'. At the back of our minds was the thought that it was a perfect time for the ANC to turn everyone's wish to reality. The ANC was not yet in power, although it was obviously just a matter of time before it took over the reins of government.

While not yet decided on how or where to start, we came across an advert for a brickmaking machine invented by an engineer, David Herbstein. According to the advert, its method of making bricks was cost-effective yet produced very strong bricks. This was guaranteed due to the hydraulic power operation of the machine. The problem was we did not have R35 000 to buy the machine or even a place and the capital to put the business in motion.

For the first time, we mulled over the offer by the municipal mayors in the FIDA party. We had to visit and see for ourselves the viability of having a business in their locations. Having been to Dobsonville and Duduza, we settled for the latter. Kebane Moloi, the mayor, was ready to hand over a portion of a plot once owned by whites who had deserted it because of the shacks encroaching towards them.

What had happened was that in the build-up to the fall of the apartheid system with all its oppressive laws, black people from the Bantustans and farms near and far were congregating in the urban areas where they had previously been barred from staying. Along with these was the younger generation from the townships, who needed places they could call their own. In the case of Duduza, their proximity to the white community made the whites feel unsafe. They were the generation who still believed that only bad things could be expected when staying close to blacks. When they fled, people took everything they could use: windows, bricks, doors, etc. The Duduza municipality salvaged one plot, and it was this plot where we were apportioned a third for business purposes.

Kebane Moloi introduced us to John Wocke of John Deere (SA), whose company was putting aside large sums of money to help develop the local communities, especially the deprived black community. The shortcoming was that they could not finance the whole project alone, so we needed another benefactor. That benefactor came in the form of the British consulate in Johannesburg. They, too, in principle, would not be able to go the whole hog without another party giving help.

So, there we were: able to come up with a business without a cent from our pockets. We named it 'A re Ageng' (Let us Build in SeTswana). John Deere even supplied us with a professional facilitator who did all the business plans and set the ball rolling. The British consulate bought us the machine and John Deere set up the building site structure and made available everything else that was needed. Our responsibility was to make sure that the business was sustainable, because after a certain time the financial assistance would cease.

At a formal settlement called Masechaba we built a show-house, which was our basic model of a house the future government could provide for the people, as opposed to 'matchboxes'. At the time the selling price – R18 000 for a 9 metre x 7 metre house with two bedrooms, a kitchen, an expansive living room and a bathroom with a toilet – was very cheap. We believed that by the time the RDP houses were rolled out, we would be ready to present our model house and take it from there.

In other developments, the Skweyiya Commission's report was handed to Nelson Mandela on 19 October 1992. It had been given access to the Stuart Commission report of 1984, the contents of which had been withheld from ANC members and the public even during the Kabwe conference of 1985. The Skweyiya Commission did not publish the findings of the Stuart Commission, but only recommended that they be published. Nevertheless, its report ended up vindicating us mutineers as not having been 'enemy agents', based on the 1984 findings of the Stuart Commission. So, all along, from the time of those years behind bars in Quatro, and being visited by OR Tambo, to the death of Sipho Phungulwa, the ANC NEC knew we were innocent, but spread malicious information aimed at discrediting us and endangering our lives. It seems telling the truth at that time would not have been convenient to the organisation, and thus it 'did not constitute the truth'.

The Skweyiya Commission concluded with these recommendations:

i. All allegations against us should be unequivocally and unconditionally withdrawn, and we deserved an unequivocal apology for the wrongs we had suffered.
ii. All who suffered maltreatment while being detained in ANC camps should receive monetary compensation for their ordeal.
iii. Medical and psychological assistance should be provided to these victims.
iv. There should be assistance in education.
v. Lost property should be compensated.
vi. An independent structure should be constituted to document cases of abuse and give effect to the recommendations made in the report.
vii. There should be investigation of all allegations of disappearance and murder.
viii. Immediate attention should be given to identify and deal with those responsible for the maltreatment of detainees.
ix. The report of a secret ANC internal investigation into the death of Thami Zulu in Zambia in November 1989 and the Stuart Commission report into the 1984 mutiny in MK should be made public.

x. The commission finally recommended the release of its report 'as soon as possible'.

What was ludicrous was that all the blame for atrocities was heaped on one person, Mzwandile Piliso, thus exonerating the rest.

The Douglas Commission report was also scathing about the ANC leadership under Tambo, which could not be excused for 'not knowing' what was going on in the organisation. It called also for those responsible for human rights abuses to be prosecuted. The recommendations of the Commission might have been validated had they been taken up by local human rights groups and if there had been a follow-up. But these groups did not have the courage to place themselves at loggerheads with the ANC. It was easy for them to shut their doors – and hearts – to our cries, only to denounce those extending a helping hand to us as 'right wing'.

A month after the Skweyiya Commission report, Nelson Mandela set up the Motsuenyane Commission to investigate the role of ANC leaders in executions, since issues such as this had not been covered by the Skweyiya Commission. The commissioners were Mr Sam Motsuenyane, Mr David Zamchiya, and Ms Margaret Burnham of the USA. It was open to the media, as opposed to the closed character of the Skweyiya Commission. The venue for the Commission was FNB Stadium in Johannesburg, and we attended in droves. At least the commissioners were drawn from independent, non-ANC people. That was a big relief and promised a fair and less biased platform for us to be heard, not least since the Skweyiya Commission's recommendation that the Stuart Commission report be published had been ignored by the ANC, and its recommendations were not heeded.

In August 1993 the Motsuenyane Commission's report was published together with the Stuart Commission report. It was blatantly clear that the ANC leadership had been at pains to withhold information about abuse in the camps. Now, after nine years of damage to us, the ANC was forced to release the report to the public. As expected, it tarnished the organisation's reputation.

The Motsuenyane Commission reported that the ANC was guilty of torture in its camps and it named specific individuals responsible for the abuses. The ANC acknowledged these findings, but felt it inappropriate to take any action against those individuals. This was due to divisions within the ANC's NEC. It was a perpetual feature masked by false unity and phrases such as 'ANC claims collective responsibility for ...', while concealing the responsibility of individuals.

To those on the receiving end of such atrocious violations, it was frustrating to hear Nelson Mandela talking of another commission of inquiry to be set up, just after the report of the Motsuenyane Commission. How many times would one be appearing at commission after commission before one's name was cleared of slander?

If one takes seriously the words of former National Commissar Andrew Masondo, 'ANC right or wrong', then it becomes simple to understand – but not necessarily accept – the logic of its 'collective responsibility' phraseology. This principle can be found in the centrist character of the organisation, whereby even the sanctity of the organisation reigned supreme and everything else, be it ethical or rational, was sacrificed. Maintaining the supreme importance – the sanctity – of the image of the national liberation movement was at the centre of every decision, at all costs.

For me, by contrast, it is through the opportunity to air the worst violations of human rights by an organisation against its members that my safety has been secured. It has been about trying to keep head above water, so each and every attempt – even writing this book – has been worth it and has great meaning to me and those like me: alive and dead.

CHAPTER 29

Easter weekend in 1993 found me hosting my girlfriend, Constance Kgakatsi, in Duduza. She had a ten-year-old son, Lebogang. We were four months into our promising relationship and all thanks to a blind date organised for us by one sister, Thelma Jabane, Derrick Makhubedu's girlfriend.

Thelma was a well-known dancer in the jazz circles of Meadowlands – a place that brings two things to mind: the apartheid regime's forced removal of black people from multiracial and vibey Sophiatown to a tribally segregated Meadowlands township, far from the city and their workplaces; and the element of jazz that has been a proud tradition reminiscent of old Sophiatown. This has been the identity that has made the place stand out from the rest of greater Soweto: the common trend that transcended tribal division and gave birth to a unified community.

It was in one of those Meadowlands jazz sessions that Thelma and I spotted each other's dancing skills. She was impressed and, seeing that I was unattached, decided to hook me up with another jazz-loving friend of hers, Constance. They were regulars at Gwangwa's Jazz Club, named in honour of the jazz legend Jonas Gwangwa. With both of us sharing a common love for jazz, I thought, who knows, this might be a match made in heaven.

From the first time we met, I loved how grounded she was. Add to that the mutual respect we had for each other and it was enough for me to conclude that we deserved each other. The signs of an everlasting happy relationship were there for both of us to see and we were going to take it to the next level even if it meant working harder towards that dream. It was easy for us to travel together anywhere and anytime, or just stay put enjoying each other's company.

Then, on the morning of Saturday, 10 April 1993, we heard on the radio that Chris Hani had been assassinated in front of his home in Dawn Park, Boksburg. The news shocked the country. A frail peace was shattered and only sanity and calmness on the part of the ANC leadership – above all Tata Mandela – was able to preserve it. No one saw it coming and, no matter how one felt towards Hani, it was an unacceptable act. In everyone's mind, I guess, were questions and more questions about the direction our country was taking. Many unanswered issues lingered in the air.

It was around midday when the weather, which had hitherto been fine, suddenly erupted into a phenomenal hell. First, a cold breeze turned into gust of wind travelling at a high speed, followed by the darkening of the sky. One could tell that a heavy thunderstorm was imminent, and I decided that we should close the windows and the door and throw a warm blanket over ourselves on the bed.

Just then the phone next to me rang. It was Constance's friend Rebecca, calling her from Meadowlands. They were still going through the preliminaries of a conversation when a lightning bolt hit the house and a bluish flame lit up the room. Connie and I were thrown off the bed and onto the floor. Thunder followed like the devil was mad with himself. I realised that I was not hurt and immediately rushed to Connie as she lay on the floor looking lifeless. Blood was oozing from one corner of her mouth and she seemed not to be breathing at all. In desperation, I tried to revive her by applying cardiopulmonary resuscitation several times, crying, 'Connie! Connie!' but getting no response from her still body. Then I looked up, closed my eyes and managed to utter these few words: 'God, please do not take Connie from me.' They came spontaneously straight from the heart, with high emotional intent and genuine faith. Something told me that however few the words were, they sufficed and I should open my eyes. I cannot find words to describe my relief and pure joy when Connie regained consciousness first by twitching her left leg and then slowly opening her eyes. I kept wiping the blood from her mouth and reassuring her.

Getting her help in hospital very fast was what was on my mind, but when I found out that the phone line had gone dead I ran to my neighbour, Sipho Ngwenya. He was the resident of the house on our plot salvaged by the Duduza municipality. Fortunately, he was at home and his phone was not affected, maybe because the source of his line was from a different pole. I prayed that, as an employee of the municipality, his urging of the emergency workers who he knew in person would yield quick results. There were other occupants staying in the big garage next to the house and the old lady there also came over after I asked her to provide us with advice and company, because I did not know what to do or not do.

In a short while the ambulance arrived and we were rushed to Pholosong Hospital in nearby Tsakane Township. All the while, I held Connie's hands and kept eye contact as though her survival depended on it.

I could never have foreseen the excitement that unfolded in front of my eyes at the hospital after the news of a survivor of a lightning strike made the rounds. Doctors and nurses could not control their curiosity and came one after the other to see for themselves while asking me questions. The point is that everyone in the Duduza and Tsakane area had heard that powerful thunder. It had been followed by silence, a little rain and then sunshine. It was while the doctors were examining Connie that I saw a blue mark the size of a ruler stretching along her left outer thigh. It was only after seeing that mark that the medical professionals were convinced.

After the necessary checks, Connie was given medical advice and discharged. Their verdict? Connie was one of a few lucky survivors. Yet I could not help blaming myself for what had happened: had I ignored the phone call, nothing of the sort would have happened. I had to cut short our long weekend plans and accompany her back home the following day.

After that incident, Connie was so subdued that her family

thought I had made up the lightning strike story to try to hide physical abuse from my side. Even Rebecca's account of the phone conversation's abrupt ending was not enough to convince them, until a local medical doctor confirmed that I was telling the truth. That somehow restored the family's trust in me.

Everything began to sink in after I returned to my house. As ongoing reports of the Hani assassination continued in the media, it dawned on me how thin a line it is between life and death. Chris Hani had narrowly escaped many attempts on his life. In 1969, he and six others had presented the Hani Memorandum to ANC leaders in Lusaka, critical of the unsatisfactory way the MK commander Joe Modise was conducting the armed struggle. Hani's and the others' lives were in peril until OR Tambo intervened; in Lesotho, an assassination attempt had also been foiled. These incidents made him an inspiration to many and gained him popularity in the ANC.

Had it not been for Margareta Harmse, a neighbour, Hani's killer might never had been apprehended; the range of the investigation could have been cast wide open, including even the organisation internally. She identified the act as criminal and thus unpardonable, whether committed by a person of the same colour as her and maybe someone with different political beliefs from hers. We should not miss the parable. She was a Good Samaritan but might be conveniently forgotten in history by those who like to use the race card when it suits their debates.

Later that week Mwezi Twala appeared on SABC TV making an unambiguous condemnation of the violent nature of Hani's death. At the end of the day, we are all human. Like many who were killed in exile and elsewhere, Hani did not deserve to be killed. Not least in memory of Sipho's murder, however, I would postulate a lack of consistency on the ANC's part in being very critical of murder by the other, compared to murder committed by the ANC of one of its own. The difference here is of colossal proportions: it is difficult to acknowledge one's own defects when the suffering and deaths were inflicted not by the apartheid system, but by the ANC. Unless this is perceived in a broad sense, then whatever Quatro stood for – the subjugation and deprivation of human dignity – will be accepted and continue unchallenged.

The ensuing climate of political turbulence could only be calmed by the wisdom of our national father, Nelson Mandela, calling for the nation not to panic and resort to violence. Somehow it brought about the lethargic resumption of peaceful talks, which took a lot of persuasion of political parties across the spectrum. From the ultra-left to the ultra-right, all ultimately agreed on holding the first ever democratic elections in South Africa.

A year after Hani's murder, the historic general elections came and went in April 1994, without incident. The ANC won convincingly, and Nelson Mandela became the first democratically elected president of the country. His cabinet, as per the 'sunset' clause suggested by Joe Slovo, comprised also ministers from the National Party and Inkatha Freedom Party (IFP), as a Government of National Unity. The interim constitution, which had been ratified by the Multiparty Negotiating Process back in November 1993, was to remain in place until a new constitution was drawn up later in 1995.

After the elections, we former MK combatants were supposed to assemble at Walmansdal military base in Pretoria for the integration of all military forces from all formations: the South African Defence Force (SADF), non-statutory forces (MK, Apla and Azanla) and the Bantustan forces – Transkei, Bophuthatswana, Venda and Ciskei – into one army, the South African National Defence Force (SANDF).

Our brickmaking business was failing to sustain itself, so it did not hurt to join the army. Hence David Makhubedu and I decided to give it a try. A visit to the ANC regional offices in downtown Johannesburg was vital to check if we were in the Certified Personnel Register (CPR). After confirming that our names were on the list, we hopped onto the next bus carrying a batch of MK combatants to a new life of integration.

PART SEVEN
MAKING A NEW LIFE

Staff-Sergeant Luthando Dyasop at
Potchefstroom's School of Artillery in 1995.

CHAPTER 30

Prior to integration, the financial assistance we ex-combatants had been receiving lapsed. What followed was a sequel to the promises made while in exile, that we were each to be given a certain amount of money to enable us to have a decent and dignified start back home. That would include having houses of our own.

These expectations of MK soldiers were not unfounded. It is a worldwide expectation for soldiers from both warring parties to expect a comfortable life after the war, and we were not immune from that. With our organisation in power, our hopes couldn't have been higher.

What struck me in Walmansdal was that the SADF, our former arch-rivals, and the former Bantustan armed forces did not undergo the gruelling tests we were about to undergo: they were home and dry. Actually, life for them changed very little. Their ranks were not queried, and their work was not interrupted. It was we, the 'non-statutory' forces, who had to grovel. I couldn't help thinking that MK should have had its own standing army before entering negotiations.

On our arrival there one other thing that was obvious to us trained soldiers was that our numbers were inflated. There were those who had been members of the local community Self Defence Units (SDUs) claiming to have been trained inside the country by MK operatives who had been infiltrated into the country. Ours was not to dispute their claim, but it was not long before the authorities questioned it because some would return from two days' leave with relatives and friends also claiming to be MK members.

One morning we woke up to find the whole camp filled with buses from all major parts of South Africa. We were all summoned to gather in front of the administrative offices. The CPR list of bona fide MK members was produced; anyone whose name did not appear on that list had to board the bus to their hometown. It was a long day that ended with almost half the camp on their way back home.

When the process of integration began in earnest, there were two options to choose from: either join the army through the process of being ranked in the corps of one's choice, or get demobilised and receive a monetary package determined by one's length of service since joining the said non-statutory force (NSF). The amount of money I could have qualified for was around R26 000 and that wasn't much. Even members of the high-end Luthuli Detachment, who had joined MK in the 1960s, were not offered a substantial enough amount to sustain them for any considerable time. Surely it was people who had bigger fish to fry who would opt for the demobilisation package. Makhubedu and I decided to join the army. Shange joined later.

There was general frenzy in the camp as everyone prepared to be ranked. I thought a CV covering my military experience would be enough, but judging from others it was not: some had been trained in the Soviet Union or the German Democratic Republic, others had been taken for short officers' courses in Zimbabwe prior to the general election, while still others were studying lectures disseminated by those who had been to Zimbabwe so as to be better ranked. It was confusing to me, so I didn't bother myself – I would present myself in the best way possible and that was that.

We first had to undergo a medical examination and then the mandatory psychometric test before facing a panel of two MK officers, two SADF officers and an officer of the British Military Advisory Training Team (BMATT) whose duty was to observe and advise.

Preparing for that fate-determining interview was daunting for most of us. Helping each other with tips on how to win over the panel seemed the only thing we could do, because we were on our own throughout the whole process. Etiquette, personal hygiene and a positive demeanour could help, but everything depended on the panel and an element of luck.

Given this quandary, it was not uncommon for us to solicit advice from some of the former SADF officers. A Lieutenant Uys was so outstandingly helpful in this regard that many gravitated towards her. Her tiny figure belied her assertive character. I soon discovered this trait of hers when I approached her, telling her of my love for art and asking if she could find me the alternative in the army where art was accommodated, as I wasn't interested in the corps available. I had with me some pictures I had drawn. She looked at them and said there was a possibility I could be taken up by a certain team of artists working in the army. She said it was worth trying and dialled them right away. I could hear her trying to convince them. They ultimately set a day when they would send someone to Walmansdal to meet me.

When that day came, I was psychologically prepared for the meeting, but no one showed up. Again, Lieutenant Uys phoned them and was given another date in a week's time. To cut a long story short, that appointment and another were not honoured either. I was left in limbo and time was wasted. On the other hand, Lieutenant Uys was fuming, insisting that we should not give up. She was raring for a battle, however long it took.

An opportunity came for me to present my dilemma to the relevant channels when the then Minister of Defence, Joe Modise, paid a visit to our base. He was accompanied by the camp's Officer Commanding (OC) and other high-ranking officers. Modise talked about integration and later fielded questions from us. That's when I made him aware of my problem of locating the artists' team in the SANDF. He did not seem to have any idea what I was talking about. The OC, on seeing the confusion, approached Modise and addressed him audibly enough for me to hear what he was saying. It was deliberate, and Modise didn't have to repeat it.

What the OC was saying to Modise was that 'It was a specialised art unit that was not affected by integration'. Modise's answer to me was, 'Man, we trained you well, go and choose any corps you are comfortable with.' Then he turned and waited for more questions. In other words, I had to forgo the hope of joining the 'specialised art unit'. It seemed that the old apartheid system continued to reign over art in the SANDF.

I woke up the next day and told myself that I would give the army a chance. I decided on infantry. Once I put to rest the dream of working as an artist in the army, I felt a certain relief. Somehow a positive feeling took over – yes, I was just a soldier who had plied his skills in the Angolan war and gained first-hand experience, so yes, infantry was the right choice. With a spring in my step, I headed to the ranking station, but first I had to let Lieutenant Uys know about the previous day's developments. That I was giving up on my initial plan was not pleasing news to her, but I assured her that her concern was appreciated, and I was grateful all the same.

The morning was still young and the queue at the infantry ranking station was not long. As I slowly proceeded to the front, I noticed something strange – the march and drill that was used was not the Soviet march and drill I was used to. I wondered when they had practised it, then I recalled that in other bases there were lots of activities going on. I suddenly felt my allegiance to the Eastern Bloc countries challenged. I doted on the East for its devotion to fighting the colonialism in Africa brought about by Western countries. Never in my wildest dream had I imagined that the compromise would go this deep.

Nothing mattered then more than that I had to face that panel and try my best to impress it. For some unknown reason, I decided to go ahead with the Soviet march and drill regardless of the consequences. I told myself that integration meant East meets West and I was going to show them how we did it, even if it was for the last time.

My unconventional entrance based on my march and drill was received with amusement, which made the ensuing interview more relaxed. Let me be forthright: I never mentioned the mutiny, incarceration in Quatro or my involvement in both. I felt it wasn't necessary. After being cross-questioned I was ranked Staff Sergeant and when I was turning to leave, the British officer commented that he didn't think I would last in the army. It must have been something he perceived, but it wasn't for me to argue, so I left.

Was I happy with the rank? Firstly, I was happy that the process was over. The suspense was over. I had given my all to achieve the rank and I needed to pat myself on my back. I deserved the rank, and I thought the panel had been fair. Yes, I was happy to be addressed as Staff Sergeant Dyasop because I had seen some of the June 16 Detachment members who had been involved in the mutiny, or were not in the good books of Mbokodo, being lowly ranked. Yes, I had had Lady Luck on my side that day.

Towards the Christmas holidays, around 16 December, President Mandela visited us in Walmansdal. As expected, there was excitement when he entered the hall. He took his time shaking our hands. He thanked us for being patient and understanding in the process of integration; wished us well in our chosen careers and hoped we had enjoyable holidays and returned to serve our country.

It was wonderful to be treated as honourable people by the most powerful man in the country, or maybe in the entire world at that time. His humility was incredible, and that earned him even more respect and love from those around him. We South Africans were the envy of many countries in the world because we had, through Mandela's wondrous magnanimity, avoided a bloodbath and our economy was still intact. He was in the hottest seat in the country in quelling anger and impatience from one section of the country while trying to address 'white fears' on the other. He was walking a tightrope with all its attendant risks.

To Mandela's detractors, those who see him as a man who sold out by agreeing to a negotiated settlement, I say they must think of the lives saved by that decision. Had he ignored the signs of a failed armed struggle and forged ahead regardless with the call for people to engage in a fight to the last, I think our generation in exile would either have been demobilised, dead, or in a hostile diaspora. It goes without saying that we Quatro inmates would never have seen our freedom. The country's stable economy had only to grow in leaps and bounds, as it had stagnated due to economic sanctions. Mandela's respect for property rights meant that interested investors' confidence in the country would be boosted. Indeed, that resulted in many people being employed and the emergence of the black middle class, which was growing fast. It took courage, in which he risked being called names while knowing that one step back is followed by two steps forward. It is in that step back that we magnify the compromises while overlooking the two steps forward that we take for granted.

CHAPTER 31

In January 1995, after returning from the Christmas break, we were taken to the School of Artillery in Potchefstroom for an instructor's course. It was for staff sergeants, sergeant majors, captains and majors. Though we were mostly in the same classes, the non-commissioned officers – staff sergeants and sergeant majors – were excluded from time to time from certain modules meant for the captains and majors. Another factor was that we were not exclusively MK as there were also Apla members among us.

We were now earning salaries according to the ranks we had been given, backdated to April 1994. That meant a large sum of money, especially for those who were highly ranked. There was a catch, though: however much the money seemed, it was nothing for people who had to build their lives from scratch. It was tough for us MK and Apla veterans from exile, although in different ways. Some felt like splashing out their money on cars first and houses later. Paying bonds and car-purchase instalments for years meant bringing home a meagre sum, which translated to slow growth in one's economic standing.

I had no intention of buying a bonded house and so I would return to our place in Duduza. Even a car to me was not that necessary as public transport between Duduza and Potchefstroom was available. Besides, I was trying to build my financial nest egg. The challenges for former exiles gaped wide before us. The ever-lingering problem of not being developmentally on a par with army colleagues from the former SADF and the former homeland armies revived our feeling that we should have be given a substantial sum of money and houses prior to integration, so as not to be burdened with paying bonds or ending up homeless, as some of us were. That problem of inequality still looms large today.

When they say, 'it's a small world', in my case nothing corroborates that expression more than the following three events.

First, my meeting Mbulelo Ndzamela at Artillery School. It was not the most pleasant experience: Ndzamela had been the driver of the car that carried Mfanelo Matshaya when he killed Sipho Phungulwa in Mthatha. Now he was a major, and so was in different barracks from mine. I never told anyone about him – not even Makhubedu – preferring to avoid unnecessary confrontation. It had been and continues to be my belief that what he and Matshaya had done was not of their own volition. Any anger directed at them was misplaced – they had been fulfilling an order from above. So, there we were, brought together again by fate, but not necessarily pitting ourselves against each other. I felt that as long as he kept to his lane and I to mine, we could coexist peacefully.

The second event also happened at Artillery School. I saw a guy I was sure I had met many years before when I was at the Wentzels' farm in Mthatha. The Wentzels' farm had employed seasonal and casual workers over the years. He was young then and employed as a farmhand but was now a major in the new SANDF. I didn't approach him, but as fate would have it we met at a Johannesburg taxi rank before the Easter holidays, both of us heading to Mthatha. We occupied the front seats of the taxi and chatted about everything like old friends. He was comfortable with that and I was ready to oblige.

It was when we reached Mthatha that the third event took place. We were to part since taxis to my location were on the other side of town while he was going to remain in Norwood – a suburb close to town. He suggested that he call friends who would drive me to my place. Within half an hour his friend arrived and he turned out to be an old acquaintance of mine. We hopped into the Kombi but he said he had to inform someone that he was taking me to the location. That someone turned out to be Matshaya.

Matshaya was asleep when we got to his home. After waking him up, he looked at us with sleepy eyes and said it was okay – I could be transported to wherever – and he turned back to sleep. Needless to say, I had a nice ride home during which I established that Matshaya ran a security company, which he had named Caculama, after the camp in Angola where he had trained. What intrigued me was the way the three of us pretended we didn't know each other, conveniently creating a facade to keep the peace. The same cannot be said of Matshaya. I was convinced, as events later proved, that he was unaware it was me who was by his bedside.

After the course was through, we were to be deployed at bases of our choice, provided there was space. I chose and found placement near Duduza. It was a base called Group 16 in the Springs jurisdiction, though nearer to Duduza. That meant I could commute to work on a daily basis, unlike others who had to stay in the barracks inside the camp.

What was peculiar about Group 16 was that it was the headquarters of commandos of the East Rand towns of Benoni, Brakpan, Nigel, Springs, Heidelberg and Delmas and also cadets from certain schools from these towns. The commandos and cadets were all white. They belonged to the old order of apartheid South Africa, when they had served as a buffer zone in outlying rural areas against any insurgence by MK and Apla, while the cadets were school children who were being militarised in a system preparing them for subsequent conscription. Having us former MK and Apla cadres working in such a place was nauseating to me because of its racist history. It had overstayed its importance and relevance. It was a discrepancy that went against the grain of our young democratic dispensation, making a mockery of it. To some extent, I felt as if I was conniving and complicit in an unethical practice, contrary to my personal beliefs and values. For us soldiers, the new interim constitution at that time was what we were, first and foremost, safeguarding. It fostered social cohesion and categorically slated all remnants of apartheid in the new political dispensation.

Though it varied from base to base, there was blatant resistance to change by former SADF white officers. The medium of communication was 80 per cent Afrikaans. Among the practices that were a slap in the face of our liberation army was that in army-based clinics only white army personnel enjoyed the benefit of medical assistance, which was also extended to their families. Blacks were not allowed to bring their wives and children for treatment. It was appalling that such an anomaly was not addressed by Joe Modise's defence ministry, thus allowing inequality to thrive.

It was in these conditions that, while I was at work in late February 1996, I received a call from home to tell me my mother had passed away. The news shattered me spiritually; it was not something I had expected. In my last phone communication with her she had been full of life, and now she was gone. I had not had a chance to bond with her after my return from exile.

I approached my immediate senior and informed him of the news and my intention to take leave. The application process is not necessarily a long one: a few signatures from the relevant persons is all it takes. Since it was still early in the week – it was a Tuesday – there was a possibility that her funeral would take place that Saturday.

Everyone signed except the acting OC. Although he had no valid reason, when I went for his signature, the OC was not prepared to sign my leave form. It wasn't that there was no one else who could do my work in my absence. It was obviously a negative racial attitude. The callousness my grief was met with really wrecked me. I was close to tears as I realised the futility of the situation. I had lost my dear mother, and what I needed was compassion. To think there were people in the army with whom we spent most of our time who could be so cold when one needed their moral support reduced me to despair.

I had decided to leave for Mthatha on the Thursday. If the delay persisted, I might end up not being able to attend my mother's funeral. I was overwhelmed with anxiety and then with anger. I told myself I was leaving on Thursday with or without the OC's consent. And I did, little knowing this was the beginning of the end of my short spell in the supposedly non-racial SANDF.

My mother was laid to rest that Saturday. It was a dignified send-off befitting someone of her social standing as an old church member and a senior citizen well known in the community. At short notice, mourners came from as far as Cape Town just to comfort us and confirm that family comes first in times of loss and sadness.

As everyone was leaving Mthatha on the Sunday, I decided to also leave that day and managed to get a taxi to Johannesburg. I couldn't have made it to work on the Monday, so I phoned and said I would report for work on Tuesday.

The taxi arrived in Johannesburg early in the morning. After disembarking from the train at Brakpan station, I missed a step and fell, landing clumsily and hurting my right wrist. It was so painful that I went to the Dunnottar Hospital near Duduza later in the morning. X-rays showed I had a dislocation and a fracture. The doctor recommended a plaster of Paris cast for me and laid me off duty for two months. He gave me a letter to hand in to my employers.

The following day I got ready for work. Being right-handed, I couldn't cope with the simplest of chores, such as polishing my boots or lifting anything. The pain was worse than ever that morning, but I managed to get to my workplace and showed them the letter. They dismissed the letter saying I should go to the camp clinic; only the clinic doctor had the authority to book me off for whatever period. They made it clear they were not happy I had been AWOL. In other words, I was to face a military tribunal and my salary would be suspended for three months, even though I would have to report for work throughout that period. If the tribunal found me guilty, I could even be sentenced to serve time in Boksburg military prison. Whichever way I considered the situation, things were not looking good for me.

There was already a queue at the base clinic but, believe me, there were white families who did not have to queue! The wives and children not only enjoyed the privilege of receiving medical attention, but were also allowed to jump the queue of black people.

When the doctor ultimately saw me and my letter he, too, dismissed it. He said that I should report for work, but only do 'light duties'. What is that?! I argued that I had pain every time I moved my wrist but that fell on deaf ears.

I decided to go back to the doctor at Dunnottar Hospital to ask about what harm might be caused by 'light duties'. In no uncertain terms, he pointed out that it was up to me: 'What's more important – your health or your work?' he asked. That rhetorical question gave me a jab. Report for duty with an arm in plaster and a sling was the last thing I would do. Furthermore, being subjected to a military tribunal and submitting to their grilling was far too degrading. I might be humble by nature, but a person must have his pride. And at that time, it was put to the test.

As I was walking home, I looked closely at my life's journey and more especially at who I really am, my values and my personality. I needed to map my way forward urgently. I decided I was leaving the army and I did not need a vocational guide to tell me that I belonged in a creative world. I couldn't help remembering the British officer in Walmansdal who foresaw that after just one meeting with me.

It was time too for me to turn my back on guns, big or small, once and for all. Although I had been brandishing them for a relatively short time, I was convinced I did not need a gun in my life. I was being true to myself. The monetary incentive of a job without spiritual fulfilment amounted to a life of betrayed dreams, with only myself to blame.

The decision to quit had its drawbacks. The uncertainty of an immediate alternative source of income posed a question, but I had to have faith and determination. Let me die trying to flaunt the gifts I have rather than have them haunt me for the rest of my life. Happiness can be found in being grateful for what one has.

I took my time the following day and, wearing my civvies, I tendered my resignation. I told them I had thought things through, and my mind was made up. There was never to be anything military in my life again, not even if you dropped me from a plane

3 000 metres from the ground with an ailing parachute, I can take that; or sent me to work on a fishing trawler in Alaska in the winter, I can take that too; but never again ask me to don an army uniform or give me a gun. My immediate seniors were alarmed by my decision. They said I hadn't finished a certain minimum period of time in the army so I couldn't resign with immediate effect; to which I said I would wait out that time as a free man at my own place. They could bring the resignation papers when that time came. And then I left.

By May, the hospital declared that my injuries had healed and it was then that the SANDF brought me my resignation form to fill in. Then came the waiting for the money due to me. It took forever, and when it came I was shocked to find it was only R4 500, more or less. Surely there must have been a mistake, I told myself, because during the time I was at home I had met one young man whose two-year contract had finished, and had asked him how much he had been paid out and what his next aims in life were. He had said in Afrikaans, 'Ek is bly' (I am happy). Now, no white person can be that happy if he had been given R4 500 or even R10 000 for that matter. He said that he was even able to further his studies at a college. The army had been his saviour! With such disparity between blacks and whites in the new South Africa's civil service it was as if we were being paid from different national budgets; it was a difficult pill to swallow, but a real one.

Leaving the army was in effect letting go of the only opportunity the ANC could ever open for us former MK members. I had messed with it and had to suffer the consequences. It is quite a paradox that peacetime in the military is full of fighting: everyone fighting for promotion, salary increases and equal rights. Yet wartime knits us together in sweet and unifying camaraderie.

CHAPTER 32

Two years after I resigned from the army Makhubedu did the same. Our passion for seeing our mission through was never dead, but rekindled with a new impetus.

The growth of our brickmaking business had an unpredictable potential. Our marketing strategy relied mainly on the imminent rollout of the grand housing project under the government's Reconstruction and Development Programme (RDP). The RDP was meant to correct the historical socio-economic imbalance inherent in South African society. It was an ambitious plan through which living standards of the 'previously disadvantaged' Africans could be raised to the same level as those of the other races. Besides housing, RDP entailed electrification, installation of running water and improvement of roads in the country's townships and the rural areas.

Though we were content with preparing for that eventuality in our area, in the meantime we made inroads into the local market with weekend door-to-door canvassing for support for our unique type of brick. In the process we became cognisant of the dire poverty in which our black people were living. The problem of unemployment and not having a decent roof over one's head were the pressing issues. Even those who were employed had the burden of taking care of the needs of an average of six people. Rampant urbanisation had led to high population density in the main cities of the country. Moreover, the youth born in these cities needed places of their own. All this resulted in many thousands of shanty towns sprouting on available land on the peripheries of every town and city. In the case of Duduza, Soul City was the name given to the squatter camp.

The new South Africa of the ANC was the land of dreams for the 'Rainbow Nation' – as we were popularly known. However, our door-to-door canvassing in the formal settlement areas around Duduza – Bluegumview, Zamane and Masechaba – produced only a clientele who could afford to buy no more than a few hundred bricks to build a backroom, thus leaving a gap in front of the yard where the actual RDP house would be built.

There was something funny about our door-to-door campaign: almost every time we introduced ourselves to a household, there would be a sharp reaction that gave us a rocky start. Unbeknown to us, there was a well-known Duduza resident with the same name – David Makhubedu – and this would lead to the inevitable question: Where are you from? The fact that we were not local worked against us to some degree. I would not put it past some people to be protective of their turf and cautious and suspicious of strangers (and impostors?) selling unique products.

This may have provided the disinterested with an excuse, but in most cases it was the female figure of the family – as the adage goes, behind every successful man is a woman – who would be the visionary encouraging her husband to come to his senses and smell the bright future of living in a formal structure. Whether it was through her wiles or nagging (from the man's point of view), her ambitions were clear: she could not settle for mediocrity. It was certainly at this juncture that our marketing paid off. But then there would be the odd John Deere employee who qualified for the company housing subsidy, coming with a house plan and asking us to furnish the bricks and supervision of the actual building. Just when we were be about to finalise the contract, the said client would hit us, and John Deere alike, with a shocker to the effect that his wife preferred a bonded house in a better residential area.

Oops! The point worth mentioning here is that chances of them succeeding were practically nil. Of course, no one is allowed to meddle in another's family affairs, so we ended up with the proverbial egg on our faces.

When the RDP housing programme actually started, we were excited, if only for a brief moment. What we had not anticipated took us by surprise. We were told of a tender system – something brought about by the new dispensation. It was expected that anyone intending to participate in any aspect of housing construction had to bid for it with other interested competitors.

What happened next was downright unfair. Out of the blue we heard that some companies won tenders. None of them were locally based. Maybe the leverage that helped them win the tender was because they were already established construction companies. The whole process of tender acquisition was flawed and it was neither transparent nor procedural. Where was justness if local stakeholders were not consulted about the product they were to receive? Was it up to their expectations? Unless one reckons with the desperation for having a house of one's own, no one will ever understand the extent to which most are prepared to accept anything, even if it is below par. The sad part is that, compared to our model, the winning models were below par. Even the apartheid four-roomed house that we in the struggle days scorned as matchboxes were, and still are, sturdier than most of those pathetic excuses for houses that we see all over the country.

The RDP houses in our area were first erected between Duduza and Bluegumview. They were so small that they acquired an apt name, amaUno (Unos), a name derived from a car of the same small size. This produced a sinking feeling in us, given our dream of instilling dignity and a sense of ownership to our citizens in need of this basic human right. The fundamental problem was that each participant in the whole process of construction had the ulterior motive of making a killing out of every available opportunity. Subcontractors sought the cheapest labour on the market who, in turn, stole and sold crucial building material like bags of cement to make up for their low pay. The result ranged from shoddy workmanship with cracks in the walls to structures actually crumbling.

The second and third phases were built concurrently near Zamane and Masechaba formal settlements. These were bigger than the Unos, but unfortunately not big enough for a standard family. Due to the great number of houses planned to be built in a small space, intense congestion was inevitable. The Department of Housing relished reminding all and sundry that RDP housing beneficiaries should be proud owners, since these houses came with title deeds, unlike those under apartheid. In fact, the department was not letting on that it was grappling with the problem of unavailability of land on which to build enough houses. Vast open spaces in Gauteng were owned by whites living in South Africa or even abroad. Under the willing buyer/willing seller arrangement, the owners were uncompromising and demanded unreasonably exorbitant payment for their land.

The land ownership question of the 1913 Land Act was obviously never discussed and addressed with forthrightness during the negotiations leading to the dawn of democracy. The problem lingers and is compounded, on the one hand, by intransigence and hoarding of land by a few who perceive compromise as reneging on privilege, which is an age-old white entitlement; while on the other hand, the ANC government brought to the equation the factors of cadre deployment, nepotism and later, in 2004, Black Economic Empowerment (BEE). BEE, in the same vein as the RDP, was meant to redress the racial disparities of apartheid. It was never successful because it benefited those who were already rich or politically connected black people, and never the 'previously disadvantaged'.

As a result of these factors, merit and competence gave way to racial and political loyalty. It is no wonder that service delivery and transformation were compromised by the process of patronage. Lack of direct political accountability to the people, or to the Treasury, meant that maladministration was to thrive indefinitely and be an everlasting feature of the new democracy. Local councils' performance indicated a constant decline in service delivery. Billions of rands, lost and wasted along the way, remained unaccounted for, while the living conditions of the poor worsened. The paradigm of willing corrupter/willing corruptee between the private and public sectors landed each lucrative deals. Some of our ANC leaders were deeply involved in this, and were not prepared to tone down their voracious appetite. In a voting system that deprives citizens of the right to appoint and recall any elected representative who has failed them – as we had called for in Dakawa – it is only through civic protests that their cries are heard, while party-nominated MPs and councillors, together with corrupt public officials, nevertheless stay in office.

One thing that should be highlighted, however, is that contrary to the widely held belief that only by being an ANC member would one automatically qualify to be the recipient of tenders, it is not so. There are many who would have hit the jackpot if they had not been principled – it takes a lot of walking the walk and talking the talk to be accepted by the other side.

Let us make the analogy of the goat that leaves its pen in the valley every morning and ascends the mountain top. Up there the grass is the lushest; the air rarefied and the views are out of this world. But it has to descend grudgingly back to its pen before sunset. This was the typical life of the politician-turned-billionaire before he walked the walk and talked the talk: every day he had to commute between his poor township home and the boardrooms in the towers of leafy suburbia to brush shoulders with the influential in the corporate world. Their lavish and the highly materialistic decadence is plainly displayed to him. It is a far cry from his dusty poverty-ridden background, and it leaves him envious of the lifestyle. All he has to do, for starters, is to renounce the fundamental principles and objectives of the organisation, be selfish, and be willing to talk the talk, which is about safeguarding the interests of capital, kickbacks, fronting and manipulation. With these conditions met, the willing corrupter/willing corruptee deal is as good as done.

One former MK member I knew from exile bid for a tender doing everything by the book. Of course, his simple demeanour, as he pitched up in sombre clothes and driving an outdated motor car, was his undoing. He failed dismally. His son, seeing his father's 'shortcomings', took it upon himself to apply the 'contemporary' approach when dealing with these issues. It involved unethical and immoral routes to acquiring tenders that ensured short cuts to quick riches. To the father, his son's immediate success was testimony to how shamefully low the organisation's morals had deteriorated. The father would not have allowed his son to do this had he known what it entailed because it was against the lofty founding principles of the liberation movement he still believed in. Talk of two factions in one family! Those who chose the opportunistic line were those who could not wait to join the social status of the white oligarchy at the expense of 'a better life for all'. By virtue of not belonging to that rogue faction, the others unwittingly belonged to another faction.

What a way for our brickmaking business to come to terms with our South African dream! Though our dream never materialised, we can hold our heads high: we never compromised quality for quantity. Our standards were high – too high for someone else with a totally different agenda.

PART EIGHT
THE TRC AND AFTER

2018, Soweto: L-R, Omry Makgoale, another Quatro survivor, centre is Sam Mngqibisa who testified at the TRC, and me.

CHAPTER 33

Following the promise by President Nelson Mandela after the report of the Motsuenyane Commission in 1993, the government set up the Truth and Reconciliation Commission (TRC), which would expose human rights violations that took place during the apartheid era. The Commission would look at both the liberation forces and the apartheid regime. This meant that the ANC had not only to make public the Motsuenyane report but open itself to more testimonies regarding those of its members who had carried out human rights violations by transgressing and abusing their powers.

According to the National Unity and Reconciliation Act (1995), these human rights violations were the following:

- Psychological torture: solitary confinement; degradation through insults;
- Severe treatment: burning; beating severely;
- Framing: labelling as an informer or traitor; spreading false information about a person a or smear campaign against a person;
- Incarceration;
- Disruption of family life: pain and suffering caused not only to the victim, but to the victim's family and loved ones.

The TRC was established in August 1995 and was headed by Archbishop Desmond Tutu, whose deputy was Alex Boraine. It started proceedings in December 1995 and those who deemed themselves victims of violations could approach TRC offices nationwide and tell their stories.

In the case of the ANC's victims, the TRC also studied the

reports of the Stuart, Skweyiya and Motsuenyane commissions of inquiry appointed by the ANC into abuses in exile, as well as that of the Douglas Commission. It also took evidence from alleged victims of abuse in the camps and from those in positions of command and authority.

In January 1996, I gave evidence to the TRC offices in downtown Johannesburg. My statement covered the conditions in the camps, the reasons leading to mutiny, the backlash from Mbokodo, the brutality of the security officers at Quatro, the suppression of democracy in Dakawa, our escape to Malawi and, lastly, the killing of Sipho Phungulwa in Mthatha by ANC operatives.

As one can imagine, it was a long and strenuous narrative. The mental and emotional strain I experience every time I tell the story is enormous. From time to time I break down and cry when some moments in my life that I had been blocking suddenly become vividly grim and my frail armour simply falls to pieces, exposing my vulnerability. One never sees it coming; it's an involuntary gush of uncontrollable emotion with tears signifying a tormented soul. Invariably one is offered water, and that's the only thing one can see coming because it is practised the world over.

But spare a moment of admiration for the person to whom I was unloading my suffering; he was supportive and understanding as we transformed from two strangers to two brothers when we emerged after hours spent in a small office. Unlike others who had said that we who had appeared at the Motsuenyane Commission should not bother to testify before the TRC because our cases had already been noted, that man insisted on my telling my whole story. I appreciated his commitment to get to the truth of the matter, no matter how uncomforting it was.

The first hearings were held on 15 April 1996 in the Eastern Cape. They were aired live on television and radio. My opportunity to appear in front of the TRC commissioners came on 25 July 1996 at Regina Mundi, Soweto. The panel consisted of chairperson Hlengiwe Mkhize, Yasmin Sooka, Glenda Wildschut, Joyce Seroke, Tom Manthata and the former political prisoner Hugh Lewin.

The hall was almost full when the proceedings commenced. I was seated with a flask of water and a glass, and alongside me sat a charming lady, courtesy of the TRC. We had never met before, but to viewers at home and my girlfriend Connie, she was my 'girlfriend' and I had a fair share of trouble because of that chance encounter. I assume she was there to keep me company during the process: a sensible gesture, given I had indicated I would be there on my own.

I had taken the oath when Ms Sooka, who was leading the evidence, said that according to the statement in front of her, I had been imprisoned by the South African police at different times before going into exile. This was not true. I still don't know where they got that from, because I never said anything like that to the man who took my statement. I told the panel I was arrested and imprisoned in Quatro, at which Sooka asked me to tell them instead about myself. For the benefit of clarity, I was ready to go through the phases of my life that I thought were worth mentioning. I started by saying I was in the class of 1976 and loved art, but my wish to become an architect had been thwarted because that was a faculty for whites only. I went on to say that this, along with other factors, had motivated me to join the ANC in Lesotho. My narration tended to be detailed and it was time-consuming to give a blow-by-blow account of the incidents leading to my incarceration in Quatro and the treatment there.

Things took a bad turn when it was clear I was not going to be allowed to talk about the assassination of Sipho Phungulwa and the attempt on my life. According to them, I had not included that in my statement. That, too, was not true. I wondered why my statement had been tampered with. I expressed my disappointment to the Commission that there had been a cover-up of the case in Transkei. Now I was seeing the pattern being passed on to the TRC. They said they would take another statement regarding that matter. I felt frustrated. Indications were that no such statement would be taken, something that I deduced from their impatience with me, telling me that I had taken more time compared with other victims, as well as the fact that my inclusion of the death of Sipho in my statement had evidently been omitted.

At that time, I had put all my hope in the TRC to expedite the case of Sipho's murder, considering that Mandela had never responded to the Motsuenyane Commission's recommendations by clearing our names. Instead, Mandela had talked of forming the TRC to look into *all* violations of human rights. Since the Motsuenyane Commission had heard me out about the death of Sipho, it was clear to me that his case was being deliberately omitted. It became obvious that the TRC was infiltrated by people who were biased towards the ANC and their influence was unavoidable. It is no secret that there were those in the ANC leadership who did not think it right for the TRC to take statements relating to ANC members who had violated human rights, and this filtered down into the TRC's work.

I left at the same time as Valli Moosa (ANC) and Tony Leon (Democratic Alliance). I overheard Leon saying to a member of the TRC that he needed to get hold of the tape, or something, of the proceedings. It was clear that the sour note on which the proceedings ended caused consternation for many. Of course, the TRC was not a substitute for the judicial process or a quick fix for everyone's problems, but I had reason to feel short-changed.

I do not know whether Tony Leon obtained whatever he had been asking for that day at Regina Mundi. The reality is that I never did get the opportunity I had been promised to submit another statement pertaining to the death of Sipho, even though I tried immediately after being dismissed. It was a bizarre failure of transparency.

I was to be in limbo for the next 21 months until the day I paid a visit to the TRC office in Johannesburg to follow up on any developments. They said they had been looking for me because I was supposed to go to Mthatha in two days' time for amnesty hearings for abusers of human rights. I wasn't to leave the offices but was later taken to Garden Court Hotel for the night and caught a flight to Mthatha the following day.

What had happened was that the TRC had submitted its report to the president. Its commissioners were suspended pending the completion of the Amnesty Committee's work. By the time I arrived at the hall outside Mthatha on 20 April 1998, the TRC report had not yet been submitted. Sipho's mother Lilian was there, accompanied by her sister Elizabeth. We had last seen each other seven years before when I had gone to pay my respects to the family in 1991. There was not enough time for us to chat and catch up on other things, as I was concerned that we should reach closure and move on with our lives. The only obstacle to that would be if we continued to harbour anger and hatred towards Sipho's killers. I beseeched them to forgive them as I had done. In that way we would free ourselves from forever seeking retribution. We had to accept that the murderers were not going to be punished and we had to be satisfied by the applicants' confession, if that was to be the case. We made a Mr Zuko Mapoma aware of our decision not to cross-examine the applicants, as long as they complied with the requirements of the Act (section 8 of the Promotion of National Unity and Reconciliation Act, 34 of 1995).

The requirements were as follows:
- The timeframe set by the Act was from 1 March 1960 – the month of the Sharpeville massacre – to 5 December 1993, the day that final agreement was reached in the political negotiations, but that was subsequently extended to 10 May 1994, the date of the inauguration of the first democratically elected president of the country;
- The incident had to be associated with political motive; and
- Representation had to be full, truthful disclosure.

The hearings in Mthatha were chaired by Judge Ronnie Pillay. Also on the panel were Advocates Leah Gcabashe SC and Denzel Potgieter. Representing the applicants was Mr NM Notununu. Mr Mapoma was directed to look after our interests, as we did not have a representative of our own.

Mfanelo Matshaya's affidavit had been co-signed by the other two, Ndibulele Ndzamela and Phumlani Khubukeli. The fourth deponent, Aga Thiya, had died. The three of them agreed that they aligned themselves with that one statement in the main affidavit.

The contents of Matshaya's affidavit were very lengthy and so it was not read out. As a result, with agreement from Judge Pillay, the proceedings went straight to the merits of the application. Matshaya was called so that Notununu could lead him. He admitted involvement in the killing of Phungulwa along with Ndzamela, Khubukeli and Thiya. The last two had been in another car. The reason for killing Phungulwa, according to him, was that 'the MK command in Transkei had gathered intelligence data that a lot of askaris had regrouped'. He described an askari as 'someone who was a member of MK who defects to the enemy – South African Police – and then starts fighting against his former comrades'.

Matshaya stressed that there was war between MK and askaris, and that askaris were their first targets because they were being used by the apartheid security police to identify members of MK. Involvement in the mutiny and being arrested by the ANC when we 'were supposed to have been shot' was why he regarded us as askaris. In addition to that, we were 'speaking against the ANC and its leadership, even the military command of the ANC'. He alleged we had called ourselves 'the new ANC' when we got back in South Africa.

When asked by Mr Mapoma if any investigation had been made to establish whether we were in fact askaris, Matshaya said there had been no investigation and repeated the above reasons. The chairperson asked him if we were in fact askaris or enemies in our own right, to which Matshaya said that merely 'defecting' from the ANC meant we were askaris. In a desperate effort to prove his point, he said we were with Patrick Hlongwane – a real apartheid state agent – in RECOC. That had nothing to do with the motive to kill Phungulwa, because Hlongwane had not yet returned from exile when they killed Sipho and RECOC had not yet been formed. Hlongwane didn't share our ideals, as he found us lenient towards the ANC and ended up forming his own organisation.

These nauseating lies sounded convincing to those in the hall, and I was becoming perturbed. I intended to add my voice to the proceedings as I had assumed there would be full disclosure of truth, but words like 'defectors' and 'askaris' were being thrown around as though those words did not constitute 'framing' us: a smear campaign, in terms of the TRC definition of gross abuse of human rights. The applicants were failing to tell the whole truth. Saying that they took the initiative and were not given orders by anyone was untrue. It was obvious they were protecting the person who gave them the order – Kaizer Mbethe. I should know, because I was there when he called Matshaya and Ndzamela. Of course, Mbethe was himself relaying an order from above. The order to kill us in public immediately after we had left the ANC office could only have come from the highest level of the ANC in Transkei.

What was astonishing was the lack of remorse displayed by Matshaya in particular. Maybe lack of remorse was not a determining factor in granting amnesty, but common sense tells me that remorse is essential in facilitating reconciliation. It was clear to me that he was proud of what he had done and was just short of demanding an Isithwalandwe Award for his cowardly act. His elevation of himself to the position of Transkei MK Command was laughable because he was just a bodyguard. Of course, he said this to corroborate the lie that no one ordered them to kill Phungulwa and me. In any army, orders come from the top structures to the lower structures. Unless it is vigilantism or a renegade army, each mission's orders can be traced back to the one who gave them.

No matter how much I tried to refute the statements by Matshaya, my words had no impact. Slander and lies filtering through the hall made me wonder whether the learned honourable judge had made any enquiries about our having appeared at the prior commissions. I found it absurd he could allow the hearing to deteriorate to the point where he said: 'I do not blame them for doing what they did, because it was part of their duty.' This was in reference to my arguing that following what Walter Sisulu told the media – that we were 'defectors' – we were vulnerable to being targeted by 'hostile forces'. In no way was I justifying what befell us.

Judge Pillay's expediency made me believe that everything happening at the amnesty hearing was consistent with the cover-up that continued from the Transkei police investigation to the unfair hearing at Regina Mundi. It was all for the convenience of the applicants – and, by implication, for the ANC government – and had nothing to do with reconciliation, justice or fairness.

The proceedings were supposed to continue the following day, but on that same day we were informed that the three had been granted amnesty. What troubled me most was that we had come with truce in our hearts and how, then, were the Phungulwa family and I to find closure? The truth is, the family was not fooled one bit. After everything was said and done and we were about to leave, Sipho's mother uttered these words: 'With what these ANC leaders ordered you to commit, nobody knows what my Sipho did when he was Chris Hani's bodyguard.' Those wise words from a mother who had lost her son, but was prepared to forgive without overlooking reality, still ring in my ear.

The contradiction here was that all along Jacob Zuma and Chris Hani were in the country fraternising with the apartheid state's top echelons. Zuma, ANC Chief of Intelligence at the time, was then the top MK commander in KwaZulu-Natal, while Hani was top commander in Transkei. So, was it right that when they were embracing the enemy, I should not set foot in South Africa? It was different strokes for different folks, revealing that political correctness can sneak its head in and win the day. Just one day, however, as events would in the end prove.

CHAPTER 34

On 24 August 1998 the TRC served notice to the ANC of its intention of publishing the findings in its final report, which were detrimental to the ANC, and that it should respond not later than in fifteen days' time (8 September). Those fifteen days were later extended to 5 October 1998.

On 19 October the ANC sent submissions to the Commission that were scathing about its competence, integrity and bona fides in respect of its findings about the ANC. It claimed that its struggle for liberation against the apartheid system was morally and legally justifiable in all respects in terms of international law.

In the early hours of the morning of 29 October 1998 – the date of the handover of the TRC report to President Mandela in Pretoria – the ANC launched an urgent application to the High Court for an interdict restraining the Commission from publishing any portion of the final report that implicated the ANC in gross violations of human rights.

In that same breath, the TRC accused the ANC – behind the scenes – of attempting to unduly influence the final findings on gross human rights violations. The High Court findings were not favourable to the ANC's urgent application. Mr Justice J Hlophe dismissed it, pointing out that the ANC was legally obliged to respond to the notice not later than the original date of 8 September and had no right to halt publication for a later date even when the original date had been extended to 5 October 1998.

The Commission had examined three categories of human rights violations in the ANC:

- Against armed combatants during the struggle;
- Against its own members outside South Africa; and
- By its supporters during the 1980s and after the ANC's unbanning on 2 February 1990.

The TRC had used a wide range of resources to compile information useful for the purpose of complying with its mission. These were not only the reports of the Skweyiya and Motsuenyane commissions, both appointed by the ANC; the TRC also used public documents from the Legal Resources Centre and the Harris and Goldstone commissions to widen its investigation.

As in the findings of the Stuart, Skweyiya and Motsuenyane commissions, the ANC was again held morally and politically responsible for a host of gross violations of human rights pertaining largely to the deaths and severe physical injuries sustained by unarmed civilians.

According to the Geneva Convention signed by OR Tambo on 28 November 1980, the ANC had an obligation under international humanitarian law as well as the applicability of Article 75 of Protocol 1 of 1977 and Common Article 3 of the Geneva Convention on the conditions and treatment of MK prisoners in their custody. Tambo had committed the ANC in his pledge when he wrote:

> Therefore, and for humanitarian reasons, the African National Congress of South Africa hereby declares that, in the conduct of the struggle against apartheid and racism and for self-determination in South Africa, it intends to respect and be guided by the general principles of international humanitarian law applicable in armed conflicts.[4]

This was binding on the ANC: the justness of the cause did not translate into the justification of any means to attain the end, although the ANC criticised the TRC for 'equating it to its apartheid

---

4 O'Malley, P. 28 November 1980. *Statement on Signing Declaration by OR Tambo*. Nelson Mandela Foundation. https://omalley.nelsonmandela.org/omalley/index.php/site/q/03lv02424/04lv02730/05lv02918/06lv02979.htm\ Last accessed 29/04/2021.

system counterpart which was defending an unjust cause'.

The impact of the final report on the history of South Africa's exile period was a big concern for ANC leaders. No moral or political justification could be found for any of its violations. As far as I am concerned, the report was fair and unbiased; there had been gross human rights violations across the political spectrum.

The report specified these violations, stating that:

> ... the ANC was found responsible for an array of gross human rights violations arising out of unplanned operations; the bombing of public buildings, restaurants, hotels and bars; the landmine campaign in the northern and north-eastern parts of South Africa; the killing of individual enemies, defectors and spies; the conflict with the IFP; violations perpetrated by supporters in the context of a 'people's war' fostered by the ANC and severe ill-treatment, torture and killing of ANC members outside of South Africa.[5]

The ANC attributed these to 'poor recce, infiltration by security officers, faulty equipment, faulty intelligence, misinterpretation of policy by their cadres and anger' on the part of individual members of MK and the 'blurring of lines' between civilian and military targets during the 1980s.

Dealing specifically with our case of so-called mutiny, the report is unequivocally critical of the heavy-handedness of the ANC military structures:

> The Commission also finds that all so-called mutineers who were executed after conviction by military tribunal, irrespective of whether they were afforded proper legal representation and due process or not, suffered a gross violation of their human rights ... The Motsuenyane Commission further finds that adequate steps were not taken in good time against those responsible for such violation.[6]

---

5 TRC of South Africa Final Report. March 2003. 6: 56. https://www.gov.za/sites/default/files/gcis_document/201409/trc0.pdf\ Last accessed 29/04/2021.
6 Ibid, page 660.

The question is, does the report make up for the disappointment I had experienced in both the hearings in Soweto and Mthatha? Being exonerated in such a resounding way is humbling. It is only disappointing that the ANC did not see it fit to apologise for its acts of cruelty to fellow South Africans. That would have brought closure and melted the tensions and emotional pain of many years.

True, it is praiseworthy that the ANC is the only liberation movement in southern Africa to have had the courage to have itself investigated numerous times and risk losing its support base. But it could have benefited itself and South Africa substantially had it given proper attention to the findings and carried out the recommendations of those commissions. Until the ANC does that, it will remain morally and ethically deficient.

I also remain a bit anxious that there was no recommendation for the return of the remains of our countrymen who died in exile. This might be a big ask, yet it is not only possible, but also imperative. No self-respecting nation leaves its own behind and has no programme in place to retrieve their remains and reunite their spirits with their spiritual home – South Africa. If such an anomaly goes unchecked, then the nation has indeed lost a big part of its soul.

That being that, given limited time and resources, the TRC had done its level best. Everything was left at the door of the TRC Unit in the Department of Justice to expedite the distribution of the funds designated by the National Treasury for reparations. The TRC had recommended R20 000 be received for four years by each victim or beneficiary. Interestingly, the state president at the time, Thabo Mbeki, unilaterally declared that a once-off R30 000 was enough. Add to this his insistence that the case of reparations laid against big multinationals that supported and profited from apartheid should be nullified.

To the survivors surely the sum was not enough; some of us needed counselling, ongoing medical care, and were mentally and physically traumatised. These were the most hard-hit survivors of a horrible period in our history. Not only were most of us from the most oppressed society, but we had hit rock bottom. If ever someone was to uplift the quality of the African people, we posed an immediate acid test. With some outstanding funds in the TRC Unit in the Justice Department still not distributed, the lack of transparency leaves victims and survivors without answers.

CODA

And so, more than two decades after the TRC, I have come to terms with the task of reorganising my life through art. I think I am on a healing trajectory, although it has not been an easy path finding the happy endings that everyone loves in any story.

After the failure of the brickmaking business presented me with the challenge of making up for lost time, it has been a life on the periphery of politics, and directly in the art world. To me, art has never been a nine-to-five job like the odd ones I had to do to survive till the following month-end's government special pension for former liberation forces. Odd jobs like beam-filling during the construction of RDP houses; signwriting the name and address of the taxi owner after it had been spray painted by my neighbour Dan; selling the merchandise of a dubious warehouse in Johannesburg for a little cash; and, later, babysitting, something which, as I will explain later, was the most rewarding of them all.

In all the jobs assigned to me, I think I have left a signature uniquely mine. Art is an individual interpretation and an intense expression of the artist's feelings towards a certain subject specially impacting on the artist at a given time. It goes way back to the time when the cavemen felt pressured to chronicle, and thus preserve through rock paintings, the life and times they were living in. Thereafter, every generation was left with an educative legacy. By the gift bestowed on us artists, we are compelled to assist in putting things in their perspective; that is, separating the truth from lies. However poignant the message is, the aesthetic element should always prevail, and the unparalleled beauty of art will make up for all the sadness of the subject.

From the onset of this century, art came to my rescue when the chips were down. Once a week in 2000 I attended art classes in Nigel under the tutelage of a very kind Johan van der Linde at his home. It was a calming session, with background music from the great classical compositions of Vivaldi ('Four Seasons'), Beethoven, Mozart, and others. We had only gone through the basics of using pencil and charcoal when I could not continue because of the unavailability of public transport back to my abode in Duduza after 8 pm. Of the six students, I was the only black person. For two hours or so, I had to foot it back home past a cemetery, an open space and two squatter camps. Each journey was a nightmarish mission, and I had to prioritise my safety and put any artistic ambitions on hold.

Then came the TRC reparations in 2002. I immediately enrolled with Intec College for a course in cartoons, but the curriculum took me through the familiar territories of painting landscape using watercolour and oils. It was when I was assigned to paint a self-portrait that I realised I did not know who the person in the mirror was; it was a different person shouting and calling for attention. I was not strong enough to face myself back then. A voice would say to me, 'Luthando, what are you trying to do to yourself, exposing your weakness?' Then and there, I decided to forgo my dream of being a cartoonist; I also realised that cartoons deal with daily pertinent political developments in a humorous way, whereas I had my own past to deal with.

Mine had been a journey less travelled and no one but me could take it to its logical end by telling it through art. But at the time I found myself reeling in a long, dark, starless night. Art and I were like day and night, and I so needed the light of day. I needed to feel my feet touching the earth. It was clear to me that the trauma of surviving Sipho's murder and my attempted murder occupied so much of my mind. Another such attempt on my life could not be ruled out, and I was eternally afraid.

It was hope – that essential ingredient that makes our lives worth living another day – that kept me going. Hope leads to action instead of inaction and through practical steps we are able to see the bigger picture with our inner eye. Connie, who had been employed as a cook at Coronation Hospital on a permanent basis in 1996, had in 2002 bought a house in Noordgesig Extension 1, Soweto, in which she was staying with her son, Lebogang. She said I could come and stay with them. I could still visit Duduza to check on my belongings, even though I had asked a homeless guy to guard the place. To some extent, that guy and I actually co-owned my place. David was married and we agreed that he could occupy the show-house we had built.

Everything seemed to be going like clockwork, what with me getting employed in 2007 as a packer at COSI Pharmaceutical Company (later renamed Pharma-Q) with the help of Connie's sister Leah (may her soul rest in peace). The company did not have a product of its own at the time, but manufactured from raw material and packaged products for, among others, Adcock Ingram, Aspen and Pfizer.

Then, on a visit to Duduza in 2008, I found new occupants at my place and in the show-house David had occupied. I was told that he had sold the house, taken the brickmaking machine and left Duduza. All my belongings were missing! I was so shocked I almost dropped dead on the spot. How could he do such a cowardly thing? This was someone I had trusted for over two decades, and then he betrayed that trust. I had been there for him when his wife passed away a year or so before and we had parted well.

I remember my sister asking me about the house during a visit to Mthatha that same year. She had been to view it during a visit to Duduza and had even met Connie. It was painstaking relating the story to her as I was still hurting. After hearing me out, she said, 'Luthando, put all your problems in God's hands.' Even though that did not make sense to me at the time, I breathed a sigh of relief after having shared my grief with someone else, little knowing that she had only a few months more to live.

Fast forward six years or so later, and David apologised profusely for his deeds. What I liked was that he never tried to put the blame on anyone or anything else. What I deduced from his apology was that, after the death of his wife, he had felt forsaken by everyone dear to him. And with an insufficient income it must have been tough. I imagined the desperation that led him to the decision to up and leave. Over the previous years I had also lost my father and both my nieces, Nondyebo and Brenda, in quick succession, which led to Connie and me taking Brenda's son Thando under our wing and becoming his guardians. So then and there I immediately empathised with David. It takes courage to apologise unequivocally and I, of all people, could not be unforgiving. Great friends like us do quarrel, but never ever end the friendship easily. Though our lives have drifted apart, I still hear from him from time to time.

In 2014 I was retrenched. Until then, I was a man incognito at the workplace. Never had I felt free to open up about my experiences in exile, not even to close acquaintances. To say that I had been involved in the glorious liberation struggle would have appeared ludicrous because I had nothing to show for it. Being a packer is a labour-intensive and low-paying job. The only consolation I found was the fact that somewhere, someone was being healed, and I had even been able to afford to get married to Connie in 2009, but that was about all.

When people who had been retrenched were offered their jobs back a year later, I declined to return. I reminded myself that I had better heed my life's calling. Besides, I looked at my life and wished that I had not walked the precarious path I had chosen: no one in the ANC top leadership had taken our side when we were whistle-blowers on our arrival home and called for close attention to be paid to the way things were being run in the ANC in exile. It was a message some did not like, and that led to us being branded dissidents and askaris.

Another part of me would dismiss my self-pitying because deep in my heart I knew someone had to muster the courage, despite intimidation and fear, to come out with the truth. No amount of words vilifying us should deter the drive for a true democratic transformation. At some point, the most crucial undertakings by humankind remain thankless – I would remind myself of that. But then the worst drawback might be when I thought the world owed me. Sometimes I felt I was a martyr entitled to anger and aggression because of my unnecessary suffering in Quatro and afterwards. But the bouts of ill-feeling only left me tired and weak. They were the weight of guns and ammunition that bring soreness to the back and waist, as suggested by the Mkatashinga song, and I was carrying those guns and ammunition, day in and day out. A time had to come when I unburdened my mind of that heavy weaponry because it was holding me back and controlling my life.

At that time, I warmly welcomed the job of being a babysitter to Lesedi, Lebogang's thirteen-month-old baby whose mother Cindy had just found employment. Here I was face to face with an innocent soul with a trusting gaze. His fragility and vulnerability to the world did not take away his resolve to take it a day at a time, whether under my supervision or not. Just being distracted by his need for attention and care, I found I could withstand the effects of the trauma of years of horror. Suddenly, my problems were no longer an emergency I could not handle and detach myself from. I said to myself, 'If I can hold on to this moment and own it, I can afford to paint a bit and write more, taking the challenge one day at a time.' This helped me slowly turn inwards.

My journey to achieve inner peace and happiness compelled me to balance the good I had done with the bad, with my conscience at its best reminding me of the worst. When I think about it, I am responsible for ending the life of the APC driver at Viana Camp in Angola, and however I might try to perceive the act as self-defence, I still wish that nobody had died on that day. I express my deepest, heartfelt condolences to the family of the deceased. In truth, we were not sworn enemies, but foot soldiers in a world of senseless wars ravaging our planet; disposable pawns killing each other in a game played by those seeking to prolong their power, or others who want to take it over. Even though I went through hell in Quatro for this deed, I realised that the vindictive punishment meted out to me had nothing to do with helping to heal anyone, and only left me numb to brutality and death.

Although it is not customary in such cases to apologise, I had to transcend my pride and ego, and pray for forgiveness. When the thought struck me as I lay on my bed face up, I felt something trickling down both sides of my face, then flooding my ears. Warm tears. I so needed help as I grappled with the fear of forgiving my soul. Was it enough to cry? I had to accept that mine had not been a perfect life. (Is there such a thing?) My exposed wound was making me vulnerable, but maybe if I do not flinch now – I thought – I might be able to control my anxiety.

Then came another surge of emotional release, the wondrous phenomenon of letting go of pain and anguish, and triumphing through brutal, honest self-examination. I knew then that anger and the blame game I had been playing were the worst punishment I had unleashed on myself since Quatro. I had wasted time counting my scars and licking my wounds. The door was open for me to exit Victimhood Village, cross the Martyrdom Bridge, and be free.

Yes, free to let myself cry tears onto my palette or paper as I paint or write the testimony of good men and women who were humiliated, tormented, tortured, even killed: my unsung heroes and heroines who should never be forgotten.

Now that the genie is out of the bottle, I cannot be silent. I know that life is give and take, and that I might not have a lot to give besides giving of myself, but that is the best thing I will ever do. In each moment, I get the feeling I am an eagle taking off to rest on its throne high up, quite far from all the earthly divides down here.

Thank you, God, that that throne is here inside of me. In the quiet, as though for the first time in my life, I listen to my heart's song as I breathe in a deep peace, forgiveness and happiness, and exhale fear, anger, trauma ... and the past.

REFERENCES

ANC takes flak for 'cast member' statement about Miners Shot Down doccie. 20 November 2015. News24. https://www.news24.com/News24/anc-takes-flak-for-cast-member-statement-about-miners-shot-down-doccie-20151124\ Last accessed 29/04/2021.

O'Malley, P. 28 November 1980. *Statement on Signing Declaration by OR Tambo*. Nelson Mandela Foundation. https://omalley.nelsonmandela.org/omalley/index.php/site/q/03lv02424/04lv02730/05lv02918/06lv02979.htm\ Last accessed 29/04/2021.

Truth and Reconciliation Commission. 20 April 1998. Amnesty Hearing: Mfanelo Matshaya and Luthando Dyasop. https://www.justice.gov.za/TRC/amntrans/umtata/umtata.htm\ Last accessed 29/04/2021.

Truth and Reconciliation Commission of South Africa Final Report, Vol 6. 2003. https://www.gov.za/sites/default/files/gcis_document/201409/trc0.pdf\ Last accessed 29/04/2021.

ACKNOWLEDGEMENTS

Special thanks to Reverend Malamb from Soshanguve, Kebane Moloi from Duduza, John Wocke and John Deere (SA). And from Aylesbury, England, Eileen Shephard for volunteering to type my manuscript and Paul Trewhela for publishing 'A miscarriage of democracy' in *Inside Quatro*.

This photo was taken in 2006 when Thando was three.
On the left is my sister, Nomzekelo.

ABOUT THE AUTHOR

Luthando Dyasop was born in 1958 in Mthatha, in the former Transkei. His inclination to art opened his eyes to the racially based inequalities in society and later to politics of the day.

In 1980 he joined the ANC and its armed wing, uMkhonto we Sizwe (MK) in Lesotho and in 1981 underwent military training in Angola. He was part of those who fought against UNITA in the Eastern Front. He was also imprisoned in the ANC's notorious jail, Quatro after they mutineered against further participation in the war.

Released in 1988 and demobilised, he was sent to Tanzania, but given his pro-democracy stance, was looking at more jail time. In 1990, they fled in two groups: one to Kenya and another, including of Dyasop, to Malawi. The Malawi group made it safely home to South Africa.

In the ensuing years until the Truth and Reconciliation Commission (TRC), the setback had forced Dyasop and the others to pursue justice and to try to clear the names of victims of human rights violation by the ANC. This is his autobiography as he now aims to carve out a niche for himself as a full-time artist. He lives in Joburg.